TRUE HEART
PRACTICES

WAYS TO SELFLESSNESS

LEADER RESOURCES EDITION

FULL COLOR

WILLIAM M. WATSON, SJ

OTHER BOOKS BY WILLIAM M. WATSON, SJ

Sacred Story:
An Ignatian Examen for the Third Millennium

Inviting God into Your Life:
A Practical Guide for Prayer

FORTY WEEKS:
An Ignatian Path to Christ with Sacred Story Prayer

Reflections and Homilies:
The Gonzaga Collection

Sacred Story Rosary:
An Ignatian Way to Pray the Mysteries

Sacred Story Affirmations

The Whole-Life Confession

My Sacred Story Missal

Understanding the Spiritual World

Forty Weeks ~ Letters From Prison

Forty Weeks ~ A Journey of Healing and Transformation for Priests

Sacred Story Press
1401 E Jefferson St, STE 405
Seattle, WA 98122
Copyright © 2019

Dedicated the Sacred Heart & Immaculate Heart

IMPRIMI POTEST
Scott R. Santarosa, SJ

IMPRIMATUR
George V. Murry, SJ
Bishop of Youngstown

Unless otherwise indicated, Scripture quotations are from the Holy Bible, New American Bible, revised edition © 2010, 1991, 1986, 1970 Confraternity of Christian Doctrine, Washington, D.C.

Cover and Book Design: William Watson, SJ (All art images are in the public domain or have been allowed use by designating authorship. If you believe otherwise, contact: admin-team@sacredstory.net

Manufactured in the United States of America
ISBN: 9781099619359

THE POWER OF TRUE HEART

Discerning a priestly vocation is not a matter of learning a craft, but of allowing the grace of God to transform our heart after Christ's own Heart. like St. Ignatius did. Despite their great desires., young men today have difficulty understanding how to do that. In a culture saturated with noise and distraction, it is harder than ever to sift through the competing voices to hear the voice of the Father, and to respond virtuously and courageously.

TRUE HEART adapts the timeless method of St. Ignatius to our own day and time. Using this program, young men and women can encounter the Risen Lord and respond to Him in a profoundly personal way in the Sacraments, prayer, and lives of virtue. Seminarians and those discerning the seminary will find that the TRUE HEART exercises and other material are useful resources in leading them to a deep daily encounter with Jesus. From this place of encounter, they will be better able to hear the Lord's call and respond as Mary did.

-Very Rev. Daniel J. Barnett – Rector
Bishop White Seminary – Spokane, WA

The Spiritual Exercises of St. Ignatius of Loyola are one of the great spiritual treasures in the Church. Ignatian spirituality has formed countless saints and holy men and women over the past five centuries. We are indebted to Fr. Bill Watson for making this spiritual treasure accessible to a new generation. It is certain to bear much fruit for many years into the future.

-Steve Bollman
Founder & President of Paradisus Dei
Author, "That Man Is You" & "The Choice Wine"

In speaking with university students and listening to their concerns, certain areas always enter into the conversation. "How do I Pray?", "How can I know what God wants me to do?", "How do I learn more about discernment?" These are areas that young adults question constantly because they have a desire to grow in holiness and faith. TRUE HEART is a very approachable program that addresses these issues and more.

I cannot wait to challenge the students and implement TRUE HEART as a semester long program at Rice University. It is set up as a turn-key program that can be led by campus ministers, chaplains or student leaders. It can also be implemented within small group communities of men, women or co-ed. I am excited for our Catholic Students to experience TRUE HEART so they in turn can experience the true love that God has for His children.

-Rev. Ray Cook, OMI
Director of Campus Ministry – Rice University – Houston, TX

In TRUE HEART, Fr. Bill Watson has created a truly unique toolkit for youth and young adult formation. I could write countless endorsements about countless aspects of the TRUE HEART program that are noteworthy, and the reader might be led to think, Davidson just wants to praise everything. SO not true. I am very critical of these types of resources, having created many, and utilized many, I know too well the myriad ways they often fall short of what is needed for formation.

TRUE HEART is simply extraordinary. I personally am so excited to have these for use with my Confirmation classes and in many other formation settings. I am grateful I am for Fr. Bill Watson's diligent and extraordinary work. I stand in awe of what Fr. Bill Watson produced—the breadth and depth blow my mind.

For those seeking a program, TRUE HEART provides a detailed, user-friendly, comprehensive curriculum. For those seeking more flexible learning modules and experiences, TRUE HEART gives you an extraordinary toolkit that can be flexibly adapted and seamlessly integrated to supplement other programs, or for use in every kind of retreat or formation experience. I have used knowledge and tools from TRUE HEART with middle school, high school, college, and young adult settings. TRUE HEART not only provides essential knowledge about the faith; it is the perfect balance of deep content and flexible implementation needed to create an authentic and engaging experience of the faith. I cannot recommend it more highly!
-Matt Davidson, Ph.D.
President, Institute for Excellence & Ethics (IEE)

The Sacred Story Institute is at the leading edge of wisdom development in both children and adults. Now the Institute and its founder, Fr. William Watson, have created a very powerful set of programs for youth and young adults called TRUE HEART. These programs--one for individual young adults and one for youth and young adult leaders--help those who use them to remain grounded in real life, discover the beauty of existence at elemental levels, face the challenges young adults face in a high pressure world, and protect their spiritual and emotional development from digital distress. I highly recommend the TRUE HEART programs.
-Michael Gurian
New York Times bestselling author of The Wonder of Boys and The Minds of Girls

In my years of work with high school students in retreat settings and teaching meditation classes, I find that the <u>TRUE HEART resources are</u> comprehensive and foundational for young adults to building stronger, long lasting experiences in the Lord as they seek purposeful direction in their lives as they are called to building the Kingdom of God. The spirituality program Fr. Bill Watson, SJ offers in <u>TRUE HEART: A Way to Selflessness</u>, invites young adults to create, sustain and live out a deeper relationship with Jesus Christ using the spiritual practices of St. Ignatius Loyola but with a modern twist.

Young adults will encounter the Lord through time proven spiritual methods such as:

- ✠ *Unplugging intentionally from technology (distractions) during periods of time daily to remain open to the spiritual sphere of life*
- ✠ *Daily prayer periods that are rooted in the Ignatian Examen*
- ✠ *Spiritual exercises that point out roadblocks to living freely the spiritual life*
- ✠ *Young adults interacting and sharing with other young adult prayer companions*
- ✠ *Experiencing night vigils modeled on the Ignatian Spiritual Exercises*
- ✠ *Engaging with trusted mentors who can guide with wisdom, experience and faith*

This time of communion with God peels away the false self of the young adult, as a companion of Jesus, and feeds their authentic self that leads to spiritual maturation.

-Andrew K. Hoelperl

Theology Department Chair – McQuaid Jesuit – Rochester, NY

True Heart Practices provides a practical Ignatian roadmap that will help young people speak, heart to heart, with our Living God. As Pope Francis continues to remind us that Christ Lives (Christus Vivit), this resource helps the reader practice the art of meditation in a vivid and relatable way.

-Jonathan Lewis

Assistant Secretary for Pastoral Ministry and Social Concerns

Archdiocese of Washington

The "'TRUE HEART' program offers resources for young adults and their formation leaders that provide simple and practical introductions to Ignatian prayer that will help all who use them to discover the deepest desire of their hearts: 'selflessness" and a daily living relationship with Jesus Christ."

-Curtis Martin

Founder & CEO of FOCUS (Fellowship of Catholic University Students)

It is not true that young adults are not interested in religion as such. Young adults are not interested in a Christianity which, in their perception, is completely irrelevant to who they are. What if we told them that it is precisely Christ that they need to understand their truest heart? TRUE HEART does this and much more! Fr. Watson's program not only awakens a passionate longing for authenticity, it actually takes you step by step, with the wise pedagogy of St. Ignatius and his sons, away from self-centeredness towards pure, selfless freedom.

My college students often ask, OK, I want to do this "Jesus thing" but what does it really mean in practice? How do you become that person God made you to be? TRUE HEART gives young people a perfect answer to this very question. I am excited for the new opportunities campus ministries around the country receive in Fr. Watson's TRUE HEART, and I wish I had had TRUE HEART 'S wonderful toolkit earlier!

-Fr. Lukasz Misko, OP

Director, St. Catherine of Siena Newman Center at the University of Utah, Salt Lake City, UT

President/Director, Dominican Liturgical Center Foundation, Krakow, Poland

*In the past God spoke to our ancestors through the prophets at many times and in various ways, but in these last days he has spoken to us by his Son… (Hebrews 1, 1-2a)". This is the core of TRUE HEART that the **Sacred Story Institute** has given us for our work with youth and young adults. TRUE HEART is a real effort to make the Word of God as near as it can be, for the new generations that hunger and thirst of an intimate encounter with their Creator. There are no magical tricks to change our lives, but the daring invitation to make fascinating treks to build a new way with the solid truths of what God has revealed to us in his Son. The TRUE HEART programs never discard the chief cornerstone, but hold fast to it, and give it a new language so it can be better heard and understood by a new generation.*
-Rev. Hermann Rodríguez Osorio, S.J.
Delegate for Mission
Jesuit Provincial's Conference of Latin America (CPAL)

As an educator I am so grateful to have a resource like TRUE HEART. This program will help students balance the connectivity they find through their devices with a deeper connection to what is going on in their hearts. TRUE HEART will help young people discover a loving God who wants to walk alongside of them in the exciting and difficult journey of adolescence. I cannot wait to have my students benefit from this program.
-Jose Oyanguren
Headmaster – St. Augustine Prep – Managua, Nicaragua

I have been privileged to work with Fr. Watson, S.J. for several years during the development of the TRUE HEART program. This life-changing guide is the culmination of years of research and study, both scholarly and with actual teen and young adult groups, in schools and parishes nationwide and in Latin America.

What gives TRUE HEART its depth and breadth is the up-to-date scientific research and day to day experiences associated with adolescents and young adults in the 21st century. TRUE HEART offers daily periods of reflection tightly woven with Scripture study leading to the desire to reach out to others from the students own awakening and new awareness.

Fr. Bill's profound and graced experiences of Sacred Story and now TRUE HEART for adolescents and young adults connects the modern trend of mindfulness practice with the ancient practice of lecio divena that has engaged my students precisely where they are and humbly sharing with them the gateway to the God of Jesus of Nazareth and the Risen Christ.

TRUE HEART exceeds one's expectations of an "all-in-one" program. It does so simply because the TRUE HEART experience provides the door through which each individual may discover God in themselves—and others—in the present moment. I cannot say the same of any other program I've tried in a thirty-plus year career in Catholic education.

I highly recommend this program for yourself and also to share with youth groups, secondary Theology Classes, school student unions working toward tolerance and equality, Newman Centers and young adult parish programs and other groups of young people searching for God now.

-Marcella M. Nesbitt

Theology Instructor — McQuaid Jesuit — Rochester, NY

TRUE HEART is a dynamic, prayerful, and timely resource for young adults to engage more deeply in a relationship with Jesus Christ. The 10-weeks of intentional prayer, quiet, and spiritual discipline will serve to open their minds and hearts to hear more clearly the ways God is speaking to them and calling them deeper. Fr. Bill says it best in the foreword- if 2% of people answer the call to participate in TRUE HEART, the other 98% will be deeply impacted by the overflow of love and devotion to Christ they develop. I do appreciate the Leader Resource Guide, as well, and would highly recommend this to leaders of young adult groups as they plan days of reflections, retreats, and other programs. Prayer is the most important way to maintain a relationship with God, and TRUE HEART offers a training regimen to instill a habit of prayer and listening to God that will be life-changing for young adults! God bless you in using TRUE HEART,

-Megan Pepin

Director of Young Adult Ministry — Archdiocese of Seattle

TRUE HEART is a brilliant pioneering effort from Fr. Bill Watson. He masterfully plays spiritual matchmaker with our youth and young adults today and invites them into the resplendent vision of St. Ignatius of Loyola's timeless wisdom for human flourishing. Fr. Watson opens the deep beauty of Ignatian practice and mindfully offers us a guided tour on how to apply its powerful relevance as a balance to our modern digital lives. Fr. Watson's work here is a profound opportunity for youth and young adults to directly encounter the footsteps of Ignatius who leads us to the heart of Jesus Christ.

The youth and young adults we share TRUE HEART with will encounter Christ's grace in personal and transformative ways they never knew were possible. To revisit the steps of Fr. Watson's process from the initial meetings with my students at O'Dea to this final stage is truly awesome.

-Tom Schutte

Theology Educator, O'Dea High School

The TRUE HEART program is a unique opportunity for young people to undergo Spiritual Exercises within their busy everyday life. Fr William skillfully adapts his wonderful Sacred Story methodologies to the needs of busy students. The author of the TRUE HEART program is very aware of the challenges young people face and so places emphasis on topics like the use of technology and the struggle with self-respect. TRUE HEART program helps to understand and deepen the experience of the sacrament of Reconciliation. It provides a great introduction to reading and meditating the Scripture.

The whole program is so constructed that it is accessible for both those who just start an intentional faith life as well as for those who want to deepen their existing relationship with God. I wholeheartedly recommend this program for Youth and Young Adult leadership teams. I also recommend it for young adults wishing to grow in their faith who also want to discern life choices in light of faith. I will use it in my own ministry.

-Fr. Marcin Szymański, OP

Associate Director of Prince of Peace Newman Center at the University of Washington

ACKNOWLEDGMENTS

TRUE HEART began with a project at Seattle's O'Dea High School in 2014. Mr. Tom Schutte, then director of Campus Ministry, asked me to visit with some of his student leadership team over the course of the year. I was to present ideas on discernment in light of Ignatian Spirituality. I wish to thank Tom and his great students for helping us shape a version of St. Ignatius' life story for this edition.

Working with Tom and his students gave us the idea for TRUE HEART We realized, in light of our meetings, that there are not many good spiritual formation resources for young adults. I discussed this challenge with several people whose evangelization instincts I trust.

The first idea to create something for young adults was to take the adult *Forty Weeks* program and redraft it for young adults. To that end, we worked with over one hundred Jesuit faculty from both Jesuit and Catholic highs across Latin America and the US to gain insights on how they would translate the experience of doing the *Forty Weeks* into ideas for a program for young adults. That Latin American part of this project was facilitated by a former SSI board member, Fr. Hermann Rodriguez, S.J. Thank you, Fr. Hermann.

After the project with Jesuit high school faculty, and when we had a working text, I asked Michael Gurian, founder of the Gurian Institute and New York Times bestseller, to work with me on the initial book concept. He worked with me on language in the exercises that would be appropriate for young adults. He also gave insights on how to pose reflection questions based on the content of the various exercises.

Once we had a working draft of the program incorporating Gurian's suggestions, we launched a beta test of these re-drafted materials in multiple high schools in the US and Latin America, several young adult ministry programs and with seminary students. I wish to thank in particular Andrew Hoelperl and Marcella Nesbitt at McQuaid Jesuit in Rochester for their help with a great group of students. Also, thanks go to Fr. Dan Barnett, rector of Bishop White Seminary in Spokane, Washington and Fr. Derek Lappe, pastor of Mary, Star of the Sea in Bremerton Washington. Also, sincere thanks to Mr. Jose Oyanguren, headmaster of St. Augustine School in Managua, Nicaragua, for his assistance on the beta text with his students and faculty.

Finally, finishing work and refining suggestions came from Matthew Davidson, Ph.D., president for the Institute for Excellence & Ethics in Malinus, NY. My thanks to Matt for his "excellent" suggestions on the final shape of the two books in the series.

DEDICATION

TRUE HEART is dedicated to every young adult who longs for meaning, authenticity, holiness and is committed to timeless truths, and who longs for faithful love in a life that will produce fruit that endures to eternity.

You are the salt of the earth. But if salt loses its taste,
with what can it be seasoned?
It is no longer good for anything but to be
thrown out and trampled underfoot.
You are the light of the world.
A city set on a mountain cannot be hidden.
Nor do they light a lamp and then put it under a bushel basket;
it is set on a lampstand,
where it gives light to all in the house.
Just so, your light must shine before others,
that they may see your good deeds
and glorify your heavenly Father.

Mt. 5: 13-16

CONTENTS

FOREWORD

A. M. D. G.

"Sacred Heart of Jesus, help me to learn perfect selflessness since this is the only path to you." These are the opening words of the *Prayer of Offering to the Heart of Jesus* written by Saint Claude La Colombière, the Jesuit confessor of Saint Margaret Mary to whom Our Lord revealed the mysteries of His Sacred Heart. In *True Heart: A Way to Selflessness*, Father William Watson, SJ, effectively makes these words his own as he charts a spiritual path from silence through self-knowledge to selflessness.

Silence prepares the way, for otherwise, the ever-increasing distractions of our age would impede our path. Noise and visual images surround us. Screen-viewing consumes much of our waking hours. Sensory overload consequently overwhelms us. Our smartphones, moreover, have outsmarted us, making us dumb. What we once retained in our memory we have now transferred to our phones and allowed them to think for us.

Keeping us wired 24/7, our cell phones have also made us more anxious and depressed. By significantly raising our stress levels, this digital cacophony is undermining our physical, mental and spiritual health. Today, the 1984 movie *The Terminator* seems oddly prophetic. For machines, that we have built, are, if you will, killing us. As a young adult today you are particularly susceptible to the adverse effects of modern technology, for you have never known a world without the Internet.

In particular, social media ironically tends to make us less social and, hence, more self-centered. Such technology-driven self-centeredness is ultimately a dead end. The way out is the way to selflessness. Father Watson's contemporary spiritual exercises in the Ignatian tradition map out for young adults a path from life-sapping self-centeredness, and the loneliness it creates, into a life-giving selflessness and connectedness to others and to the Lord.

The Christian tradition has always prized silence where the soul communes with its Creator. But today, more and more, neuroscientists, medical professionals, Silicon Valley technicians and non-religious organizations have also begun to acknowledge the benefits to be gained from meditation and "mindfulness."

They encourage us to find technology-free spaces for the sake of our well-being. Father Watson himself invites young adults to find a quiet, technology-free place apart from this world's constant distractions in order to gain self-knowledge in Our Lord's company.

He counsels you to unhook "from technology so that you can hear your heart" (from the *Introduction*). This unhooking entails being still and knowing the God who has created us in His own Image. Jesus Himself, the visible Image of the invisible Father, shows us the way to authentic self-knowledge.

On this account, Father Watson invites you to speak prayerfully with Jesus and indeed to imitate Jesus' own nocturnal prayer by keeping vigil during the quiet hours of the night when, in the silent sanctuary of your heart, spiritual discourse becomes most intimate.

A true heart pulsates with pure love. But sadly, if we are honest with ourselves, we will have to admit that our loves are not always pure. They are, in fact, quite often self-seeking. Even the saints lamented the times when they had fallen short in their ardent desire to love God with an undivided heart. That is why Saint Claude La Colombière himself prays: "Teach me what I must do to attain the purity of your love, the desire for which you have inspired in me. I feel powerless ever to succeed in this aim without a very exceptional light and special help that I can only expect from you." Jesus alone gives us the grace of pure love. In giving us that grace, He also calls us to cooperate with it.

Cooperating with His grace, we enter deeply into His love for us, the source of all pure love. The experience of His selfless, crucified love unmasks our self-centeredness and moves our wounded hearts to contrition. Sorrow for our sins is the necessary first step toward true repentance and conversion. Such frank self-knowledge also entails an honest admission of our own inability— or, in Saint Claude's words, our powerlessness—to break free, alone and unaided, from all that binds us interiorly.

Here again, we pray with Saint Claude: "Accomplish your will in me, Lord. I know that I resist it, but it seems to me that I would truly like not to resist. It is you who will have to do it all, divine Heart of Jesus Christ." Yes, Christ's grace alone paves the pathway to freedom.

This journey to selflessness, this journey to discover our true heart in the True Heart of Jesus, leads us "to rest and find a new way to live our life" (from the *Introduction*). Whereas self-centeredness is always a matter of our turning away from God, the journey, to which Father Watson invites his readers, entails an ever more complete turning toward God. Only in that "turning toward," which begins in grace, does Jesus' light dispel our darkness and the peace, that He alone can give, abide within us.

This world's "peace" only anesthetizes us and nothing more. The blue light shining from the screens, that we hold in our hands or before which we sit, saps our energy rather than restores our strength. It hypnotizes rather than illuminates.

By diverting its gaze from these seductive rays, the true heart finds peace when it beholds Christ and bathes in His light. The true heart gladly acknowledges before Jesus in the words of Saint Claude La Colombière that "the glory of my sanctification will be yours alone, and it is for that reason alone that I wish to desire perfection." What is this desired perfection? It is to rest in God. As Saint Augustine of

Hippo eloquently observes in his *Confessions*, because God has created us for Himself, our hearts remain restless until they rest in Him. Truly, in the end, only the selfless heart experiences enduring peace.

True Heart: A Way to Selflessness is a journey worth taking. For those of you who undertake it wholeheartedly, it will turn out to be a marvelous, spiritually life-giving adventure.

These spiritual exercises are indeed a treasure map to a treasure buried in the field of your innermost self. That treasure, placed there by God in whose Image we have been created, is the gift of Christ's peace experienced both in time and for all eternity.

Father Joseph Carola, S.J.

Gregorian University, Rome, 21 January 2019
Memorial of Saint Agnes, Roman Virgin and Martyr

INTRODUCTION

THE TRUE HEART JOURNEY TO SELFLESSNESS

Be Still and Know That I am God, the Psalmist prays (Ps. 46:10). That is easier said than done. Being still and silent in our modern technological age is, in fact, nearly impossible. Yet it is at the very core of the Christian vocation.

It is said that for the first five years, the Pythagorean School Initiates took an oath of silence, and were referred to as hearers. The idea was that in order to *know thy self* and gain wisdom, one first had to be silent and listen.

True Heart does not ask you to take five years to know yourself by the spiritual discipline of being silent. We offer instead ten weeks of time for you to reset and find a new way to live your life and listen to your heart...your true heart.

Our programs are not for everyone. In fact, we focus on trying to reach those who are ready for a challenge and willing to commit their time to open up to God. It is this minority that will impact the majority and change the world. You will know in your heart, your true heart, if you are one of that number.

St Ignatius Loyola awoke to his true heart at the age of thirty. He was given the grace to see how two different sets of fantasies, portraying two possible directions his life could take, were fundamentally different from each other. The first set of fantasies he described as "vain" and were focused on his ego and achieving fame (self-centered). The second set of fantasies he described as "holy" and focused on serving Christ and doing good works (selfless).

Both the self-centered and selfless fantasies entertained him while he actively fantasized their possibilities. But one day he was given grace to notice a difference. When he set the self-centered fantasies aside, he felt dry and dissatisfied. When he set the selfless fantasies aside, he felt peaceful and content. He was given to understand that the selfless fantasies that left him peaceful and content were his "true heart," and from that day forward he pursued those dreams and fantasies.

There are a million stories in each life but each life only has two possible directions: towards God and the light (selflessness) or away from God and the light (self-centeredness). The goal of the various True

Heart exercises is to help youth and young adult leaders help others understand the two fundamentally different directions one's life might take. Only one direction can make you feel content and peaceful. Only one direction is your True Heart.

To help young adults of all ages understand their True Heart, Sacred Story Institute created the ten-week True Heart program set spiritual exercises. Nearly half the allotted time for spiritual exercises is simply designed unhooking from technology so individuals can hear the voice of the Holy Spirit in their hearts. Why is that important? Listen to the words of Pope Francis:

It has become countercultural to choose a lifestyle whose goals are even partly independent of technology, of its costs and its power to globalize and make us all the same. Technology tends to absorb everything into its ironclad logic, and those who are surrounded with technology "know full well that it moves forward in the final analysis neither for profit nor for the well-being of the human race", that "in the most radical sense of the term power is its motive – a lordship over all."[1] As a result…our capacity for making decisions, a more genuine freedom and the space for each one's alternative creativity are diminished.[2]

In this Resources Edition for True Heart, we have taken all the different spiritual exercises and broken them down into components that can be used for retreats, prayer experiences or other needs youth and young adult ministers, retreat planners, religious education coordinators and others might want for pastoral planning needs.

Holy Wings: I choose the image of wings to evoke the freedom that living one's True Heart will bring to those who journey this path. They also symbolize one's spiritual nature and the guidance on this journey from one's personal guardian who draws all light and strength from Christ, the original True Heart.

---

[1] Romano Guardini, *Das Ende der Neuzeit*, 63-64 (*The End of the Modern World*, 56).
[2] Laudato Si, 81.

SCRIPTURE AND THE HEART

Use these scripture passages and the statements on how they connect to the heart for prayer exercises in any context you find helpful. The power of the passages is that they all describe the human heart. For exercises where people are trying to find their True Heart, these exercises are very valuable.

Remember, it is a profound challenge to know our true heart. Jeremiah says in 17:9, "More tortuous than anything is the human heart, beyond remedy; who can understand it?" It is much easier to know our sensual desires but these don't reveal our true identity as children of the Father. We must enter the private place in our hearts where the Holy Spirit resides in our soul. It is only there that we will discover our true heart.

You can print the statement along with the scripture passages, have people pray with them for five, ten, fifteen, thirty minutes or longer and then write some personal reflection in a journal for future reference. Use this text as an opener.

Take a moment to ask God for this grace: 'Lord, open me to the knowledge of my own heart.' The heart is where the important work of prayer takes place. The mind reveals facts but the heart reveals the truth, your innermost being. The "heart" is the word used in Scripture for the most important aspects of the human condition.

Seek knowledge of the heart and ask God for the grace to open a pathway to your heart. Seek, also, knowledge of God's heart, present in Christ's Sacred Heart. This grace will help to unite your heart to the heart of Christ.

Prayerfully listen to the passage(s) below and "listen" to how the statement(s) strikes your own heart. Discover how it impacts, stirs you, gives you hope. Notice if it feels like it is "just for you."
Jot down in your journal the reason(s) you think it is meaningful for you.

Say out loud: "Lord, open me to the knowledge of my heart."
Every day, pay close attention to what your heart senses and believes.

✠ The heart reveals the state of corruption caused by sin (Read: Gen 6:5; Jer 17:9-10; Mt 15:8-9)

✠ The heart is where the process of conversion and forgiveness takes place
(Read: Ez 36:26; Mt 18:35; Rom 2:29)

✠ A True Heart enables one to see God (Read: Mt 5:8).

✠ The heart is the center of compassion (Read: Lk 7:13).

✠ The heart is the vessel holding the secrets that illuminate the true meaning of life
(Mt 6:21; Lk 24:32;).

✠ The heart is defined as the center where God judges human thoughts, words and deeds
(Read: Heb 4:12-13).

✠ The heart perceives love as the ultimate end, gift, and purpose of being (1 Cor 13).

✠ The testimony of Christ in Scripture speaks to the heart's desire for innocence
(Read: Mt 11:28-30.).

✠ Christ gives the conviction that He can be found in hearts who seek Him (Read: Lk 11:9-11).

You can use the prayer-poem attributed to Fr. Pedro Arrupe, SJ, to accompany any or all of these exercises as a capstone spiritual exercise. It is about the most important thing in the world: falling in love forever!

FALLING IN LOVE

NOTHING IS MORE PRACTICAL THAN
FINDING GOD, THAT IS THAN

FALLING IN LOVE

IN A QUITE ABSOLUTE FINAL WAY.
WHAT YOU ARE IN LOVE WITH,
WHAT SEIZES YOUR IMAGINATION,
WILL AFFECT EVERYTHING.
IT WILL DECIDE
WHAT WILL GET YOU OUT OF BED
IN THE MORNING,
WHAT YOU DO WITH YOUR EVENINGS,
HOW YOU SPEND YOUR WEEKENDS,
WHAT YOU READ, WHO YOU KNOW,
WHAT BREAKS YOUR HEART,
AND WHAT AMAZES YOU WITH
JOY AND GRATITUDE.
FALL IN LOVE, STAY IN LOVE,
AND IT WILL DECIDE EVERYTHING.

PEDRO ARRUPE, SJ

Holly Monroe Calligraphy

At the end of your reading, write in your journal what would make you selflessly fall in love "in a quite absolute, final way?"

Would it be a type of person, a commitment, a mission or something else that would lead you to selflessness in love?

Write your responses below or in your journal.
What amazed you about your response(s)?

Sacred Story Institute © 2019

PRAYING WITH SCRIPTURE
MARK'S GOSPEL

ON PRAYING WITH SCRIPTURE[3]

The Second Week of the *Spiritual Exercises* is focused on the public life of Christ. St Ignatius, in his wisdom, often chose passages that reflect the how following Christ can lead individuals into conflict with the ways of the world. We chose in *True Heart* to emphasize this cultural tension in the selections from Mark's Gospel as one between self-centeredness and selflessness. Let us consider how these sections from Mark might be employed by pastoral guides in various settings.

---

[3] Image of St. Mark originally from: https://citydesert.files.wordpress.com/2014/11/mark-coptic.jpg

First, you can use any individual exercise to teach individuals how to pray with a Gospel passage. Fr. Nigro's method unlocks a sure way for individuals to enter any Gospel passage and begin to find their true heart in the contemplation of Holy Scripture.

A second way to use the exercises is thematically. If you are doing a retreat or want a focusing exercise, take one of the specific themed passages from Mark and allow individuals to pray with it, journaling afterward to see how the passage spoke to their hearts. Group sharing of fruits can accompany this sort of exercise.

A third way to use these exercises is as a unit. You can build a retreat weekend or a series of evening meetings and go through all the exercises in order to help your people enter into the story of Jesus. This can be a very formative way to help people draw close to the Living Christ and to let him touch their lives through his own.

Please share with us other fruitful ways you successfully used the exercises in this section.

The wisdom below on praying with Scriptures comes from Fr. Armand M. Nigro, S.J., a renowned retreat master and a good friend of the author. You can share this resource with individuals or groups you work with on how to pray with Scripture and it might be beneficial for the selections we have chosen from Mark's Gospel as well.

GOD SPEAKS TO US FIRST

This fundamental truth makes it possible for us to pray to God. He has been concerned for each of us long before we became concerned for ourselves. He desires communication with us. He speaks to us continually, revealing Himself to us by various modes:

✠ through Jesus Christ, His Word:
✠ through the Church, the extension of Christ in the world (because we are joined together in Christ, God speaks to us through other people.);
✠ through visible creation around us, which forms the physical context of our lives. (Creation took place in and through His Son, and it is another form of God's self- revelation.);
✠ through the events of our lives;
✠ through Holy Scripture, a real form of His presence. This is the mode of communication we are most concerned with in prayer.

GOD INVITES US TO LISTEN

Our response to God's initial move is to listen to what He is saying. This is the basic attitude of prayer.

What you do immediately before prayer is very important. Normally, it is something you do not rush into. Spend a few moments quieting yourself and relaxing, settling yourself into a prayerful and comfortable position. In listening to anyone, you try to tune out everything except what the person is saying to you.

In prayer, this can be done best in *silence* and *solitude.* Select a favorite passage from Holy Scripture, 5 to 10 verses. Put a marker in the page. Try to find a quiet place where you can be alone and uninhibited in your response to God's presence. Try to quiet yourself interiorly. Jesus would often go up to the mountain by Himself to pray with His Father.

In an age of noise, activity, and tensions like our own, it is not always easy or necessary to forget our cares and commitments, the noise and excitement of our environment. Never feel constrained to blot out all distractions. Anxiety in this regard could get between ourselves and God.

Rather, realize that the Word did become flesh -- that He speaks to us in the noise and confusion of our day. Sometimes in preparing for prayer, relax and listen to the sounds around you. God's presence is as real as they are.

Be conscious of your sensations and living experiences of feeling, thinking, hoping, loving, of wondering, desiring, etc. Then, conscious of God's unselfish, loving presence in you, address Him simply and admit: "Yes, you do love life and feeling into me. You do love a share of your personal life into me. You are present to me. You live in me. Yes, You do."

God is present *as a person,* in you through His Spirit, who speaks to you now in Scripture, and who prays in you and for you.

Ask God the grace to listen to what He says. Begin reading Scripture slowly and attentively. Do not hurry to cover much material.

If it recounts an event of Christ's life, be there in the mystery of it. Share with the persons involved, e.g. a blind man being cured. Share their attitude. Respond to what Jesus is saying.

Some words or phrases carry special meaning for you. Savor those words, turning them over in your heart. You may want to speak or recite a Psalm or other prayer from Scripture. Really mean what you are saying.

When something strikes you, e.g.,

✠ You feel a new way of being with Christ. He becomes for you in a new way (e.g., you sense what it means to be healed by Christ.)
✠ you experience God's love,
✠ you feel lifted in spirit,
✠ you are moved to do something selfless,
✠ you are peaceful,
✠ You are happy and content just to be in God's presence,

This is the time to ---- *PAUSE*.

This is God speaking directly to you in the words of Scripture. Do not hurry to move on. Wait until you are no longer moved by the experience.

Don't get discouraged if nothing seems to be happening. Sometimes God lets us feel dry and empty in order to let us realize it is not in our power to communicate with Him or to experience consolation. God is sometimes very close to us in His seeming absence (Ps. 139:7-8). He is for us entirely in a selfless way. He accepts us as we are, with all our limitations -- even with our seeming inability to pray. A humble attitude of listening is a sign of love for Him, and a real prayer from the heart.

At these times remember the words of Paul: "The Spirit, too, comes to help us in our weakness, for when we cannot choose words in order to pray properly, the Spirit himself expresses our plea in a way that could never be put into words." (Rom. 8:26-27.)

Relax in prayer. Remember, God will speak to you in *God's* own way: "Yes, as the rain and snow come down from the heavens and do not return without watering the earth, making it yield and giving growth to provide seed for the sower and bread for the eating, so the word that goes from my mouth does not return to me empty, without carrying out *my will* and succeeding in what it was sent to do." (Isaiah 55:10-11.)

Spend time in your prayer just being conscious of God's presence in and around you. If you want to, speak with Him about the things you are interested in or wish to thank Him for, your joys, sorrows, aspirations, etc.

SUMMARY OF THE 5 "P'S"

1. *Passage from Scripture.* Pick one and have it marked and ready.
2. *Place.* Where you are alone and uninhibited in your response to God's presence.
3. *Posture.* Relaxed and peaceful. A harmony of body with spirit.
4. *Presence of God.* Be aware of it and acknowledge and respond to it. If nothing happens, turn to the
5. *Passage from Scripture.* Read it very slowly aloud and listen carefully and peacefully to it.

(5. cont.) Read *aloud* or *whisper* in a rhythm with your breathing -- a phrase at a time -- with *pauses* and *repetitions* when and where you feel like it.

Don't be anxious, *don't* try to look for implications or lessons or profound thoughts or conclusions or resolutions, etc. Be content to be like a child who climbs into its father's lap and *listens* to his words and his story. When you finish, remind yourself that God continues to live in you during the rest of the day.

Sacred Story Institute © 2019

Gospel of Mark Chapter One:
The Call of the First Disciples

Read the text from Mark One below (or in your Bible). In place of the sentence that says: "Jesus said to them," read it with your name in place of "them." I have provided the original passage and then, just below it, the passage with the names left blank so that you can insert yours and others name.

As he passed by the Sea of Galilee, he saw Simon and his brother Andrew casting their nets into the sea; they were fishermen. Jesus said to them, "Come after me, and I will make you fishers of men." Then they abandoned their nets and followed him.

He walked along a little farther and saw James, the son of Zebedee, and his brother John. They too were in a boat mending their nets. Then he called them. So they left their father Zebedee in the boat along with the hired men and followed him.

Reflection:
Fill in your name and others who come to mind.

As he passed by the Sea of Galilee, he saw _____ casting a net into the sea.

Jesus said to _____, "Come after me, and I will make you fishers of men."

Then _____ abandoned the net and followed him.

He walked along a little farther and saw _____, the son/daughter of _____ who was in a boat mending nets. Then he called _____ so _____ left the other workers and followed him.

Hear Jesus' call. In your imagination, do you follow Jesus?

The others had to leave some people behind. In your imagination do you have to leave anyone behind to follow the call to be with Jesus?

Sacred Story Institute © 2019

As always with True Heart, feel free to write notes in your journal, or speak aloud your thoughts, if seeing the words on paper, or hearing them spoken, will help you discern your truth. Also, feel free also to discuss this exercise with a spiritual companion or mentor.

Sacred Story Institute © 2019

Gospel of Mark Chapter One:
The Cure of a Demoniac

Then they came to Capernaum, and on the Sabbath he entered the synagogue and taught. The people were astonished at his teaching, for he taught them as one having authority and not as the scribes.

In their synagogue was a man with an unclean spirit; he cried out, "What have you to do with us, Jesus of Nazareth? Have you come to destroy us? I know who you are—the Holy One of God!"

Jesus rebuked him and said, "Quiet! Come out of him!" The unclean spirit convulsed him and with a loud cry came out of him. All were amazed and asked one another, "What is this? A new teaching with authority. He commands even the unclean spirits and they obey him." His fame spread everywhere throughout the whole region of Galilee.

Reflection:
Pope Francis has affirmed that Satan is a real spiritual entity who seeks the destruction of people and creation. Many of us read books like *The Lord of the Rings* because it accurately depicts a spiritual world of good and evil.

Now re-read the Gospel portion and notice how, by entering into the wilderness at the beginning of his ministry, Jesus was prepared to be victorious in this battle—that includes the in battle inside each of us.

Ask Jesus to master any evil and self-centeredness you experience in your life. Know that he has the power to help you. Say aloud, "Jesus, I trust in Your power to help me be more selfless."

Feel and think the feelings and thoughts that come to you in this exercise and write down any you wish to write down in your journal.

Gospel of Mark Chapter Four
Parable of the Lamp

He said to them, "Is a lamp brought in to be placed under a bushel basket or under a bed, and not to be placed on a lampstand? For there is nothing hidden except to be made visible; nothing is secret except to come to light. Anyone who has ears to hear ought to hear."

Reflection:

In this passage can you see that Jesus has invited you to your True Heart training because he wants the light of Christ living in you to bring hope to the world?

Read it again. Find yourself in the "them" so that now you read it this way:

He said to me, "Is a lamp brought in to be placed under a bushel basket or under a bed, and not to be placed on a lampstand? For there is nothing hidden except to be made visible; nothing is secret except to come to light. Anyone who has ears to hear ought to hear."

Listen to Jesus speaking about your life as a "lamp" and tell him what kind of light you want it to bring to your friends and the world. How is the light of selflessness different from that of self-centeredness? Maybe let this be what you write in your journal.

Gospel of Mark Chapter Five
The Woman with a Hemorrhage

There was a woman afflicted with hemorrhages for twelve years. She had suffered greatly at the hands of many doctors and had spent all that she had. Yet she was not helped but only grew worse. She had heard about Jesus and came up behind him in the crowd and touched his cloak.

She said, "If I but touch his clothes, I shall be cured." Immediately her flow of blood dried up. She felt in her body that she was healed of her affliction.

Jesus, aware at once that power had gone out from him, turned around in the crowd and asked, "Who has touched my clothes?" But his disciples said to him, "You see how the crowd is pressing upon you, and yet you ask, 'Who touched me?'" And he looked around to see who had done it.

The woman, realizing what had happened to her, approached in fear and trembling. She fell down before Jesus and told him the whole truth. He said to her, "Daughter, your faith has saved you. Go in peace and be cured of your affliction.

Reflection:

Can you feel the wisdom of this passage? Jesus comes to anyone who will be willing to accept his healing and mercy. Let him touch anything in your life that needs physical, emotional or spiritual healing.

Believe in his power and ask him to heal you from self-centeredness and transform your heart to selflessness. Feel him touch your life and believe in him. As you feel this power and grace, discern each part of you that needs his healing.

Write down or speak aloud what patterns of self-centeredness you need Jesus to heal.

Gospel of Mark Chapter Six
The Rejection at Nazareth

He departed from there and came to his native place accompanied by his disciples. When the Sabbath came he began to teach in the synagogue, and many who heard him were astonished. They said, "Where did this man get all this? What kind of wisdom has been given him? What mighty deeds are wrought by his hands! Is he not the carpenter the son of Mary, and the brother of James and Joset and Judas and Simon? And are not his sisters here with us?" They took offense at him.

Jesus said to them, "A prophet is not without honor except in his native place and among his own kin and in his own house."

So he was not able to perform any mighty deed there apart from curing a few sick people by laying his hands on them. He was amazed at their lack of faith.

Reflection:
In his life, Jesus was rejected many times because he was true to his heart and mission. Those who fought against him did not welcome him or his mission. Did he take it personally or did he let rejection bring him closer to God?

When have you felt rejected for being true to your heart and mission in life? By whom?

Describe three incidents in the last year. Was it because you were being selfless and true to your heart and mission or were you acting on self-centeredness?

Can you pray for those who reject you?

Sacred Story Institute © 2019

If we approach rejection with discernment, we can see why we were rejected, get past blaming the other person, and learn from the rejection so that we become increasingly true-of-heart and more selfless. Because nurturing wounds makes us more self-centered.

As you preach this gospel to yourself, in your heart, listen for Jesus' voice preaching to you. Let his gospel make you stronger, more loving, selfless and wiser young adult.

The Gospel of Mark Chapter Eight
The Blind Man of Bethsaida

When they arrived at Bethsaida, they brought to him a blind man and begged him to touch him. He took the blind man by the hand and led him outside the village. Putting spittle on his eyes he laid his hands on him and asked, "Do you see anything?" Looking up he replied, "I see people looking like trees and walking." Then he laid hands on his eyes a second time and he saw clearly; his sight was restored and he could see everything distinctly. Then he sent him home and said, "Do not even go into the village."

Reflection:

Can you feel in this passage the greatness of the revelation that Jesus is Lord of all creation?

Imagine the passage with *you* as the blind person. You are not physically blind but feel blind to important things in life about selflessness and self-centeredness that you can't clearly see.

What are the self-centered patterns that you are blind to but want to see more clearly?

Ask Jesus to lay his hands on the eyes of your heart to feel his press upon your real heart.

Tell him aloud you believe he can help you see and thank him for hearing your request for sight.

Gospel of Mark Chapter Eight
Peter's Confession about Jesus

Now Jesus and his disciples set out for the villages of Caesarea Philippi. Along the way he asked his disciples, "Who do people say that I am?" They said in reply, "John the Baptist, others Elijah, still others one of the prophets." And he asked them, "But who do you say that I am?" Peter said to him in reply, "You are the Messiah." Then he warned them not to tell anyone about him.

Reflection:

What thoughts and feelings arise for you in reading this passage? Ponder them.

Then re-imagine the passage taking place with a large crowd of people that you know and who know you. See Jesus come up to you and ask you to say in front of the crowd who he is.

What would you say about Jesus in front of your friends and how do you think they would react?

Play it out like a movie in your imagination but notice your thoughts, the thoughts and reactions of others and the reaction of Jesus to your statement about him.

Sacred Story Institute © 2019

Gospel of Mark Chapter Eight
The Conditions of Discipleship

Open your heart to The Gospel Story of the One who holds you and all creation in being. Jesus is real and wants to become part of your daily life. He wants a relationship with you. He waits to be your hope, your forgiveness and your peace. Ask the Holy Spirit open your heart to Jesus' story which is The Word of God

He summoned the crowd with his disciples and said to them, "Whoever wishes to come after me must deny himself, take up his cross, and follow me. For whoever wishes to save his life will lose it, but whoever loses his life for my sake and that of the gospel will save it.

What profit is there for one to gain the whole world and forfeit his life? What could one give in exchange for his life? Whoever is ashamed of me and of my words in this faithless and sinful generation, the Son of Man will be ashamed of when he comes in his Father's glory with the holy angels."

Reflection:
As you reflect on this passage, see Jesus come up to you and ask if you will follow him.

Tell him the one self-centered thing you think you must deny to freely follow him.

Tell him what you think the cross is in your life that you must selflessly carry to be his follower.

 Sacred Story Institute © 2019

Gospel of Mark Chapter Nine
The Transfiguration of Jesus

After six days Jesus took Peter, James, and John and led them up a high mountain apart by themselves. He was transfigured before them, and his clothes became dazzling white, such as no fuller on earth could bleach them. Then Elijah appeared to them along with Moses, and they were conversing with Jesus.

Then Peter said to Jesus in reply, "Rabbi, it is good that we are here! Let us make three tents: one for you, one for Moses, and one for Elijah." He hardly knew what to say, they were so terrified. Then a cloud came, casting a shadow over them from the cloud came a voice, "This is my beloved Son. Listen to him."

Reflection:

The story of the transfiguration of Jesus and the glory revealed is a sign of the coming resurrection when Christ's glory will transform "transfigure" all creation and us as well. Can you feel this eventuality in your heart? It will be the final victory of selflessness over self-centeredness.

Stand with Jesus and hear the Father say it about you: "This is my beloved child." Can you hear and feel your Father's love?

What self-centeredness in your life do you want the Father to "transfigure" so that you can be a more selfless True Heart?

Be specific and ask for the grace to be beautifully transformed. Write in your journal how you desire to be transformed.

Sacred Story Institute © 2019

Gospel of Mark Chapter Nine
Temptations to Sin

"Whoever causes one of these little ones who believe [in me] to sin, it would be better for him if a great millstone were put around his neck and he were thrown into the sea. "If your hand causes you to sin, cut it off. It is better for you to enter into life maimed than with two hands to go into Gehenna, into the unquenchable fire. "And if your foot causes you to sin, cut it off. It is better for you to enter into life crippled than with two feet to be thrown into Gehenna. "And if your eye causes you to sin, pluck it out. Better for you to enter into the kingdom of God with one eye than with two eyes to be thrown into Gehenna, where 'their worm does not die, and the fire is not quenched.'"

Reflection:

Jesus uses exaggeration to make a point. He is not really suggesting one cut off their body parts. But he is making the point that sin is destructive and we must fight it with discipline and his grace.

Imagine Jesus coming up to you and asking what self-centered behavior you need "cut out of your heart and life" so that you have the freedom to selflessly follow him. Remember as you ask that you can't do this, but He can.

Ask these questions of Jesus until you have listed for him everything that needs to be cut, plucked out, and changed in your life. Ask for his help and believe he has the power to change you! Write in your journal what you asked Jesus to cut out of your heart.

Gospel of Mark Chapter Eleven
The Authority of Jesus Questioned

They returned once more to Jerusalem. As he was walking in the temple area, the chief priests, the scribes, and the elders approached him and said to him, "By what authority are you doing these things? Or who gave you this authority to do them?" Jesus said to them, "I shall ask you one question. Answer me, and I will tell you by what authority I do these things. Was John's baptism of heavenly or of human origin? Answer me."

They discussed this among themselves and said, "If we say, 'Of heavenly origin,' he will say, '[Then] why did you not believe him?' But shall we say, 'Of human origin'?"—they feared the crowd, for they all thought John really was a prophet. So they said to Jesus in reply, "We do not know." Then Jesus said to them, "Neither shall I tell you by what authority I do these things."

Reflection:

Jesus is the son of the Eternal Father. Yet, the religious authorities of his time saw him as being possessed by an evil spirit and they refuse to respect his authority. The most selfless person to have ever lived is accused of being the very embodiment of self-centeredness. As he faces these misconceptions, Jesus is the model of both the courage and humility that signify real strength and authority.

Have you ever stood by Gospel values and had people challenge why you believe something? Has it created fear in your heart?

Remember one occasion when you stood your ground and one occasion when you caved into the pressure of others. What can you learn from these two experiences? Write a sentence below or in your journal. Ask Jesus to be a selfless True Heart, strong and courageous in the face of outside pressures.

Gospel of Mark Chapter Twelve
Parable of the Tenants

He began to speak to them in parables. "A man planted a vineyard, put a hedge around it, dug a wine press, and built a tower. Then he leased it to tenant farmers and left on a journey.

"At the proper time he sent a servant to the tenants to obtain from them some of the produce of the vineyard. But they seized him, beat him, and sent him away empty-handed. Again he sent them another servant. And that one they beat over the head and treated shamefully. He sent yet another whom they killed.

"So, too, many others; some they beat, others they killed until he had only one other to send, a beloved son. He sent him to them last of all, thinking, 'They will respect my son.' "But those tenants said to one another, 'This is the heir. Come, let us kill him, and the inheritance will be ours.' So they seized him and killed him, and threw him out of the vineyard.

"What [then] will the owner of the vineyard do? He will come, put the tenants to death, and give the vineyard to others. "Have you not read this scripture passage: 'The stone that the builders rejected has become the cornerstone; by the Lord has this been done, and it is wonderful in our eyes'?"

"They were seeking to arrest him, but they feared the crowd, for they realized that he had addressed the parable to them. So they left him and went away."

Reflection:

The Good News of the Gospel proclaimed by Jesus is constantly getting him in trouble with the religious authorities. He tells these authorities a parable about how the prophets of the Old Testament were beaten or killed by their ancestors. Upon hearing the parable they wanted to arrest Jesus on the spot, but they were afraid.

What modern-day selfless prophets do you see in your country or the world who are putting their lives at risk to proclaim the Gospel? What are they proclaiming and how is the message being received? Can you imagine selflessly standing up for something that would bring you the same condemnation? What in your life do you need to sacrifice to stand with Christ as a modern-day prophet? Write it down in your journal.

Say in your heart, "Be not afraid." Say these words when confronted by situations that call you to selflessly take a stand for the Gospel.

The Gospel of Mark Chapter Twelve

The Greatest Commandment

One of the scribes, when he came forward and heard them disputing and saw how well he had answered them, asked him, "Which is the first of all the commandments?"

Jesus replied, "The first is this: 'Hear, O Israel! The Lord our God is Lord alone! You shall love the Lord your God with all your heart, with all your soul, with all your mind, and with all your strength.'
The second is this: 'You shall love your neighbor as yourself.' There is no other commandment greater than these."

The scribe said to him, "Well said, teacher. You are right in saying, 'He is One and there is no other than he.' And 'to love him with all your heart, with all your understanding, with all your strength, and to love your neighbor as yourself' is worth more than all burnt offerings and sacrifices."

And when Jesus saw that [he] answered with understanding, he said to him, "You are not far from the kingdom of God." And no one dared to ask him any more questions."

Reflection:

The Greatest Commandment Jesus repeats is something every Jew would know. It is central to the Torah; *Sh'ma Yisrael Adonai Eloheinu Adonai Eḥad* - "Hear, O Israel: the LORD is our God, the LORD is One."

As a Jew and a prophet, Jesus connects this Commandment with a second Commandment that must be in place if one really says "I love God": loving one's neighbor as oneself. To love God and to love others moves us from self-centeredness to selflessness.

Sacred Story Institute © 2019

Can you remember an experience in your life where you felt a real love of God or another person that let you feel the joy of selflessness? Remember it and write a single sentence below or in your journal. Can you remember a time when selflessly "loving your neighbor" who might have been very self-centered was difficult for you? Write this person or group down and write or speak aloud why it was or is hard for you to love them.

As you reflect, ask God for strength of heart to love others more selflessly as he loves them. God loves everyone, even if they disappoint me or are self-centered. That is a great truth Jesus taught us.

 Sacred Story Institute © 2019

Gospel of Mark Chapter Twelve
The Poor Widow's Contribution

He sat down opposite the treasury and observed how the crowd put money into the treasury. Many rich people put in large sums. A poor widow also came and put in two small coins worth a few cents.

Calling his disciples, he said to them, "Amen, I say to you, this poor widow put in more than all the other contributors to the treasury. For they have all contributed from their surplus wealth, but she, from her poverty, has contributed all she had, her whole livelihood."

Reflection:

Take a moment to think of those who have made the greatest selfless sacrifices in life for you. It might appear as if they have done almost nothing, but they have done a lot, haven't they?

Why did it look like no real selfless sacrifice was being made by this parent, mentor, or friend?

Can it be that your discernment process was not well established so you missed how deeply this person was sacrificing selflessly for you?

What is the greatest selfless sacrifice you have made in your life? Have others seen it? Has that sacrifice been invisible to them?

If you were to selflessly give up your whole livelihood like this woman, what would you put in that collection basket? Write it down in your journal.

SPIRITUAL AFFIRMATIONS

The Affirmations are thumbnail sketches in spiritual discernment inspired by St. Ignatius of Loyola. They can be a tremendous spiritual resource for your life. Most of them are lifted from St. Ignatius' Rules for the Discernment of Spirits; called Rules for Weeks One and Two in the *Spiritual Exercises*. Week One Rules are more appropriate for understanding how to discern the different spiritual signatures of God and "the enemy of human nature" (St. Ignatius' name for Satan) on the sensual level of life. Week Two Rules are designed to help with understanding the different spiritual signatures of God and the enemy of human nature at the spiritual level and in our intellect.

I have taken the substance of St. Ignatius' "Rules" for both Week One and Week Two of his *Spiritual Exercises* and translated Ignatius' discernment guidelines into affirmative statements. Learning their wisdom can provide hope and encouragement on your spiritual journey through this life to Christ's eternal kingdom. You can also avoid much suffering and grief as you learn the predictable ways evil manifests in your life history—your story—and learn to resist the spiritual assaults and deceptions that move you away from the pathway of light—of selflessness.

Because the Affirmations are so important and so beneficial to our spiritual journey, we examine each one and build a prayerful meditation around it to help individuals better understand its meaning for their own True Heart. The Affirmations were written for the book, *Forty Weeks: An Ignatian Path to Christ with Sacred Story Prayer*. Yet they are beneficial for any person of good will seeking to better understand the signals that point to the path of light and resist those that lead to the path of darkness.

In preparation for our Affirmations journey, I invite you to reflectively pray over one Affirmation each week and let its wisdom gradually sink into your mind and heart. All of them are valuable and important and each individual Affirmation will have specific significance at different points in your faith journey. The meaning and value of certain ones will strike your heart immediately while others may not make any sense at all. Don't worry! All of them will eventually make sense and their meaning will only deepen as your spiritual journey unfolds.

For pastoral events or retreats, use the Affirmations singly or in groups of two or three. They can be printed up and handed out for prayer and reflection exercises. In using them, invite those you are giving them to pay attention to those that speak to their hearts. Have them journal or ask God *why* they are meaningful for their own True Heart. St. Ignatius always wants us to ask God for the grace of understanding. So don't be shy! Tell the Lord: "this touches my heart - help me to understand why it is important for me in my life." Note too, the ones that make no sense at all on your first pray-through. Ask that God's Holy Spirit keep you open to the graced wisdom they can offer further down the road of your True Heart journey.

Lord Jesus, you promised to always be with each of us and with the Church until the end of the age. I pray that you keep me awake to the many helps you provide to me along the journey of life, especially the discernment wisdom in the Affirmations. May this series of spiritual lessons help me to open more fully to Your Creation, Presence, Memory, Mercy and Eternity alive in my heart.

The just rejoice and exult before God;
They are glad and rejoice.
Sing to God, chant praise to his name;
Whose name is the Lord.
(Psalm 68: 4-5)

MY TRUE HEART
TAKES A LIFETIME TO CREATE

It is a cliché to say that life is not over till it is over. I doubt anyone would disagree with this fact. Yet often ignored is the fact that we have to work daily on our spiritual growth. Or more precisely, we must work daily to open to the Artist who can transform our lives into a True Heart.

Think of your life as a work of art. The powerful image from Jeremiah 18 about the potter and the clay speaks to this: "…Indeed, like clay in the hand of the potter, so are you in my hand, house of Israel." In this passage, God reminds Israel that a potter can destroy a bad work of art and rebuild a new one from the original clay. While that might seem a bit harsh to contemplate, we can view the potter and clay image through the lens of Christ Jesus who has come to restore what was lost.

Christ can take our lives, daily undermined by the weight of bad decisions, selfishness, and our own sin and weakness, and transform all of it into blessing. God, in Jesus, is the artist and it will take a complete lifetime for the Lord to work His miracles of grace and selflessness in our True Heart. We will always be in need of the merciful forgiveness of the divine artist in Jesus. Once we see that Jesus needs to work daily in our lives, we understand why "my True Heart takes a lifetime to create."

Lord Jesus, you never tire of being our Savior and you never get discouraged with our failures and weaknesses. We give you thanks for your great patience with us and we pray that we allow you, daily, to create my True Heart by your love and grace so that we may praise you in Creation, Presence, Memory, Mercy and Eternity.

Teach us to number our days aright,
That we may gain wisdom of heart.
Return, O Lord! How long?
Have pity on your servants!
(Psalm 90: 12-13)

BE NOT AFRAID:
FEAR COMES FROM
THE ENEMY OF MY HUMAN NATURE

The phrases, "be not afraid" and "fear not" are two of the most common phrases in scripture. Fear enters human history after our fall from grace. We did not know fear in our state of original innocence. But we gave in to the temptation of "the knowledge of good and evil" and thus, much of our lives are now consumed by fear.

Instilling fear in our hearts is the principal role incarnate evil plays in our lives. The more we fear, the less we trust God. Evil even tricks us into being afraid of God, so we will not turn to God when our need is greatest. We fear God's judgment of us and so we remain isolated and consumed by grief.

We must constantly challenge the fear that rules our lives. We must awaken to the fact that fears just below the surface of consciousness are designed to manipulate our choices and decisions so that we avoid what can bring us hope and peace. We oftentimes do not recognize when we make or avoid choices due to fear. We must awaken to evil's strategy of using fear to manipulate us at every possible point in our lives. We must live in trust of God and be not afraid.

Always examine fears and the way they seek to manipulate you. The fear may be focused on giving up some sensual habit that undermines your human nature or a spiritual fear about approaching Confession. God is not the author of fear. Evil is the author of fear. Awaken to fear's destructive ways and be not afraid. Trust in the Lord always!

Lord Jesus, help us unmask the fears that control our hearts and keep us from the joy of more fully serving you. Teach us what we fear and teach us not to be afraid. We thank you for conquering the author of fear so that we may praise you in
Creation, Presence, Memory, Mercy and Eternity.

Have mercy on me, O God, in your goodness;
In the greatness of your compassion wipe out my offense.
Thoroughly wash me from my guilt
And of my sin cleanse me.
(Psalm 51: 1-2)

THE PATHWAY TO GOD'S PEACE AND HEALING RUNS THROUGH MY HEART'S BROKENNESS, SIN, FEAR, ANGER AND GRIEF

The human story is forever transformed when our first parents made the choice to turn their hearts from God. This sin, apart from ending our immortality, broke our hearts and robbed us of peace. The world of perfect relationship ended and the world of broken relationships began. When perfect relationship ends, the relationships our hearts were made to receive are opened to grief, shame, anger and death.

But God would not tolerate the destruction of His beautiful creation nor the beautiful creatures made in the Divine image. He inaugurates the grand rescue operation that culminates in the birth of the Messiah. The Lord Jesus enters into our broken world and into the chaos and darkness of the evil occasioned by our choice to reject God. Indeed, He bears the full weight of the destruction of the relational world and is consumed by it as He enters our experience of abandonment: "...And about three o'clock Jesus cried out in a loud voice, 'eli, eli, lema sabachthani?' Which means, 'my God, my God, why have you forsaken me?'" (Mt 27: 46).

If you want to be holy, you must allow the Divine Physician to enter into your sinfulness, brokenness, fear, anger and grief—all that relates to the imperfect, unbeautiful and shameful dimensions of your human story. It is the Divine Physician's intention to transform the ugliness of our sin and grief into blessings and peace. The Father transformed the scandal of the cross into our resurrection. Christ will transform the scandal and shame of our brokenness into our joy and our hope.

Lord Jesus, give us the courage to let you into the brokenness of our hearts and history. By your grace working in the wounds of our lives, we believe you will transform them into a true heart and in this we may praise you forever in
Creation, Presence, Memory, Mercy and Eternity.

He raises up the lowly from the dust;
From the dunghill he lifts up the poor
To seat them with princes,
With the princes of his own people.
Praise the Lord who lifts up the poor.
(Psalm 113: 7-8)

GOD RESOLVES ALL MY PROBLEMS
WITH TIME AND PATIENCE

The enemy of human nature is fond of using our impatience to generate great worry and anxiety. When we are worried and anxious, we turn our eyes away from the Lord. We focus almost exclusively on our problems, whether they are great or small. We forget all the times the Lord has rescued us in the past. We think, "why is this happening to me? Where is God?" The enemy's strategy, shrewdly implemented, is to keep us focused on the difficulty of any situation, seeing only its seeming hopelessness. This strategy keeps us from turning to the Lord who, in time, rescues us; always, always, always, rescues us!

When you find yourself getting tied up in knots over your problems, turn to God and praise the Lord for all the times you have been rescued in the past. Thank Christ Jesus, and tell him, "you are my Savior, you always help me. I trust you to help me resolve these problems. Please keep me patient as your grace works. Keep my heart focused on your love and fidelity. Lord, I thank you for the marvelous way you will resolve this present crisis. Thank you!"

Lord Jesus, you have been our refuge from one generation to the next.
You are faithful to your people and the church. You never leave us.
Make us turn to you in our trials
that we may praise you forever in
Creation, Presence, Memory, Mercy and Eternity.

Be still before the Lord; wait for him.
Wait a little, and the wicked will be no more;
Look for them and they will not be there.
But the poor will inherit the earth,
Will delight in great prosperity.
(Psalm 37: 7, 10-11)

I WILL HAVE DIFFICULTIES IN THIS LIFE

The grandfather of all modern self-help books is M. Scott Peck's *The Road Less Traveled*. It took five years to become a New York Times bestseller but once it did, it stayed on The List, often at #1, for 694 weeks, a record for The List. The opening line of the book is, "Life is difficult." Obviously, the message struck a chord with millions of people, and the message that self-discipline is required to tackle life's challenges did too. People, Peck once said, try to avoid difficulties and it only makes life more difficult.

It should be noted that the book also challenged the prevailing mood that life should not be difficult. We can often be upset that we have difficulties in life, but they are present nonetheless. We either choose to avoid them or deal with them. The original sin guaranteed that life would be difficult. Yet the advent of God's saving mission in Christ provides a super-guarantee that through those difficulties, grace and love will triumph.

We never face our difficulties alone. We have Christ, daily present to us in the power of the Holy Spirit and in the Eucharist. Both forms of "presence" bring us hope and comfort. He promised to stay with us "until the end of the age," and His promise is true (Mt 28: 20).

Lord Jesus, you endured all the pains and
difficulties of life to free us from the burden of sin.
Thank you for your gift of presence to us.
May we seek you often in the Eucharist and by helping our
brothers and sisters in distress,
so that one day we may all praise you in
Creation, Presence, Memory, Mercy and Eternity.

"Will the Lord reject us forever, never again show favor?
Has God's mercy ceased forever?
The promise to go unfulfilled for future ages?"
I will recall the deeds of the Lord; yes, recall your wonders of old.
I will ponder all your works; on your exploits I will meditate.
(Psalm 77: 7-8; 12-13)

THERE ARE JUST TWO WAYS TO COPE
WITH MY DIFFICULTIES
ONE LEADS TO LIFE, ONE TO DEATH
I WILL CHOOSE LIFE

The Lord's labor of love to rescue and redeem humanity begins by calling a people and giving them the code of our true human nature. The code of the Ten Commandments is a gift to help them discern truth from falsehood in all their relationships. Once given the law of true relationships, they are cautioned: *I have set before you life and death, the blessing and the curse. Choose life, then, that you and your descendants may live, by loving the Lord, your God, obeying his voice, and holding fast to him. For that will mean life for you, a long life for you to live on the land which the Lord swore to your ancestors, to Abraham, Isaac, and Jacob, to give to them.* (Dt 30: 19-20).

Life is difficult, as we all know. But knowing the right path to choose in the face of life's difficulties is often less complicated than we think. There may appear to be thousands of options, but in fact, there are only two options for each decision. We can choose life or death. We can choose love or retribution. We can choose forgiveness or hate. We can choose humility or pride. We can choose selflessness or selfishness. We can choose to turn towards God or to turn away. We can choose hope or despair.

We affirm that we have a choice in each and every decision. Let us always see the choices that lead to life and ask God for the grace to open to the light.

Lord Jesus, you have been our hope from one generation to the next. You never leave our side.
Strengthen us to always reject choices that lead to death and choose instead those that lead to life so
that each decision in my true heart opens to
Creation, Presence, Memory, Mercy and Eternity.

The Lord has made his salvation known:
In the sight of the nations he has revealed his justice.
He has remembered his kindness and his faithfulness
Toward the house of Israel.
(Psalm 98: 2-3)

"IMPOSSIBLE" IS NOT A WORD
IN GOD'S VOCABULARY

Throughout scripture, numerous stories testify to *this* truth: in the end, no obstacle can stand against God's mercy, truth, justice, peace and love. Sin, betrayal, deceit, treachery, imprisonment, slavery, captivity, injustice, barrenness, poverty, natural disasters, sickness and even death—nothing can prevent the love of God from reaching its fulfillment for our salvation.

When we pray the Rosary, we remember that with God, all things are possible: *Then the angel said to her, "do not be afraid, Mary, for you have found favor with God...for nothing will be impossible for God.* (Lk 1: 30-31, 37).

It is of vital importance that we hold fast to this biblical faith in God's power. We must remember that nothing is impossible for God, especially when we face those situations that appear from our perspective, unsolvable. I think this faith in God's triumphant love is why Pope Francis has such affection for "Mary, the untier of knots." God, working through Mary and many other parts of the body of Christ, does indeed untie all knots—no matter how twisted and tight!

Consciously bring your most "unsolvable and impossible" situations to God—all selfishness. Surrender them with absolute faith and confidence that God will help you. Activate your faith ahead of time and praise God's power and victory over these situations—your hope will increase and your spirits will be lifted up. Do not be afraid, for nothing is impossible for God!

Lord Jesus, you endured all the pains and difficulties of life to free us from the burden of sin. Thank you for your gift of presence to us. May we seek you often in the Eucharist, and recognize you in our distressed brothers and sisters, so that one day we may all praise you in Creation, Presence, Memory, Mercy and Eternity.

The Lord is your guardian; the Lord is your shade;
He is beside you at your right hand.
The sun shall not harm you by day, nor the moon by night.
(Psalm 121: 5-6)

Sacred Story Institute © 2019

TRUE HEART LEADS TO MY FREEDOM AND AUTHENTICITY, BUT DOES NOT ALWAYS MAKE ME FEEL HAPPY

Jesus told us that if we "remained in [His] word", we would be true disciples: *you will know the truth, and the truth will set you free.* (Jn 8:32). Each of us has had a faith-inspired experience of a truth that challenges previously held convictions. The new "true belief" or "true practice" that we have discovered brings freedom. But it can also bring discomfort because it upsets our established patterns.

Think of the call of Simon Peter (Lk 5:1-11). The fisherman "sees the truth" that Jesus is Lord in the incident of the miraculous catch of fish. But in this true vision, he also sees himself as he is: *depart from me Lord, for I am a sinful man.* Jesus brings Peter freedom to see rightly, which reveals his true lack of freedom.

Following Jesus to live a life as True Heart leads to my authenticity and freedom. But it might also bring discomfort as the light of Christ shines brightly on the places in my life history—my beliefs and practices—that need reform and change.

We must never confuse the true peace of following the Lord with the false peace or shallow happiness of clinging to beliefs and practices that, even though familiar, are not serving our true freedom. We must shoulder the discomfort of spiritual growth that brings us freedom and thank the Lord for calling us to live authentically and selflessly.

Lord Jesus, give us patience with our spiritual growth. Let us not be discouraged by the spiritual and emotional discomfort when you call us to grow in freedom and authenticity. Give us happiness and true peace as we grow into living our lives as a true heart. Gives us the true freedom that opens us to Creation, Presence, Memory, Mercy and Eternity.

The Lord confronts the evildoers, To destroy remembrance of them from the earth.
When the just cry out, the Lord hears them, And from all their distress he rescues them.
(Psalm 34: 16-17)

MY LIFE'S GREATEST TRAGEDIES
CAN BE TRANSFORMED INTO
MY LIFE'S MAJOR BLESSINGS

It is important to listen to the phrasing of this Affirmation. The "can" in "can be transformed" does not limit the *capability* of God. It indicates the possibility of transformation that relies on *my cooperation* with God's grace. There is nothing that God cannot transform. No tragedy, disaster or hopeless case is beyond God's power. But the "can" indicates that God needs my active faith and cooperation to work His miraculous transformations.

As difficult as it might be at the time of some personal misfortune or tragedy, we must have the presence of heart to turn to God and call upon His graces to bring light out of darkness. But we are invited to go even further than this. We should begin to thank God for the ways in which these events, that seem like "the end of the world," will be transformed to my benefit by the miraculous grace of God.

If we begin with the "sacrifice of praise" at the moment of some misfortune, we begin to activate our faith in the God for whom "nothing is impossible" (Lk 1:37). Our spirits can be lifted up, even in great misfortune, and we can be restored to a measure of interior peace and hope. Be not afraid: *I have told you this so that you might have peace in me. In the world you will have trouble, but take courage, I have conquered the world.* (Jn 16: 33).

Lord Jesus, I affirm that you are the Lord of life. All sickness, disasters, and misfortunes—yes even death itself—are transformed by your redeeming love. Give me the grace to open my heart to you, especially at times of great misfortune, so that you can work your miracles of grace in my life and the lives of those I love. May even the greatest misfortunes eventually be transformed into your Creation, Presence, Memory, Mercy and Eternity.

The Lord is faithful in all his words
And holy in all his works.
The Lord lifts up all who are falling
And raises up all who are bowed down.
(Psalm 145: 13,14)

TIMES OF PEACE AND HOPE
ALWAYS GIVE WAY
TO TIMES OF DIFFICULTY AND STRESS

Times of spiritual blessing and peace are to be savored. They should call forth from us joy in God's abundant goodness. We need to very consciously attend to the blessings we are receiving. We grow in faith when we make a point of thanking God for the blessings of hope, peace, joy, love, reconciliation, selflessness and whatever else we might be enjoying as *gifts* from the Lord.

When we are clothed by blessings and grace, we can hardly remember times of difficulty or pain. They are swept away by joy (Jn 16: 21). These times of abundant blessing and peace, although they point to our final destiny, are never permanent in this life. We do well to remember in times of blessing that all is a gift from God. We do well also in these moments to ask God for strength and fortitude for the next time of difficulty that lies in the future.

By honoring God in times of abundance and reminding ourselves to hold fast in times of future stress, we entrust our whole life to God. And we are ensuring that when misfortune again makes itself felt, we will not be undone by it. For we have already reminded ourselves that all is gift from God. It is this same God who will one day make that joy and peace permanent.

Lord Jesus, may we never fail to praise you in times of great joy, blessing and peace for it is you who are our anchor in this life. Keep our hearts anchored in you so that whether we experience joy or sorrow, we know you are our source and end—our
Creation, Presence, Memory, Mercy and Eternity.

My steps have been steadfast in your paths,
My feet have not faltered.
I call upon you, for you will answer me, o God;
Incline your ear to me; hear my word.
(Psalm 17: 5-6)

TIMES OF DIFFICULTY AND STRESS
ALWAYS GIVE WAY
TO TIMES OF PEACE AND HOPE

Anyone who has been sick with the flu or a severe cold knows how sickness diminishes one's perspective and limits it to the present misery. When we try to recall the feeling of health in the midst of our sickness, it seems completely foreign! Just as physical misery destroys our perspective, so does spiritual distress. When we suffer a loss of faith, hope and love, we can feel like life has ended—that it was never good and will never be good again!

The enemy of our human nature seeks to instill fear during these times of spiritual desolation. Jesus knows we will be susceptible to rash judgments and he wants us not to lose hope. So during these times of "spiritual desolation" we must consciously turn our hearts and minds to God. We must make an act of faith that grace, light, hope and peace will return and that God has not forgotten us. We must activate our spiritual energies and even though we don't feel hopeful, we must make a firm act of faith that hope, peace, and joy will return.

Lord Jesus, let us know that you walk beside us in times of trial and temptation. When our hope has fled, be our stronghold. Make us turn our hearts to you and give us the conviction that you will give us a future of hope and peace. Even though we may feel a loss of faith, hope and love, let us remember that you have never allowed us to be tested beyond our strength. May we turn our hearts to you in all our troubles, you who are our
Creation, Presence, Memory, Mercy and Eternity.

"Be still and know that I am God!
I am exalted among the nations, exalted on the earth."
The Lord of hosts is with us;
Our stronghold is the God of Jacob.
(Psalm 46: 10-11)

I WILL NOT TIRE OF ASKING GOD FOR HELP
SINCE GOD DELIGHTS IN MY ASKING

The first Sunday Angelus address of Pope Francis was delivered to the people of Rome on March 17, 2013. It was the Lenten season and the Pope was speaking about God and forgiveness. He said:

"Let us not forget this word: God never tires of forgiving us, never! 'So, father, what is the problem?' Well, the problem is that we get tired, we don't want to, we get tired of asking forgiveness. Let us never get tired. Let us never get tired."

The Lord never tires of us asking for forgiveness. We have emphasized this truth in a different Affirmation. But it is not limited to forgiveness - the Lord never tires of us asking for help, no matter what the need is!

At times, I am amazed at how often I forget to ask God for help. Yet when I do, God always, always, always helps. Many times the Lord helps me in unexpected ways, but it is always better than what I had expected.

Why do we fail to ask for God's help? Sometimes, we may think that others' problems are much more pressing than ours and we don't want to "bother God". This is a very common thought, but I suspect that this excuse is a form of false humility. At other times, we may be angry with God for the difficulties we face. This anger blocks us from requesting God's help. Still other times, we may feel hopeless - as if nothing will be able to help us. We give up hope and so do not ask for help.

No matter what excuses we use, we must resist our false humility, our anger and our loss of hope and always, always, always ask God to help us. God delights in helping us and His heart goes out to us in our need. Daily ask God for help and begin thanking God daily for hearing your prayer, and for the wonderful fidelity He will display in coming to your rescue.

Lord Jesus, may we always ask for your help and so more fully experience your love in Creation, Presence, Memory, Mercy and Eternity.

I rejoiced because they said to me,
"we will go up to the house of the Lord."
And now we have set foot
Within your gates, O Jerusalem.
(Psalm 122: 1-2)

THE URGE TO STOP
TRUE HEART PRACTICE
ALWAYS COMES BEFORE
MY GREATEST BREAKTHROUGHS

Early in his conversion, St. Ignatius was confronted with two distinct *discouragement temptations* that he recorded in his autobiography. One was wondering how he could keep to a path of Christian living for the remainder of his life. The other was disgust for his overly zealous religious practices that were exhausting him.

The first discouragement was linked to the panic of giving up his former vices; the second discouragement was linked to his pride in light of his inability to master his sinfulness by only his own effort. The first was a temptation linked to sensual sin and the second was a temptation linked to spiritual sin.

As your own conversion deepens, you will confront similar discouragements. Some will be inspired by the fear of surrendering past pleasures, others will be linked to anger and frustrations at how slowly you find change happening in your life.

Both temptations are "designed" by the enemy of human nature to turn you away from God and the practice of your faith. Be on the lookout for such temptations and resist them! The fact you have them are clear signs that you are on the right track, and by God's grace, are achieving significant spiritual growth.

Lord Jesus, keep us alert to the temptations of discouragement used by human nature's enemy.
Give us the grace to hold fast by your grace to the practice of prayer and spiritual disciplines.
May our fidelity in times of temptation and discouragement lead us to you in
Creation, Presence, Memory, Mercy and Eternity.

Pray for the peace of Jerusalem!
May those who love you prosper!
May peace be within your walls,
Prosperity in your buildings.
(Psalm 122: 6-7)

GOD GIVES ME INSIGHTS,
NOT BECAUSE I AM BETTER THAN OTHERS,
BUT BECAUSE I AM LOVED

Those engaged actively in their spiritual growth frequently experience graced insights of understanding and wisdom that move them forward in holiness. Some of these insights are profound. Yet we must not allow these gifts to cause pride. God helps us along the way because God loves us and because we need it, not because we are better than others. Be ever watchful for spiritual pride. It is the greatest threat to our spiritual growth!

And remember, if you want to be holy, be prepared not to feel holy. The more our authentic holiness grows, the more aware we become of our fragility and sinful nature. It is just one of the rules of the Christian spiritual life.

Lord Jesus, keep us grateful for the graces of the Father. May we not confuse these loving gifts as signs that we have achieved holiness but rather recognize them as aids in our path toward holiness. Keep pride far from our hearts so that in all things we remain open to you, in Creation, Presence, Memory, Mercy and Eternity.

May his name be blessed forever;
As long as the sun his name shall remain.
In him shall all the tribes of the earth be blessed;
All the nations shall proclaim his happiness.
Justice shall flourish in his time,
and fullness of peace forever.
(Psalm 72: 17)

THE INSIGHTS AND GRACES I NEED
TO MOVE FORWARD IN LIFE'S JOURNEY
UNFOLD AT THE RIGHT TIME

The last words of Jesus in Matthew's gospel always bring me great joy: *Go, therefore and make disciples of all nations, baptizing them in the name of the father, and of the son, and of the holy spirit, teaching them to observe all that I have commanded you. And behold, I am with you always, until the end of the age.* (Mt 28: 19-20.)

Each of us must learn as we advance in our spiritual lives that the Lord never leaves us orphans. We learn, gradually and not without anxiety, that the Lord always gives us what we need, and at just the time we need it. Learning to trust the Lord and to resist doubt is part of the purifying fires that burn away our self-centeredness. We must also learn, as we are called to make disciples of all nations, that the Lord will give us the resources we need for the task.

I remember a story of Mother Theresa of Calcutta on one of her visits in the United States. A Catholic non-profit organization was strapped for cash and told mother about their problems. She asked them who their patron was and they said St. Joseph. She asked them if they had requested his help and they said, "no." On her inspiration and embarrassed they had so little faith, they prayed to St. Joseph and the money they needed was donated the next day. The Lord watches out for us in our personal lives and in all our apostolic works. His grace and blessings will always come through.

Lord Jesus, may we always take the necessary spiritual risks. May we learn to trust
that you will provide the grace and support we need at each step of the way.
Move us beyond our complacency and always come to our aid so we can praise you in
Creation, Presence, Memory, Mercy and Eternity.

The Lord God keeps faith forever,
Secures justice for the oppressed,
Gives food to the hungry.
The Lord sets captives free.
(Psalm 146: 6-7)

MY PERSONAL ENGAGEMENT WITH TRUE HEART ACCOMPLISHES, THROUGH CHRIST, A WORK OF ETERNAL SIGNIFICANCE

In 1985, the American pop artist Andy Warhol said: "In the future, everyone will be world-famous for 15 minutes." Of course, the pop artist was speaking about the disposability of modern life and the ease of capturing the world's attention for short-lived fame.

How different is the focus in scripture where in 1 John 2:17 we hear: "Yet the world and its enticement are passing away. But whoever does the will of God remains forever." It is easy to lose sight of the truth that our holy actions—love, forgiveness, charity, kindness, patience, long-suffering and self-sacrifice, apparently so unimportant to the world, are the only actions that will endure to eternity.

Taking time to pray daily and open our hearts to God can feel like a waste of time and appear insignificant in the face of all the pressures and responsibilities of life. Yet when we open to Christ daily in prayer to receive the grace to align our thoughts, words and deeds with Christ, we will "produce results" that endure to eternity.

We must recover a sense of this holy *delayed gratification* and realize our true treasure lies in the world to come. When we work for fruit that endures, we will be eternally famous in the Kingdom of the Father and eternally cherished by Christ Jesus our brother and Lord.

Lord Jesus, help us to judge wisely the things of this earth and to place our hope
in the true gifts of the Kingdom to come so we can praise you in
Creation, Presence, Memory, Mercy and Eternity.

The Lord's are the earth and its fullness;
The world and those who dwell in it.
For he founded it upon the seas
And established it upon the rivers.
Let the Lord enter; he is king of glory.
(Psalm 24: 1-2)

INSPIRATIONS CAN HAVE A DIVINE OR A DEMONIC SOURCE I PRAY FOR THE GRACE TO REMEMBER HOW TO DISCERN ONE FROM THE OTHER

All of us are familiar with the cartoon image of a person with an angel on one shoulder and a devil on the other. Each "spirit" is whispering into the person's ear, and presumably with a different message for the individual in question.

The work of spiritual discernment (and it *is* work) calls us to awaken to the two different types of inspiration and notice the directions in which they lead. Those whisperings are not periodic but constant, each seeking to influence our thoughts, words and deeds—one for life and one for death.

This Affirmation invites us to "remember" how to discern one from the other. We say "remember" because God has placed the truth in our hearts: *For this command which I am giving you today is not too wondrous or remote for you. It is not in the heavens, that you should say, "who will go up to the heavens to get it for us and tell us of it, that we may do it?" Nor is it across the sea, that you should say, "who will cross the sea to get it for us and tell us of it, that we may do it?" No, it is something very near to you, in your mouth and in your heart, to do it.* (Dt. 30: 11-14)

Therefore, learning right from wrong is a process of prayerful remembering, for God has placed in our hearts the truth we need to follow to find life and hope.

Lord Jesus, give us the presence of mind and heart to cultivate a deep remembering of your love in our hearts. May your grace help us to learn discernment so that in everything we may praise you in Creation, Presence, Memory, Mercy and Eternity.

Behold, thus is the man blessed who fears the Lord.
The Lord bless you from Zion:
May you see the prosperity of Jerusalem
All the days of your life.
(Psalm 128: 4-5)

CHRIST, WHO HAS WALKED BEFORE ME, SHARES MY EVERY BURDEN

Suffering, whether it is spiritual, psychological or physical is intensified when the one who suffers feels alone, as if no one else understands what they are experiencing. This terrible sense of isolation is the result of sin's fracturing of relationship.

The divine creator knew the terrible suffering that would result if the beloved children divided their hearts and broke relationship with God. Fully anticipating this devastation, the enemy of human nature soothed with deceptive assurances: *You certainly will not die! God knows well that when you eat of it your eyes will be opened and you will be like gods, who know good and evil.* (Gn 3: 4-5).

God responds to the cataclysm of sin's suffering and loneliness by fully entering into the suffering created by our own rejection of God's love. The one "for whom and through whom" all creation was made, in an act of supreme love and humility, choose to be born as one of us and to take on the full cost of our sin.

The Lord Jesus wanted us to know, even in the depths of our suffering, that love has come to rescue us and His sacred heart fully understands what we endure. He does not want us to ever feel alone in our suffering, for He is by our side.

Lord Jesus, no matter what we suffer in our lives, give us the presence of mind and heart to always invite you in to our hearts and ask for your help. You know the full depth of our suffering - give us the knowledge of the gift of your love, that we may praise you in
Creation, Presence, Memory, Mercy and Eternity.

For he shall rescue the poor when he cries out,
And the afflicted when he has no one to help him.
He shall have pity for the lowly and the poor;
The lives of the poor he shall save.
(Psalm 72: 12-13)

CHRIST, WHO HAS WALKED BEFORE ME, WILL HELP ME RESOLVE EVERY CRISIS

The visitation to Mary proclaims God's power to bring about the new heavens and the new earth. The angel Gabriel announces to the world at the fullness of time that the miraculous power of God is coming into the world. The heart of the announcement is this: "For nothing will be impossible for God." (Lk 1: 37)

We must remember at all times that no matter what happens, and no matter how impossible the problems we face, that promise: "nothing will be impossible for God." Christ has promised to resolve all problems by His power and grace and by our patience. We must nurture our faith and give Christ the room to work miracles. Our belief in God's power strengthens us and gives us hope. Faith is a verb and we need to thank God in Christ for the amazing ways He saves us, the church and the world.

Begin again your habit of praise today because Christ, who has walked before all of us, will resolve every crisis to the glory of His Father.

Lord Jesus Christ, we praise you, for you have done wonderful things. Thank you for being our savior and walking ahead of us. Thank you for your promise that for you, nothing will be impossible. Please deepen our faith in your promise so that in everything we may praise you in Creation, Presence, Memory, Mercy and Eternity.

The God of glory thunders,
And in his temple all say, "glory!"
The Lord is enthroned above the flood;
The Lord is enthroned as king forever.
(Psalm 29: 9-10)

CHRIST, WHO HAS WALKED BEFORE ME, KNOWS MY EVERY HOPE

The Lord Jesus knows all our hopes because He is the source of those hopes. He will bring them to pass. Whenever we think that love is not possible, that we will never contribute anything of value to the world, that our time and our luck has run out - whenever we succumb to this darkness, we must find that spark of hope deep in our hearts and realize that God will be faithful. God *will* be faithful and our hope is not in vain. For Christ who has walked before me, knows my every hope, and will bring them to pass in ways unimaginable.

St Therese of Lisieux wrote that the very fact that we have holy desires means that God intends to fulfill them. In other words, God has placed those holy desires in our hearts and they will come to pass because of God's power. This simple message has always deeply moved me and given me hope when I am tempted to doubt. This assurance awakens me to the falsehood of my fears and to the truth of God's promise to save, to bind up, to bring about for all of us a new heaven and a new earth.

Lord Jesus Christ, you are the source and the ultimate object of our hope. Thank you for guaranteeing that our hearts desires will be fulfilled by you. Thank you for being our savior. Let us always hold fast to hope and in this we will find you always in
Creation, Presence, Memory, Mercy and Eternity.

I have waited, waited for the Lord,
And he stooped toward me and heard my cry.
And he put a new song into my mouth,
A hymn to our God.
(Psalm 40: 2)

CHRIST, WHO HAS WALKED BEFORE ME, KNOWS EVERYTHING I SUFFER

During the cold war, an American Jesuit named Walter Ciszek was captured by the Soviets and charged as a spy. He suffered for years in solitary confinement. They interrogated him night and day until after four years, he broke down and signed a confession that he was guilty.

Fiercely proud, he had built his identity on not signing the confession. When he finally broke, he was devastated and filled with darkness and despair. He slowly began to consider Christ in Gethsemane and his own aloneness and abandonment. Suddenly, Fr. Ciszek felt comforted and realized that Christ understood his suffering.

There is no human suffering that Christ has not personally tasted. We experience great abandonment in those moments when it seems no one can understand our own unique circumstances and pain. Yet, Christ was born, lived and died so that we would never be alone again—so that we would be forgiven and one day find life eternal with him. Christ has walked before us so that we would know that in all things, He understands our grief, suffering and pain, and even in these, is close to our hearts.

Lord Jesus Christ, out of love for us, you have taken on all the suffering of the world. You have done this willingly, so that we would be freed from all that separates us from you. Thank you for undergoing death so that we can have life. Help us to know that there is nothing in heaven or on earth; nothing above or below; no principality or power that can ever separate us from your love. Be our Creation, Presence, Memory, Mercy and Eternity.

The Lord is my light and my salvation;
Whom should I fear?
The Lord is my life's refuge;
Of whom should I be afraid?
(Psalm 27: 1)

CHRIST, WHO WALKS BEFORE ME,
WILL ALWAYS LEAD ME HOME TO SAFETY

An Affirmation is something declared to be true; a positive statement or judgment. It is not an opinion. When we affirm "Christ who walks before me will always lead me home to safety," that is a fact—a guarantee.

A close friend of mine, Wanda Spasowski, told me a story. Wanda was the wife of the Polish ambassador to the United States under both Presidents Kennedy and Reagan. At a very difficult time in her life, she felt overwhelmed by all the events happening in her marriage and in the Polish nation. She was at the breaking point.

Wanda had a deep faith and had been through many other trials. She reached out to Christ through the intercession of Our Lady of Czestochowa, patroness of Poland. She was able to get through the crisis and know that the Lord was always by her side.

Wanda's experience is the same as mine. Never in my life have I been denied help and assistance from the Lord. No matter the trial or crisis; things always end up better than I could have ever possibly hoped for, according to the Lord's timing.

I take great comfort in this truth: that Christ, who suffered everything that we do, knows what we can and cannot endure. He will always rescue us when we call to Him. He is faithful and suffered, died and rose again so we would have faith in His care. He wants us to reach out to Him in every crisis and always have faith in His power to rescue us. He died so we could find our way home.

Lord Jesus Christ, you walked the way of life and suffering before us so we would know we are never alone. We affirm our faith in you that you will rescue us in every crisis and difficulty and will always lead us home to safety. Increase our faith in you so that in all things, we may hope in your Creation, Presence, Memory, Mercy and Eternity.

Lift up, O gates, your lintels;
Reach up, you ancient portals,
That the king of glory may come in!
(Psalm 24: 7)

I WILL STRIVE TO CURB TEMPTATIONS
TO REACT TO PEOPLE AND EVENTS

In the foreword to *Sacred Story: An Ignatian Examen for the Third Millennium,* Jesuit priest George Aschenbrenner wrote:

"The most dangerous issue confronting our culture is to learn to deal with violent sudden and explosive impulses. Though we can unhealthily try to squelch these strong feelings, such violent explosives simmer in all our hearts and flail out often beyond our control. Without realizing such explosive power resides within us or without an ability to control such eruptions, we all face disaster.

Learning to control these violent impulses is the greatest challenge facing our families, our culture and our world. Facing, learning and helping to control these activities can be the most important issue for the examen. In years gone by, often children learned from parents and family how to deal with these attacks. But so much of our family structure has now fallen apart – and all of us are now available to deadly disaster.

The Ignatian *Examen* can provide a faithful human education for simmering emotions, unreflective thoughts and explosive impulses. This is the deep-seated heart of Ignatian examen. Never automatic, it requires gutsy work and tough decisions if we are to avoid the deadly disaster that faces us all."[4]

Lord Jesus Christ, help us to curb our temptations to react to persons and events.
Give us the grace to control our tongues and to guard our hearts so we can
grow in faith, hope and love so live more fully your
Creation, Presence, Memory, Mercy and Eternity.

Light shines through the darkness for the upright; He is gracious and merciful and just.
Well for the man who is gracious and lends, Who conducts his affairs with justice.
(Psalm 112: 4-5)

---

[4] William M. Watson, SJ, *Sacred Story: An Ignatian Examen for the Third Millennium* (Seattle: Sacred Story Press, 2012), xxviii-xxix.

I WILL ASK MYSELF WHAT CAUSES MY ANGER AND IRRITATION AT PEOPLE AND EVENTS

Filmmaker Alfred Hitchcock was famous for developing the aerial shot to give dramatic perspective to a movie scene. This camera angle is often called a "bird's eye view." When you find yourself in the grip of the anger and irritations of daily life, consider rising up to get an aerial shot of your situation. Move out of the heat of the moment. Rise above and step outside yourself to see the situation that is causing your displeasure and resentment with a "bird's eye" perspective.

Stepping outside our aggressive moods takes presence of mind and heart. We are so used to just "feeling" the anger and irritations that we must make a decision to remove ourselves from the passion of the moment and watch ourselves dispassionately.

When you step outside the scene of the moment of passion, you can then ask yourself what is causing you to be upset, angry and irritated. The very act of removing yourself from the scene to watch it "from above" will have the effect of diffusing the emotions so that you can ask for God's grace to enlighten the "eyes of your mind" as to the cause of your anger and irritation. Bring God into the conversation so you can seek the grace of enlightenment.

Try it! You will be amazed by what you discover and how this simple "Affirmation" put into practice will help you advance in your selfless True Heart journey. Appropriately enough, another name for the cinematic angle of "bird's eye view" is "God's eye view"!

Lord Jesus Christ, your gaze is compassion and love. Help us to step outside ourselves when we are angry and irritated so that we can be enlightened by your grace to understand our negative moods.
Help us to stop and ask your help so that each day we can open more to
Creation, Presence, Memory, Mercy and Eternity.

Instruct me, o Lord, in the way of your statutes,
That I may exactly observe them.
Give me discernment, that I may observe your law
And keep it with all my heart.
(Psalm 119: 33-34)

I WILL SEEK TO IDENTIFY THE
SOURCE OF MY ANGER AND IRRITATION

Thomas Merton identifies anger as one of the two capital sins that are the most difficult to purge and control. To complicate matters, many people can also be disconnected from the sources of what makes them angry or lustful.

A different Affirmation encourages one to turn to Christ and ask for enlightenment as to the immediate cause of a particular anger one experiences in the present moment. This Affirmation asks one to seek the original causes, where they exist, of present anger that can be triggered by the undetected and unresolved original wounds in our lives.

This process of spiritual and emotional excavation is something that takes time. It can only be accomplished by God's grace working in union with our openness to that grace. We must never tire of asking God to help us remember the sources of these original events so that we can better "avoid the near occasions" of the sins they prompt.

Yet we know that God will do the hard work we can't do ourselves. The impact of original sin in our lives is something we will never eliminate but with God's help, we can move toward greater and greater understanding and freedom. God is the one who turns our life into a selfless True Heart.

Lord Jesus Christ, you are present to us at each moment of our lives and see our entire history. Help us, with your grace to unlock the history of sin and darkness in our history so we can grow in freedom and peacefulness. Give us the grace of forgiveness so that in all our thoughts,
word and deeds we can open to your
Creation, Presence, Memory, Mercy and Eternity.

As far as the east is from the west,
So far has he put our transgressions from us.
As a father has compassion on his children,
So the Lord has compassion on those who fear him.
(Psalm 103: 12-13)

I WILL GIVE THANKS FOR WHAT ANGERS AND UPSETS ME FOR IDENTIFYING THEIR SOURCE WILL HELP TO SET ME FREE

Other Affirmations address the issue of identifying the angers (and lusts) in our lives to minimize their destructive influence. This Affirmation invites you to see the angers and upsets that you experience as opportunities for grace and healing.

We humans are gifted with sense perceptions that are physical, spiritual and emotional. We automatically pull away from hot objects because we know they will burn us. Spiritually, we can become sensitive to inspirations from sources of light and darkness. From this we learn which to avoid and which to welcome.

We can also take our most difficult emotions such as anger, and use them as moments of self-understanding and healing. The things that make us angry can provide valuable information about what frightens, hurts or damages us. Paying attention to the emotion when it erupts and thanking God for the "emotional perception" it provides, can help you unlock its secrets.

Here is one way to go about this process. First, distance yourself from the immediate emotional reaction by turning to God and thanking God for the gift of your emotional self-awareness. Second, ask God for the grace to understand the origin of the angers so that you can better see the outlines of your life story. Third, ask for deep healing and forgiveness. This forgiveness is both for those individuals you need to forgive, and individuals whose forgiveness you need to seek when your various angers have become destructive instead of instructive.

Lord Jesus Christ, thank you for the gift of emotional self-awareness. For even those things that anger us can open our hearts to your grace and deepen our self-understanding. Help us always turn to you in our anger and thank you for the ways you transform them into moments of healing and peace,
so that in all things we can live
Creation, Presence, Memory, Mercy and Eternity.

With God is my safety and my glory, He is the rock of my strength; my refuge is in God.
Trust in him at all times, O my people! Pour out your hearts before him.
(Psalm 62: 7-8)

I WILL STRIVE TO
LISTEN, WATCH AND PRAY;
LISTEN, WATCH AND PRAY.
I WILL LISTEN, WATCH AND PRAY!

I believe Jesus' request for the disciples to stay awake in Gethsemane, to "watch and pray," and St. Paul's exhortation to the Romans to "wake from sleep" are spiritually linked.

"So you could not keep watch with me for one hour? Watch and pray that you may not undergo the test The spirit is willing, but the flesh is weak." (Mt 26: 40-41)
You know the time; it is the hour now for you to awake from sleep. For our salvation is nearer now than when we first believed. (Rm 13: 11)

Jesus invites His disciples to stay awake to "see" their salvation being accomplished in His surrender to the Father's will. He wants the disciples to stay awake and watch so they will have an example to imitate in their own lives.

Despite its importance, it can be very difficult to "stay awake." Sin and the burdens of life can weary us and cause us to fall asleep. It is hard for us to "see" our lives truthfully and this is why we need to surrender our burdened hearts to God.

St. Paul, therefore, exhorts the Romans to awake from sleep so that they can see the nearness of salvation. St. Ignatius' daily examen (which we pray as *True Heart prayer*) is a call to "wake up." Ignatius wants us to see our lives, the world, and the Lord Jesus with clear eyes. We are invited daily to listen, watch and pray. In our simple daily prayer, we can respond to the exhortation of Christ, echoed by Paul, that we may be more fully awake!

Lord Jesus Christ, give me a persevering spirit so that I can always listen to your voice, watch your example and pray for your help. Help me always to listen, watch and pray so that I can fully awaken to Creation, Presence, Memory, Mercy and Eternity.

Give me back the joy of your salvation,
And a willing spirit sustain in me.
O Lord, open my lips, And my mouth shall proclaim your praise.
(Psalm 51: 12, 15)

EVERYONE HAS BEEN MORTALLY WOUNDED SPIRITUALLY, PSYCHOLOGICALLY, AND PHYSICALLY BY ORIGINAL SIN AND THE LOSS OF PARADISE

We do well to reflect often on God's gifts. God gifted us "originally" with immortality. We were created to share everlastingly in God's love, the love of each other and the amazing cosmos God fashioned. How we could have turned from God and rejected the gift is captured in the phrase: *the mystery of iniquity*.

The spiritual choice to turn away from God's pure love to the love of self is what we call the original sin. The gift of immortality was replaced by the "new normal:" fractured consciousness, broken hearts, violence, murder, depression, disease and death.

The perfect relationship between body, mind and spirit was made possible by our free choice to be fully united with God. When we turned away, all that made us immortal was fatally destabilized. This Affirmation states that we have all been mortally wounded—spiritually, psychologically and physically. We can reflect on the perfect relationship between these three integral dimensions of the human person as the locus of this mortal wound. For sin ultimately destroys relationships. Sin attacks the heart of God's gift—perfect relationship and perfect love.

Only God, in Christ, can restore what was lost. And so, in love, Christ enters into the history of the world's brokenness to undo what was undone. We must admit the full truth of what was lost if we are to ever fully turn to the source of our salvation.

Lord Jesus Christ, help me to know and honestly admit my brokenness and the loss
of my original immortality so that I can turn to you with all my heart
and awaken anew through your love and grace to
Creation, Presence, Memory, Mercy and Eternity.

Instruct me, O Lord, in the way of your statutes,
That I may exactly observe them.
Give me discernment, that I may observe your law and keep it with all my heart.
(Psalm 119: 33-34)

62 Sacred Story Institute © 2019

JOURNEYING WITH CHRIST TO THE ROOTS OF MY SINS AND ADDICTIONS WILL HELP BREAK THEIR GRIP

This Affirmation continues the good news of the Divine Physician's healing graces in our lives. It can be customary for each of us to avoid a conscious awareness of our own sins and addictions. We fear them, or they embarrass us, or they make us feel powerless or pained or hopeless.

Whatever the reasons we might avoid these parts of our lives, we need to allow Christ the divine physician to enter them with His light and healing graces.

Ignoring the darkness within does not make it go away: quite the contrary. Avoiding our darkness only gives it more control, eroding our hope and intensifying fear, embarrassment, powerlessness and pain.

If the original sin was the act of us turning away from God, the way back to God is to look honestly at our sin, with Christ by our side as divine healer and savior of souls. We are not to fear: "There is no fear in love, but perfect love drives out fear because fear has to do with punishment, and so one who fears is not yet perfect in love" (1 Jn 4:18).

Lord Jesus Christ, enter my darkness and powerlessness and help me untangle the sin
and addiction in my life. I know with you by my side that I have nothing to fear,
for in your love and mercy I can open to
Creation, Presence, Memory, Mercy and Eternity.

Come, let us bow down in worship;
Let us kneel before the Lord who made us.
For he is our God,
And we are the people he shepherds, the flock he guides.
(Psalm 95: 6-7)

I WILL NOT WASTE TIME WORRYING
ABOUT MY SINS AND FAILURES

To grow in faith requires us to put on the mind of Christ when contemplating our sins and failures. First, to "put on Christ" entails that I admit my sin, for to deny it is to "call God a liar" (1 Jn 1: 8-10). Second, to "put on Christ" requires that I have hope and faith in Him to heal me and forgive me.

When we constantly fret and worry over our sins and failures, we move away from faith in God. We need to confront this damaging and fruitless type of worry because it destroys our hope and only serves the enemy of our human nature.

We could use humor and remind ourselves that "guilt is the gift that keeps on giving." Constant guilt is a form of worry that reveals less a "holy conscience" and more a self-centeredness and effort at self-salvation. Although it is rarely conscious, when we constantly feel guilty, we act as though this suffering from guilt is all the penance we need. It is a tragic, twisted pride that enslaves us.

Lord Jesus Christ let me have the honesty to know my sin and the maturity of faith to trust you completely as my hope and my salvation. Break any and all patterns of worry and guilt that block my faith in you so that I can open each day to
Creation, Presence, Memory, Mercy and Eternity.

The Lord is my shepherd; I shall not want.
In verdant pastures he gives me repose;
Beside restful waters he leads me;
He refreshes my soul.
(Psalm 23: 1-2)

I WILL USE MY TIME WISELY AND ASK GOD TO HELP ME UNDERSTAND THE SOURCE OF MY SINS AND FAILINGS

Other Affirmations suggest how we must resist obsessive worry about our sins and failings. The Lord's desire is always to help us, not scold us. When we imagine Christ as a harsh schoolmaster, we have not understood His mission or the mercy He comes to lavish on those who have been devastated by sin's effects… and we waste precious time!

We must instead work with the Lord who wants to help us grow. We must remember that He is infinitely patient with our failings and weaknesses. All Christ wants is for us to keep trying, to not lose hope and not waste time fretting!

When we allow our faith to mature, we realize that Christ is our fortress and our rock. We must use our time to speak to Christ from our hearts and ask His help to grow in understanding and freedom.

We cooperate with Christ who is mercy and graciousness when we ask Him to help us in this process of freedom. He will hear our prayers and help us along the way. Jesus is not the cop in the rearview mirror! Jesus is the captain of our hearts and the one who died for us so that we can have life, and have it abundantly! (Jn 10:10).

Lord Jesus Christ, let me use all of my time asking for your help to understand my life. You are the only one who can unlock the mysteries of my heart. I affirm you are loving and forgiving and want to help me grow in freedom. Let me believe this more deeply each day,
so that all my time is well-spent opening to you in
Creation, Presence, Memory, Mercy and Eternity.

If you, O Lord, mark iniquities, Lord, who can stand?
But with you is forgiveness, that you may be revered.
For with the Lord is kindness and with him is plenteous redemption;
And he will redeem Israel from all their iniquities.
(Psalm 130: 3-4, 7-8)

I WILL TRUST THAT CHRIST CAME TO HEAL ALL MY WOUNDS

Merriam-Webster defines "trust" this way: assured reliance on the character, ability, strength, or truth of someone or something. When we say that we trust that Christ can heal my wounds, it means that we have assurance that He has the strength and the ability to do so!

When we say that Christ has come to heal "all" my wounds, we mean the spiritual, physical, and emotional wounds of our lives. It is our spiritual wounds that are the most important because they are the root of all other wounds. Remember in the scripture how Jesus confounded the scribes with the case of the paralytic: *He said: "which is easier, to say, 'your sins are forgiven,' or to say, 'rise and walk'? But that you may know that the son of man has authority on earth to forgive sins"—he then said to the paralytic, "rise, pick up your stretcher, and go home."* (Mt 9: 5).

We may want the Lord Jesus to only heal our physical or emotional ailments, but He came for a much greater healing—our full spiritual renewal in Him so that we can once again share eternal life. He is indeed, the Divine Physician. Christ is also the "firstborn of all creation" and the "firstborn from the dead" (Col 1: 15, 18).

Lord Jesus Christ, I believe, help my unbelief! Let me trust more fully in your healing love and never be afraid to surrender my sins in thoughts, words and deeds to you for healing. I affirm that you have the power to heal me and that because of your passion, death and resurrection, I can rise with you to new life. Increase my trust so that I can live with you in
Creation, Presence, Memory, Mercy and Eternity.

They divide my garments among them,
And for my vesture they cast lots.
But you, O Lord, be not far from me;
O my help, hasten to aid me.
(Psalm 22: 18-19)

I ALONE CONTROL CHRIST'S ABILITY
TO TRANSFORM MY LIFE INTO A TRUE HEART

It is a fact that love is only possible if it can be freely rejected. Without the freedom to reject love, every relationship would be one of slavery. But since we are made in God's image and likeness, the freedom to love (or not) is our very birthright.

It is vital to remember this freedom. Ultimately the choice is ours, whether we will allow Christ to transform us from selfishness to selflessness—into a true heart. Christ will never force us to accept Him in our hearts. Not to invite Love into our lives is sure death, but it is up to us to decide. Because we are made in Love's image and likeness, we will never be happy apart from a relationship with God but we have the freedom to say "no" to it. As St. Augustine said in the Confessions: "O Lord our hearts are restless until they rest in thee."

We also have the freedom to make that "no" definitive. We know this is possible because Jesus said that to willfully sin against the Spirit is a sin that cannot be forgiven (Mk 3: 28-29; Mt 12: 30-32). Sin can be "unforgivable" only because we have the freedom to reject the Spirit. This willful hardening of one's heart was something that Jesus noticed not in the tax collectors and sinners but in the religious leaders—the scribes and the Pharisees. Their hardness of heart manifested itself in their frightening assertion that the mighty works of Jesus came from Satan (Mt 12:22-32).

Let us affirm that we hold the power over what happens in our lives and that we have the power to allow Christ to enter our hearts and by His grace, turn all sadness, darkness, sin and death into life— True Heart. Let us daily say "yes" to Christ so that in all things we can participate with Him in Creation, Presence, Memory, Mercy and Eternity.

*The stone which the builders rejected
Has become the cornerstone.
By the Lord has this been done;
It is wonderful in our eyes.
(Psalm 118: 22-23)*

Sacred Story Institute © 2019

THE PROCESS FOR CHRIST TO TRANSFORM MY LIFE INTO TRUE HEART BEGINS WHEN I ASK FOR THE GRACE TO HONESTLY NAME MY SINS AND ADDICTIONS

Opening our hearts to Christ is a choice only we can make. Christ wants us to open to His love as our creator who now recreates us as our healer, forgiver, redeemer and savior. This means we must bring to Him those parts of our lives that need healing. These are the things from which only He can save us—our sins and sinful addictions—and death!

We must be ever-vigilant in this mission of opening to Christ. We must resist the fear that keeps us from honestly naming sin and addiction for what they are: sources of death and slavery. Yet we must not be afraid of our sins and addictions. Christ Jesus is not afraid of them nor does He take offense at those who honestly turn to Him for healing. He honors our courage by forgiving and strengthening us.

The Sunday after Easter has been very appropriately named Divine Mercy Sunday. The death and resurrection of Christ has unleashed upon the world the healing graces that can and will bring about the new heavens and the new earth (Is 65: 17; Rev 21: 1). Let us take courage and bring our sins and addictions to the Divine Physician who died so we might "have life and have it more abundantly" (Jn 10: 10).

Lord Jesus Christ, with you by my side, give me the courage and grace to honestly look at my sins and addictions. Help me not to be afraid, for fear comes only from the enemy of my human nature. You love me and only want to heal me. Be my divine physician and flood your mercy in all my wounds so that in you I can be restored in Creation, Presence, Memory, Mercy and Eternity.

"The right hand of the Lord has struck with power; the right hand of the Lord is exalted. I shall not die, but live, and declare the works of the Lord."
(Psalm 118: 16-17)

THE PROCESS OF CHRIST
TRANSFORMING ME INTO A TRUE HEART
CONTINUES WHEN I INVITE HIM
TO ILLUMINATE MY SELFISHNESS

It is one thing to ask God for the grace to honestly name my sins and addictions. It takes even greater courage to ask that my concealed narcissistic pride be unmasked. Narcissism is incredibly deadly because it makes me both god and center of the universe (Gn 3:5). Ignatius struggled mightily with this narcissism. As he discovered, it infects even the religiously pious and those who aspire to holiness. For evil most effectively conceals itself in a mantle of righteousness.

Narcissism is always about a refusal to worship the one God and instead to worship oneself—it is selfishness. Outside of a faith context, self-centeredness can manifest in the obsession over a temporal good (power, beauty, wealth, prestige, etc.). This form of narcissism can also tempt the religious person! But a person of faith is more likely to be tempted to self-salvation. Narcissism manifests by efforts to fulfill the law "perfectly" - therefore eliminating the need to rely on God as savior and redeemer.

Whatever form our self-centered narcissism takes in my life, it must be "revealed" to me by the God who knows my true heart and who seeks to free me from the pride that this "original sin" wrought in human history. I must ask God to show me the very specific way I seek to be my own god and how I need to repent and open myself to my true heart and the true God!

Lord Jesus Christ, I affirm that you and you alone are Lord of my life and of the world. You are the firstborn of creation and the firstborn from the dead. Only you are God. Every knee will one day bend to you as Lord and savior of all (Phil 2:10). Grant me the courage to ask for a gracious and compassionate illumination of my narcissism, so that I can find my way to you in Creation, Presence, Memory, Mercy and Eternity.

Therefore my heart is glad and my soul rejoices, My body, too, abides in confidence;
Because you will not abandon my soul to the netherworld,
Nor will you suffer your faithful one to undergo corruption.
(Psalm 16: 9-10)

Sacred Story Institute © 2019

ONLY GOD'S GRACE AND MERCY
CAN CREATE MY TRUE HEART

We come to this Affirmations with one final admission. We have a profound temptation to make ourselves god. The reason we do this is because it takes humility to admit we cannot save ourselves. It takes a lifetime of courage to daily face the fact that we need the Lord as savior and redeemer. This means that daily we must take up our cross and follow the Lord. This is Good News! Listen again to the words from Luke's gospel:

Then he said to all, "if anyone wishes to come after me, he must deny himself and take up his cross daily and follow me. For whoever wishes to save his life will lose it, but whoever loses his life for my sake will save it. What profit is there for one to gain the whole world yet lose or forfeit himself?" (Lk 9:23-25)

We cannot be holy apart from God. Holiness consists of daily admitting my need of a savior and turning to the true savior of the world—the TRUE HEART.

In this turning to God, I admit my weakness and self-centeredness. Weakness is the cross I must daily carry to stay in communion with Christ and His mission of reconciliation for the world. And self-centeredness is the issue I need help overcoming so that I can admit my weakness. There is a freedom in this because when I learn that I cannot save myself, this is the moment when I fully turn to the one who wants to carry me to new life. There are a number of sayings that capture this reality: "Let God;" or "Let Go and Let God;" or "Let God be God!"

Jesus is the Good Shepherd who seeks out what is lost and brings us home. I do not have to climb the mountain of the Lord alone. I don't have to save myself! God, in Christ, will create my True Heart!

Lord Jesus Christ, you are mercy, you are the TRUE HEART of the universe. In you I place all my fears, all my sins and all my failings. I affirm that it is you who will create my True Heart. Help me turn to you daily and unburden myself from seeking my own salvation. In all things, be for me Creation, Presence, Memory, Mercy and Eternity.

You spread the table before me in the sight of my foes; You anoint my head with oil; my cup overflows. Only goodness and kindness follow me all the days of my life; And I shall dwell in the house of the Lord for years to come.
(Psalm 23: 5-6)

SAINT IGNATIUS CONVERSION EXERCISE

St Ignatius Chapel, Seattle University

St. Ignatius' Autobiography is his personal testament of how God transformed a self-centered person into a selfless servant of Jesus Christ. He resisted writing it for years and close to his death, allowed Gonçalves da Camera, his house minister, to write the story as Ignatius dictated it to him.

The first two years of Ignatius' conversion process compromise a significant portion of this rather short work. For *Forty Weeks ~ An Ignatian Path to Christ with Sacred Story Prayer*, we included a longer three-part re-telling of these first two years of his conversion.

We discovered that people find hearing about Ignatius' sinful past and seeing how God worked with that "sinner" to transform him into one of the greatest saints in the world brings tremendous hope to those who feel "beyond redemption." As the saying goes, every saint has a past and every sinner a future. So often we view saints as perfect people on holy cards. They seem unrelatable to our own lives and present unattainable goals for us "regular" people.

Dorthey Day, the founder of The Catholic Worker said once when a bystander said she was a saint: "Don't dismiss me so easily." What she meant is that the bystander was excluding their responsibility for seeking their own holiness before God.

St. Ignatius himself said close to his own death that he did not think there had been in the history of the Church one who had sinned so much and also who had been given so many graces.

We included the longer version of St. Ignatius' story in our version of *Forty Weeks For Prisoners*. It has given so much hope to those who are incarcerated and whose lives are marked by violence, darkness and hopelessness.

This is a shortened and simplified version of St. Ignatius' story for both *True Heart* and *True Heart Practices*. Helping us with this process was Mr. Doug Schutte, former director of Campus Ministry and theology instructor at O'Dea Catholic High School in Seattle, along with a group of his upper-class student faith leaders. They slowly prayed through the longer story and helped us simplify it for a young adult audience.

This two-part exercise can be used in multiple ways, in various settings: as a stand-alone exercise or accompanying other exercises in this book. Consider for example how a weekend or day-long retreat might incorporate this exercise with the two autobiographical exercises in Chapter 11. You could have your group pray with St. Ignatius' story and do the Reflection Questions for Journaling Exercises each of the two parts presents.

The Philippine Jesuits released a movie of St. Ignatius's early story. It is called: St. Ignatius: Solider - Sinner - Saint. If you are using this particular exercise, you might consider combining it with this movie.

You could then do one or both of the autobiographical exercise on self-centeredness and selflessness as a way for individuals you are working with to move from Ignatius' story to their own developing life story. As the autobiographical exercises present, conclude with having the individuals in the group write out a life-plan for prayer, spiritual development (sacraments, daily and weekly Mass and Reconciliation) to resist a life of self-centeredness and embrace one of selflessness.

St. Ignatius' Story Part One: A Life Upended

St Ignatius Chapel, Seattle University

A Self-Centered Person

Until his thirtieth year, Ignatius Loyola was unconscious of the sacredness of his life. Instead, he was sincerely devoted to life's pleasures and vanities. He was a gambling addict, sexually self-indulgent, arrogant, hotheaded and insecure. In short, he was very self-centered and narcissistic.

By our contemporary measures, Ignatius' family was dysfunctional. Was Ignatius a possible candidate for sainthood? It did not look promising. But God does not judge by human standards. It is in God's mercy to pursue all who have fallen asleep through sin, addiction and selfishness. God judges the heart. With unbounded grace and patient mercy, God reaches into the ruins that sin causes and makes of our hearts true and transforms our lives into *Sacred Stories*.

Ignatius, with all his narcissism, psychological problems and sinful vices, was awakened by God's great love. A failed military campaign that left him with a shattered leg forced him into a lengthy convalescence back at Loyola castle, his family home. Ignatius' time of recuperation provided an opportunity for Christ to shine a light on much more serious and life-threatening wounds that were spiritual, emotional and psychological in nature.

These more serious wounds were gradually evolved from a destructive, sinful narcissism. Contributing to his problems were the facts that Ignatius' mother died when he was an infant and his father died when he was sixteen and his family had a history of infidelity and violent behavior. Even his brother who was a Catholic priest had five children. Human families and the family of the Church have always had problems.

For thirty years Ignatius' narcissism had rendered him unconscious to his true human nature and oblivious to his life as *a True Heart*. The pleasures he indulged in and the power he wielded functioned like a narcotic to numb the pain of his hidden spiritual and psychological wounds. His sinful vices and self-indulgent pleasures blinded him to his authentic human nature. Yet God saw his life could be fruitful if Ignatius awakened to his conscience.

God's grace reached into the sinful and chaotic heart of Ignatius' life and awakened in him a desire for innocence. His long-buried aspirations for living authentically suddenly became his prime motivation. He noticed it first while recovering from his wounds at Loyola. He became aware of new desires and a different energy while he daydreamed in reading stories of Christ and the saints. Pondering the saints' lives he imagined himself living a different, selfless life.

He compared these new daydreams to his former vain, narcissistic daydreams. The old daydreams drew energy from a life of sin, addiction and vice. The new daydreams of selfless generosity produced their own very different energy. Ignatius noticed a significant difference between the two sets of daydreams and the energies they created in his heart. The vain fantasies entertained him when he was thinking about them. But he noticed that when he set them aside, he felt him empty and unsatisfied.

The new holy daydreams also entertained him when he was thinking about them. Yet when he set these aside, he remained content and felt an enduring calm and quiet joy. By paying close attention to the different moods these two energies created in his heart, and discerning their difference, Ignatius discovered and popularized spiritual discernment and created a system of spiritual disciplines that transformed his life and the history of Christian spirituality. Here is his discovery in a graphic chart:

Hearing the Voice of Conscience

Ignatius discovered that the new, selfless aspirations were influenced by Divine inspirations. He further discovered that these inspirations reflected his true human nature. He discovered too that the vain fantasies deadened his conscience. His narcissistic daydreams led him away from enduring peace because they masked his true heart. The old daydreams and fantasies were powerful, ego-affirming, and familiar but ultimately left him empty and unsatisfied.

Ignatius was awakened to the emotional wisdom and spiritual truth of his new daydreams. He became aware of the significant damage that his old lifestyle had done to both himself and others. What had been awakened in him was the divine gift of conscience. With an awakened conscience, Ignatius experienced profound regret and sorrow for having wasted so much of his life on self-indulgent pleasures and fantasies—seductions that could never bring him lasting peace and satisfaction. He began to understand that living in pleasure and fantasy destroyed his True Heart and silenced his deepest desires.

Divine inspiration inspired Ignatius to seek forgiveness for wasting his life and his innocence. Grace enabled Ignatius to take responsibility for his sins against God and his True Heart. Divine inspiration provided Ignatius with the desire, energy, and courage to renounce the thoughts, words, and deeds of his sinful habits. Grace, received through the Sacrament of Reconciliation, heightened Ignatius' consciousness and enabled him to imagine a new path for his life and new ways to express his gifts and talents.

As usually happens when people respond to the grace of conversion, Ignatius' new aspirations confused and disconcerted many of his closest family members and friends. Nonetheless, he acted on these aspirations. Ignatius was now able to understand a path to God, a *pattern of conversion* to his true heart that countless thousands would imitate.

REFLECTION QUESTIONS FOR JOURNALING EXERCISES

--What would this kind of conversion feel like to you, now, in the third millennium?

--Have you felt grace before? When? Describe that feeling and that incident in your journal.

--Have you felt something very passionately that confused the people close to you? As you look back on it, was that feeling something you regret now? Was it something you realize has helped form you into who you are?

--Explore that incident and that feeling and maybe let it be your journal entry tonight.

--In light of St. Ignatius's story, briefly describe one pattern of self-centeredness and one pattern of selflessness that you note in yourself.

St Ignatius' Story Part Two:
A Journey to a Selfless True Heart

St Ignatius at Montserrat, Evie Hone Artist (Manresa Retreat, Dublin)

Ignatius in Control

Ignatius' decisive and enduring commitment to his conversion launched him directly into the center of his heart's brokenness and the pride masking those wounds. After leaving home Ignatius traveled to Montserrat and spent three days reviewing his life. It was at this time that he made a general confession of all his past sinful deeds. In this written confession Ignatius consciously detailed his sinful attitudes, behaviors and passions: gambling addiction, sexual self-indulgence, arrogance, and violent outbursts of temper. It took all three days to write the story of his past life.

But Ignatius started to confess and re-confess past sins multiple times, never feeling he had gotten to the bottom of his immoral deeds. This excruciating spiritual and psychological torment lasted for months. He was so anguished by his obsessive guilt that numerous times he wanted to commit suicide by throwing himself off the cliff where he prayed.

Finally, exhausted and disgusted with his efforts, he realized he intensely despised the spiritual life he was living. Ignatius had an urgent and compelling desire to "stop it!" Reflecting on the temptation to walk away from his new Christian life, Ignatius received an insight that the burdensome, destructive habit of re-confessing past sins was rooted in pride to try and save himself. This pride forced him to his knees. On seeing this he "awoke as if from a dream," and was given the grace to stop the habit. It is here that Ignatius admits his powerlessness to save himself and surrenders control of his life to God—he becomes selfless. This opposite of pride is selflessness.

This traumatic crisis taught Ignatius a most vital lesson about counter-inspirations. The willpower and resolute commitment to live virtuously for the rest of his life could be manipulated and turned against him by means of subtle *inspirations*. What seemed like a holy, pious, and noble practice—a serious approach to confession—evolved into a damaging habit that made him loathe his spiritual life, and in frustration, *inspired* him to abandon it. He learned that the counter-inspirations of the enemy of his human nature could act like "an angel of light." These inspirations appear holy but when followed, they end in disaster, turning one from God and toward a self-centered pride to stay in control your life.

God led Ignatius through this distorted evolution back to the lost innocence of his true human nature—his true heart of selflessness. To get there Ignatius had to confront his pattern of spiritual and psychological distortions signified by his self-centered pride. It was a mighty castle that he had built on the shifting sands of a child's wounded innocence, on a child's lonely, broken heart. God provided Ignatius the inspiration and grace to allow that castle to crumble. The shattering of his powerful defenses and the unmasking of his self-centered, narcissistic pattern proved to be the tipping point of Ignatius' entire conversion process. Ignatius' conversion from his anti-story of selfishness and his full awakening to his selfless *True Heart* was not a single event but rather a gradual process. His full evolution from a vain egomaniac to a selfless saint took the rest of his life.

A proud, dissolute, insecure, self-centered narcissist finally found peace and contentment in God's full love, acceptance, mercy, and forgiveness. Interestingly enough, this happened in and through Ignatius' sinful, self-centered pride and perhaps even because of them! What marred his early life became the very source of his strength and sanctity—his *True Heart*. Ignatius discovered, like St. Paul, that in his weaknesses and sin, he was strong in Christ (2 Cor 12:10). The same conversion from self-centeredness to selflessness awaits us all.

CLOSING REFLECTION/JOURNAL EXERCISE FOR SAINT IGNATIUS' STORY

Recall the two parts of St. Ignatius' *True Heart* narrative.

1) What spontaneously evoked *anxiety* in me about my own self-centeredness as I listened to St. Ignatius' story? I will reflect on <u>why</u> my anxiety was provoked and the particular type of self-centeredness I discovered. In my notebook, I will record what evoked my anxiety and why.

2) What spontaneously evoked *inspiration* and hope in me about my own selflessness as I listened to Ignatius' conversion story? I will reflect on <u>why</u> I was inspired or hopeful and the particular type of selflessness I discovered. In my notebook, I will record what inspired me and why.

3). "Like Ignatius, have I discovered the one area of my life that convinces me, <u>beyond any doubt</u>, that I cannot save myself, and must rely on God to save me is_____."

GUIDED GOSPEL MEDITATIONS

The Spiritual Exercises of St. Ignatius comprise four weeks of disciplines that help one making them draw close to Christ and one's own interior, spiritual world. We adapted the structure of St. Ignatius' Gospel contemplations for the 10-week *True Heart* program. One meditation was placed as the final exercise of each of the weeks that was thematically linked to the content of that week of the journey.

A fair number of the meditations close with what St. Ignatius called a Colloquy. That is a fancy word for a "conversation." The colloquies are a powerful way for people of any age to learn how to dialogue with the Blessed Mother, Jesus and the Father in words from the heart. This is how the Lord wants us to communicate with him and all our heavenly intercessors—from the heart.

The colloquy structure also encourages the spiritual exercise of "asking" for the graces we need in our lives, but specifically in each meditation for unique graces linked to the exercise at hand. We must get in the habit of asking God for help. It lets us know what we need by voicing it aloud and it increases our humility by letting us in on the secret truth that we need God's graces...because we can't save ourselves.

For *True Heart Practices*, we have pulled all ten meditations and placed them contiguously in this section so they can be used individually. They can be applied for the many different pastoral situations in any ministerial context. Youth and young adult ministries will be able to print and give them to people to do on their own, in groups on retreats or evening exercises. They can also be presented as a guided meditation where the leader reads the text and has the group do the mediation by listening to it and "contemplating" on the theme.

You might want to try different ways of applying it in this guided format. Consider having your group do the guided meditation before the Blessed Sacrament. You slowly read the various sections and then allow time for individuals to do a short journal entry after each section. You might want to consider playing instrumental music during the times people are contemplating. Or you could do the whole meditation with musical interludes and then have folks write a journal entry at the end of the whole exercise.

You might even want to consider having a single meditation be a whole evening, morning or afternoon exercise. Extend the length of time for each of the five parts of the meditations and conclude with journaling and sharing of graces at the end of each section. Take a break between sharings and do the next section and so forth.

Let us know other ways you are able to adapt the exercises by sharing with us on our Sacred Story Institute FACEBOOK page for TRUE HEART PRACTICES. You can find there an online community of leaders to help us build out a "best practices" for this resource.

ALONE WITH JESUS

Jesus Goes Up Alone on a Mountain to Pray—James Tissot (1836-1902) Brooklyn Museum

Do only one section at a time. Do not read ahead but stay with each section until you feel inclined to move on. Spend 15-45 minutes on this meditation

I. Let yourself be mindful of the presence of Christ Jesus in the Blessed Sacrament. Spend a minute or two to get in a position of prayer that allows you to relax but at the same time stay alert. As you repose in this way, ask God to keep you open to your own life and God's love for the whole retreat. As a way of asking for this grace of openness, pray the Triple Colloquy below. Stay with this as long as you are able to remain engaged in this prayer. Move ahead as your heart suggests. Rest with Jesus as his disciples might have at the end of a day of ministry and preaching.

II. "Now it was about this time that he (Jesus) went out into the hills to pray: and he spent the whole night in prayer to God." (Lk. 6:12)

Imagine the kind of place Jesus went to so he could be alone. Spend some time to create in your own imagination the location as you envision it. Pay attention to all things: the color of the evening sky and stars, the rocks and vegetation, the trees and the views from the hills, what the evening air felt like. Place yourself in the scene at a distance from Jesus so he cannot detect your presence. Move on when your heart suggests.

III. After a while, imagine Jesus notices you alone in that place. Watch as he approaches you and see him sit quietly next to you. He knows you are beginning a journey and after a while, he asks you why you have decided to come. What do you say to him as asks you this? Spend some time telling him your hopes and fears. You know he understands what you are saying and the depth of your desires and concerns. The two of you just sit quietly in each other's presence. Stay here for as long as you like. Before you leave the place, ask him for the grace to stay open to what he wants for you to receive from the retreat.

IV. As you walk down the hill, go back to your room slowly praying the words of the Our Father.

First Colloquy, or conversation, will be with Mary. Speak with Mary, using your own words, asking her to obtain from her Son the grace of selflessness to be open to the Spirit working inside you. When you finish this conversation, pray the Hail Mary slowly, thinking of the words and the person to whom you are praying.

Second Colloquy, or conversation, will be with Jesus. Speak directly to Jesus, asking him to request his Father for the same graces as above. When you finish your conversation, pray the Anima Christi slowly, thinking of the words and the person to whom you are praying.

Soul of Christ, sanctify me. Body of Christ, save me. Blood of Christ, fill me. Water from the side of Christ wash me. Passion of Christ, strengthen me. O Good Jesus, hear me. Within thy wounds, hide me. Permit me not to be separated from thee. From the wicked foe, defend me. At the hour of my death, call me, and bid me come to thee that with thy saints I may praise thee forever and ever. Amen.

Third Colloquy, or conversation, will be with God the Father. Ask the Father directly in your own words to give you the graces as described above. When you finish, pray the Our Father, thinking of the words and the person to whom you are praying.

TEMPTATION IN THE WILDERNESS

Temptation in the Wilderness by John St. John Long, 2814 Photo ©Tate
https://www.tate.org.uk/art/artworks/long-the-temptation-in-the-wilderness-t04169

Do only one section at a time. Do not read ahead but stay with each section until you feel inclined to move on. Spend 15-45 minutes on this meditation

I. Gather in what your senses are experiencing. Breathe in the Spirit of God. Breathe out whatever is troubling, distracting, or burdensome. Be aware of all the thoughts and feelings coming from the day so far.

II. Talk to Jesus in your own words about your desire for this particular grace: "that I may come to know and believe God the Father as the source of my greatest freedom in being selfless and that I may come to understand more clearly the source of my greatest un-freedom in being self-centered. Stay with this for as long as you like. Don't feel compelled to move on unless your heart suggests.

III. Imagine yourself accompanying Jesus away from the Jordan River, out into the wilderness. This is the first time you have decided to go away, apart from your family and friends. This is your first attempt to spend such a lengthy time in prayer and silence with your God. You are both filled with the Holy Spirit -- yet it is not long before you are faced with the insidious seduction of the spirit of evil and darkness. See and experience the events as they happen. Notice everything about what is happening to Jesus and yourself. Do not move to the next section unless your heart suggests.

Open your Bible and enter the scene of the story in Luke 4: 1-13 See, feel, touch, and smell everything about the story because Scripture is a "living word."

IV. ASK THE LORD FOR HIS STRENGTH AND GUIDANCE in facing the temptations and the ways your spirit is not free to be a True Heart. Specifically for the:

THE BREAD which represents the material possessions and comforts that you feel you need for status and security;

THE POWER of independence, self-sufficiency and pride which keep you, not God, as the center of your life, for not realizing your need for God as the source of your freedom and life;

THE VANITY of self-centeredness which subtly manipulates or exploits others;

ASK THE LORD FOR HIS HELP in letting go of what binds you; of what keeps you trapped in self-centeredness, from freely loving others, from freely giving your heart to God, and from freely being your truest self.

V. Bring your own prayer period to a close by praying the Triple Colloquy of St. Ignatius for this particular meditation.

TRIPLE COLLOQUY OF SAINT IGNATIUS

First Colloquy, or conversation, will be with Mary. Speak with Mary, using your own words, asking her to obtain from her Son the grace to surrender comfort, self-sufficiency and self-centeredness and to be open to the Spirit working inside you. When you finish this conversation, pray the Hail Mary slowly, thinking of the words and the person to whom you are praying.

Second Colloquy, or conversation, will be with Jesus. Speak directly to Jesus, asking him to request his Father for the same graces as above. When you finish your conversation, pray the Anima Christi slowly, thinking of the words and the person to whom you are praying.

Soul of Christ, sanctify me. Body of Christ, save me. Blood of Christ, fill me. Water from the side of Christ wash me. Passion of Christ, strengthen me. O Good Jesus, hear me. Within thy wounds, hide me. Permit me not to be separated from thee. From the wicked foe, defend me. At the hour of my death, call me, and bid me come to thee that with thy saints I may praise thee forever and ever. Amen.

Third Colloquy, or conversation, will be with God the Father. Ask the Father directly in your own words to give you the graces as described above. When you finish, pray the Our Father, thinking of the words and the person to whom you are praying.

JESUS ACCUSED OF BEING THE DEVIL

Christ and the Pharisees by Ernst Karl Zimmermann

Do only one section at a time. Do not read ahead but stay with each section until you feel inclined to move on. Spend 15-45 minutes on this meditation.

I. Begin this meditation by asking Jesus to be with you. Ask Jesus to give you the graces he feels will be best for you during this time of the night vigil and this time of training. Specifically, ask for the grace to know how the religious leaders of Jesus' day could have mistaken him and his message as satanic. Pray to understand how the values of Jesus can be seen as evil and hateful in our own time. Use the *Triple Colloquy* below to ask for these graces.

II. Open your Bible to the twelfth chapter of Matthew, verses twenty-two to thirty-two. Before you read, plan to read it slowly so you can visualize the scenes as they really happened; only place yourself in the scene to see and feel the profound tensions between Jesus and the religious leaders. Notice all the details of the people, the smells, the sounds, etc. Keep aware of all the thoughts and feelings you had entering this meditation; only now let yourself be distracted by the events as they unfold before you.

Watch Jesus perform his act of curing the possessed man, restoring his sight and hearing. How does the crowd react? How does the man cured thank Jesus? Why are the religious leaders so angered by Jesus' act of mercy? What are the tensions you feel in the crowd between Jesus, his followers and those denouncing him? How do the leaders react when Jesus speaks to them about blasphemy against the Holy Spirit?

III. Pay attention to your reaction to the events that have unfolded before you. See the man leave the presence of Jesus. Walk up to Jesus from your place in the crowd. You are present before Jesus so no one else in the crowd can hear you. Speak to Jesus about what you have just seen and heard. What do you say? What does he say? What invitation does he extend to you?

IV. Ask Jesus if there is anything you have confused as evil or hateful that is actually holy and good. Tell him why you are confused. What does he tell you? What do you say in return? What is Jesus' response? Stop and listen. What are you thinking and feeling?

V. Conclude your prayer with the Triple Colloquy of St. Ignatius.

TRIPLE COLLOQUY OF SAINT IGNATIUS

First Colloquy, or conversation, will be with Mary. Speak with Mary, using your own words asking her to obtain from her Son the grace to follow her Son selflessly in every act and decision of your life. When you finish this conversation, pray the *Hail Mary* slowly, thinking of the words and the person to whom you are praying.

Second Colloquy, or conversation, will be with Jesus. Speak directly to Jesus, asking him to request his Father for the same graces as above, i.e., that you may selflessly follow Jesus. When you finish your conversation, pray the *Anima Christi* slowly, thinking of the words and the person to whom you are praying.

> *Soul of Christ, sanctify me. Body of Christ, save me.*
> *Blood of Christ, fill me. Water from*
> *the side of Christ wash me.*
> *Passion of Christ, strengthen me.*
> *O Good Jesus, hear me.*
> *Within thy wounds, hide me. Permit me*
> *not to be separated from thee.*
> *From the wicked foe, defend me.*
> *At the hour of my death, call me,*
> *and bid me come to thee that with thy saints*
> *I may praise thee forever and ever. Amen.*

Third Colloquy, or conversation, will be with God the Father. Ask the Father directly in your own words to give you the graces so you may selflessly follow His Son. When you finish, pray the *Our Father,* thinking of the words and the person to whom you are praying.

PEACE, BE STILL

Peace, Be Still by Arnold Frieberg

Be open to all thoughts, feelings, and ideas you have coming from the day. Spend some time talking with God about the things you think significant. Stay here as long as you are comfortable. **Be Alone.**

I. Begin this meditation by asking Jesus to be with you. Ask Jesus to give you the graces he feels will be best for you during this time of the night vigil and this time of training. Specifically, ask for the grace to know the good you desire and how you can be tempted to believe that Jesus is not working in your or love you when you feel your weakness and sinfulness. Pray for the grace to know why you can feel bad when God is actually energizing your conscience to know your True Heart. Use the *Triple Colloquy* below to ask for these graces.

II. Open your Bible to the fifth chapter of Luke, verses one to eleven. Before you read, plan to read it slowly so you can visualize the scenes as they really happened; only place yourself on the boat as one of the disciples. Notice all the details of the people, the smells, the sounds, etc. Keep aware of all the thoughts and feelings you had entering this meditation; only now let yourself be distracted by the events as they unfold before you.

* What is Peter's dilemma? Can you sense what he may be feeling as he speaks to Jesus and asks him to leave him? What is Jesus' response? What does Jesus offer him? Speak to Peter after he is invited by Jesus to be a fisher of people. What is his joy or confusion? What does he say?

III. Pay attention to your reaction to the events that have unfolded before you. See the man leave the presence of Jesus. Walk up to Jesus from your place in the crowd. You are present before Jesus so no one else in the crowd can hear you. Speak to Jesus about what you have just seen and heard. What do you say? What does he say?

IV. Ask Jesus if there is anything in your own life that would prevent you from being a disciple of his. Ask Jesus about any particular things in your own life that cause you shame and make you think Jesus could not or does not love you. What do you say? What is Jesus' response? Stop and listen. What are you thinking and feeling?

V. Pray: *Take, Lord, and receive all my liberty, my memory, my understanding, and my entire will; all that I have and possess. You have given all to me. To you, Lord, I return it. Everything is yours; dispose of it according to your will. Give me only your love and your grace. That is enough for me. Amen!*

TRIPLE COLLOQUY OF SAINT IGNATIUS

First Colloquy, or conversation, will be with Mary. Speak with Mary, using your own words asking her to obtain from her Son the grace to follow her Son selflessly in every act and decision of your life. When you finish this conversation, pray the *Hail Mary* slowly, thinking of the words and the person to whom you are praying.

Second Colloquy, or conversation, will be with Jesus. Speak directly to Jesus, asking him to request his Father for the same graces as above, i.e., that you may follow Jesus selflessly. When you finish your conversation, pray the *Anima Christi* slowly, thinking of the words and the person to whom you are praying.

Soul of Christ, sanctify me. Body of Christ, save me. Blood of Christ, fill me. Water from the side of Christ wash me. Passion of Christ, strengthen me. O Good Jesus, hear me. Within thy wounds, hide me. Permit me not to be separated from thee. From the wicked foe, defend me. At the hour of my death, call me, and bid me come to thee that with thy saints I may praise thee forever and ever. Amen.

Third Colloquy, or conversation, will be with God the Father. Ask the Father directly in your own words to give you the graces so you may selflessly follow His Son. When you finish, pray the *Our Father,* thinking of the words and the person to whom you are praying.

THE RICH YOUNG MAN

Artist Unknown

Be open to all thoughts, feelings, and ideas you have coming from the day. Spend some time talking with God about the things you think significant. Stay here as long as you are comfortable. ***Be Alone.***

I. Begin this meditation by asking Jesus to be with you. Ask Jesus to give you the graces he feels will be best for you during this time of the retreat and this time of prayer. Specifically, ask for the grace to know the good you desire and how you can be tempted to choose the kinds of things in life that don't bring you peace and happiness. Use the *Triple Colloquy* on the back to ask for these graces.

II. Open your Bible to the tenth chapter of Mark, verses seventeen through thirty-one. Before you read, plan to read it slowly so you can visualize the scenes as they really happened; only place yourself in the crowd. Notice all the details of the people, the smells, the sounds, etc. Keep aware of all the thoughts and feelings you had entering this meditation; only now let yourself be distracted by the events as they unfold before you.

What is the dilemma of this person? Can you sense what he may be feeling as he speaks to Jesus and asks him the questions he does? What is the man really looking for? Why does he leave so sad? Stop the man and ask him what he is thinking and feeling as he leaves Jesus. What does he say?

III. Pay attention to your reaction to the events that have unfolded before you. See the man leave the presence of Jesus. Walk up to Jesus from your place in the crowd. You are present before Jesus so no one else in the crowd can hear you. Speak to Jesus about what you have just seen and heard. What do you say? What does he say?

IV. Ask Jesus what specific type of self-centeredness in your own life would prevent you from being a disciple of his. Ask Jesus about any particular type of self-centeredness in your own life that you think may cause you to walk away sad from him like the person you just witnessed. What do you say? What is Jesus' response? Stop and listen. What are you thinking and feeling?

V. Pray the Triple Colloquy of St. Ignatius when you are done with the meditation.

TRIPLE COLLOQUY OF SAINT IGNATIUS

First Colloquy, or conversation, will be with Mary. Speak with Mary, using your own words asking her to obtain from her Son <u>the grace to follow her Son selflessly in every act and decision of your life</u>. When you finish this conversation, pray the *Hail Mary* slowly, thinking of the words and the person to whom you are praying.

Second Colloquy, or conversation, will be with Jesus. Speak directly to Jesus, asking him to request his Father for the same graces as above, i.e., that you may follow Jesus. When you finish your conversation, pray the *Anima Christi* slowly, thinking of the words and the person to whom you are praying.

Soul of Christ, sanctify me. Body of Christ, save me. Blood of Christ, fill me. Water from the side of Christ wash me. Passion of Christ, strengthen me. O Good Jesus, hear me. Within thy wounds, hide me. Permit me not to be separated from thee. From the wicked foe, defend me. At the hour of my death, call me, and bid me come to thee that with thy saints I may praise thee forever and ever. Amen.

Third Colloquy, or conversation, will be with God the Father. Ask the Father directly in your own words to give you the graces so you may follow His Son. When you finish, pray the *Our Father,* thinking of the words and the person to whom you are praying.

THE LOST SON AND THE DUTIFUL SON

Le Retour du fils prodigue, Michael Martin Drolling (Wikimedia Commons)

Spend fifteen to forty-five minutes on this meditation. Do only one section at a time and do not read ahead. Do not feel compelled to finish the whole sheet. Stay with each section until your heart suggests moving on. **Be Alone.**

I. Gather in what your senses are experiencing. Breathe in the Spirit of God. Breathe out whatever is troubling, distracting, or burdensome. Be aware of all the thoughts and feelings coming from the day so far.

II. Talk to Jesus in your own words about your desire for this particular grace: that I may come to know lifestyles that give life and those that do not. Ask Jesus for a discerning heart that you may choose the path of life and always turn away from the path of death. Stay with this for as long as you like. Don't feel compelled to move on unless your heart suggests.

III. We read in the story of the lost son and the dutiful son that both the life of self-centeredness and the life of self-righteousness are wrong. Both the son who broke all the Commandments and the one who self-righteously followed them all, were both lost. Lifestyles that have the appearance of

Sacred Story Institute © 2019

goodness can be as death-dealing as those that openly violate Gospel values. In Luke chapter fifteen, verses eleven to thirty-two, read the very familiar Gospel story of these two sons and the father who loves them. Visualize their lives as you read the story and see the emptiness and self-centeredness from which they both suffered.

As you watch their lives, see if you have in your own life any of the temptations of the lost or the dutiful son. Listen to their lives and your own. Most especially, feel the embrace of the Father who loves you and will always welcome you home—even when you have strayed from his house and have been lost in self-centeredness.

Then watch the crowd as Jesus tells the story. Who in the crowd do you see living a life of self-indulgence and who a life of legalistic duty? See and experience the events as they happen. Notice everything about what is happening to Jesus and yourself. Do not move to the next section unless your heart suggests.

Pray with Luke 15: 11-32

IV. ASK THE LORD FOR HIS HELP in letting go of the self-centeredness that binds you; of what keeps you from freely coming home if you have strayed, or from accepting the joy of those who have been lost but now are found by the Father's Mercy. Pray that Jesus makes you a selfless True Heart.

V. Following the meditation, bring your own prayer period to a close by slowly praying the *Our Father*, listening to the words in your heart as you pray.

JESUS WALKS ON THE WATER

Jesus Walking On Water by Rebecca Brogran at jtbarts.com

Sacred Story Institute © 2019

*Spend fifteen to forty-five minutes on this exercise. Do only one section at a time and do not read ahead. Do not feel compelled to finish each piece of this. Stay with each section until your heart suggests moving on. Do not read or write after this meditation except perhaps a short journal entry. **Be Alone.***

I. Gather in what your senses are experiencing. Breathe in the Spirit of God. Breathe out whatever is troubling, distracting, or burdensome. Be aware of all the thoughts and feelings coming from the day so far.

II. Talk to Jesus in your own words about your desire for this particular grace: that you may learn to overcome self-centeredness, dread, fear and panic and follow him in selfless faith no matter the storms that rage.

III. Open your Bible and pray with Matthew chapter fourteen, verses twenty-two through thirty-three. Jesus is instructing his disciples that he is the Lord of all Creation and everything is under his command. He is showing his disciples that they must learn to walk in faith by keeping their True Hearts fixed on him and him alone.

Visualize the disciples terrified of Jesus as he walks towards their boat during a raging storm. See the darkness and feel the storm and boat at the point of sinking. See and feel the great fear in the disciples. See also the great love that Peter had for Jesus that leads him to ask Jesus to let him be with him.

Notice: Peter is scared but perseveres but there is still more to learn. When he takes his eyes off of Jesus, he begins to succumb to fear and starts to sink. Notice Jesus rescue him and rebuke him for this lack of faith. Watch and Pray.

IV. ASK THE LORD FOR HIS HELP. Now see yourself with the disciples in the boat. Ask Jesus to let you come to him across the water—to walk by selfless faith. Tell him your fears of walking by selfless faith and ask for the specific help you need to step out of the boat. Mention to him your fears and the patterns you've been remembering in this lesson. What does Jesus say to you? What invitation does he extend to you? What help does he give? As you close, say with the other disciples on the boat: "Jesus, you truly are the Son of God!"

V. Following the meditation, bring your own prayer period to a close by slowly praying the *Our Father,* listening to the words in your heart as you pray.

THE BEHEADING OF ST. JOHN THE BAPTIST

The Beheading of St. John the Baptist by Pierre Puvis de Chavannes

*Spend fifteen to forty-five minutes on this training. Do only one section at a time and do not read ahead. Do not feel compelled to finish the whole exercise. Stay with each section until your heart suggests moving on. Do not read or write after this meditation except perhaps a short journal entry. **Be Alone.***

I. Gather in what your senses are experiencing. Breathe in the Spirit of God. Breathe out whatever is troubling, distracting, or burdensome. Be aware of all the thoughts and feelings coming from the day and week so far.

II. Talk to Jesus in your own words about your desire for this particular grace: that I may learn to love him so much that I would, if the time came, selflessly offer my very life for him and his Leadership in the world. Pray for the grace to be more in love with Christ and his light, than to fear those who follow the enemy in darkness. Pray for the grace to give your life's blood for Christ the King. Stay with this for as long as you like. Don't feel compelled to move on unless your heart suggests.

III. Open your Bible and pray with Matthew chapter fourteen, verses one through twelve. As you read, be aware of this: John the Baptist was the greatest prophet in Israel's history. He is the pivot point between the old and new Covenants. He, like you, was known by Christ in his mother's womb. From the moment Mary visited Elizabeth and the child John leapt, he was blessed by Christ to be the herald of the Lamb of God coming into the world. Like Jesus said, "of those born of women, none is greater than John."

Now see John imprisoned for challenging Herod's marriage. See the party as it unfolds and the hatred and jealousy of Herodias' mother. See this courageous prophet in the fullness of his manhood through the pledge of a coward who succumbs to the hatred of his wife. Be at the party. Watch events as they unfold. See, smell, sense all that is happening. Feel Jesus' Spirit from afar sensing what is happening to his herald and champion.

What is in Jesus' heart as he feels John's life ended? Watch and pray. See and experience the events as they happen. Notice everything about what is happening to Jesus and yourself. Do not move to the next section unless your heart suggests.

IV. ASK THE LORD FOR HIS HELP. You are with Jesus as the news is brought to him of John's murder. Hear Jesus say to you: "The least in the Kingdom is greater than John. Do you still want to be my follower knowing the price? What do you say to Jesus? What then, does he say to you in return? Listen.

V. Following the meditation, bring your own prayer period to a close by slowly praying the *Our Father,* listening to the words in your heart as you pray.

THE PHARISEE AND THE TAX COLLECTOR

Basilica di Santapollinare Nuovo, Ravenna Italy, 6th Century

Spend forty-five minutes on this training. Do only one section at a time and do not read ahead. Do not feel compelled to finish the whole vigil quickly. Stay with each section until your heart suggests moving on. Do not read or write after this meditation except perhaps a short journal entry. Be Alone.

I. Gather in what your senses are experiencing. Breathe in the Spirit of God. Breathe out whatever is troubling, distracting, or burdensome. Be aware of all the thoughts and feelings coming from the day so far.

II. Talk to Jesus in your own words about your desire for this particular grace: that I may come to know that a True Heart is always humble and never proud in a self-centered way.

Pray to Jesus in very personal words that he gives you the knowledge you are loved, even in your sinfulness and weakness. Pray for the grace to know that Jesus our TRUE HEART, learned obedience by suffering on and the path of humility. Stay with this for as long as you like. Don't feel compelled to move on unless your heart suggests.

III. Open your Bible and pray with Luke chapter eighteen, verses nine to fourteen. Jesus is instructing his disciples whom he wants to be True Hearts and leaders. He must show them that a true leader is always humble and never proud. Visualize the disciples listening to Jesus and the imaginary scene in the temple describes. Does Jesus make the story serious or humorous? How is he trying to get his disciples to see what real leadership is about in how he describes the story? See and experience the events as they happen. Notice everything about what is happening to Jesus and yourself. Do not move to the next section unless your heart suggests.

IV. ASK THE LORD FOR HIS HELP. Imagine that you are with the disciples as Jesus relates the story of the Pharisee and the tax collector. Now imagine that Jesus turns to you in the crowd and repeats the very last line of the story: "Everyone who exalts himself will be humbled, but the person who humbles oneself will be exalted."

How does Jesus say this to you? Does he challenge you or is he praising you? What do you feel as you hear Jesus speak this truth to you? Stop, listen and understand. When you are done, turn to Jesus and say: "Please, Lord, make me a selfless, True Heart."

V. Following the meditation, bring your own prayer period to a close by slowly praying the *Our Father*, listening to the words in your heart as you pray.

THE BAPTISM OF JESUS

The Baptism of Christ by Jacopo Tintoretto

Spend forty-five minutes on this training. Do only one section at a time and do not read ahead. Do not feel compelled to finish the whole vigil in each intricate part. Stay with each section until your heart suggests moving on. Do not read or write after this meditation except perhaps a short journal entry. **Be Alone.**

I. Gather in what your senses are experiencing. Breathe in the Spirit of God. Breathe out whatever is troubling, distracting, or burdensome. Be aware of all the thoughts and feelings coming from the day so far.

II. Talk to Jesus in your own words about your desire for this particular grace: that I may always submit to my True Heart and live in humility so I can be one with Jesus and also his disciple--beloved of the

Father. May I not be afraid to follow the vocation/mission of selflessness I know in my True Heart for which I have been baptized. May I know in my True Heart that Jesus wants me as his disciple so he can honor me one day in his Kingdom before the Father. Stay with this for as long as you like. Don't feel compelled to move on unless your heart suggests.

III. Open your Bible and pray with John chapter one, verses twenty-four through thirty-four and Matthew chapter three, verses twenty-one and twenty-two. Watch John and Jesus as the events you read unfold. See the crowd. What is their mood? Are they young and old? Be in the crowd watching this pivotal moment in the life of Jesus. See Jesus in the river and watch him as the water is poured over his head and body and notice the expression on his face and on the face of John who baptizes him. Can you sense what Jesus is thinking and feeling? What John is thinking and feeling? What the assembled crowd is thinking and feeling?

IV. ASK THE LORD FOR HIS HELP. After the descent of the Holy Spirit, notice that Jesus sees you in the crowd and invites you to be with him in the Jordan. He reaches out to take your hand. He tells you are beloved to him and he wants you as his disciple. He wants you to live selflessly like himself.

Imagine it just like this. See Jesus take the seashell from John and with water from the Jordan, pour it over your head and body. See how he looks to heaven and tells his Father: "Father (put your name here) is to be with me in my mission. Confirm (put your name here) in the vocation you have placed in (put your name here) True Heart."

How do you feel now? What is the exact vocation/mission of selflessness he has placed on your True Heart? Listen to Jesus' words as he defines your vocation with you—your way of following him into service for others. Let him take both your hands and speak to you from his heart to yours. As he does, feel your common vocation with Jesus: to selflessly bring the Father's light and salvation to the world.

V. Following the meditation, bring your own prayer period to a close by slowly praying the *Our Father*, listening to the words in your heart as you pray.

SPIRITUAL AUDITS

Created by Asierroomero--Freepic.com

Created by Asier_relapagoestudio – Freepik.com

In our book, *Forty Weeks*, the first section leading up to the making of a Whole-Life Confession has many different types of spiritual audit exercises. The goal of the audits is to help individuals assess the spiritual, psychological and emotional dimensions of their life story.

Many people have a limited perspective on the integrated elements that make up their personalities—the various dimensions of their human nature in both is graced elements and in those areas where it is darkened by original sin.

We are all called by our Christian baptism to integrity of life but that requires we possess a conscious awareness of who we are before Christ. As a spiritual director and confessor for over thirty-five years, and as one who prays regularly and sees a confessor and spiritual director monthly myself, I know it is a constant challenge to maintain that integrity and conscious awareness.

That is why we developed these various audit exercises; to help individuals understand themselves better. The audits draw on the Ten Commandments, virtues and vices, addictive elements of the personality, human psychology, and persons and events in our life history that have shaped or misshapen us. The audits also provide integrating exercises that help synthesize the various different audits in order to help individuals make connections in their lives between all the complex dimensions of the human personality—our sacred story.

The pastoral uses of these various audit exercises are many. They can be used individually or in combinations or as a whole. They can comprise an entire retreat weekend, a series of evening exercises over weeks or months or as a day-long retreat experience which has Reconciliation service or an accountability exercise as its conclusion.

In TRUE HEART, the exercises lead up to the writing of a Whole-Life Confession. You can also use them for that purpose over an extended period of weeks or again in the context of a weekend retreat.

We encourage pastoral leaders to do the audits yourselves as a way to understand their usefulness and to gain insights on how they can be strategically employed for the spiritual growth and holistic human development of those you serve.

For the exercises on the Seven Capital Vices, we have incorporated three different artists. The first two artists go by the name of Dahlig and Procrust. Dahlig is a woman from Poland and Procrust (alias) a man from Russia. I have not been able to reach either through the site where they host their art. I use both of these artists for one set of the reflections because they represent a male and female version of what the vices "look like" that I think will appeal to youth and young adults who are used to the cyber and gaming world. The other set of reflections have a more classic art style in the engravings by Pieter Bruegel.

ANALYTIC CHARTS

To fully exploit the Spiritual Audits, they are best used as a group. This way, you can use the Analytic Charts at the end of the section to help people get a fuller picture of the key issues they face in growing in selflessness and preventing self-centeredness. Look over the exercises to get a full appreciation of how they work and how you might use them in the most beneficial ways for your work or ministry.

Take fifteen minutes and ask for Spirit's inspiration to move you deeper into Jesus' story as it connects to your own life story.

To help you in this task, ask in words *from your true heart,* to discover or remember the most intimate and/or meaningful name for God the Father, Son and Spirit that you have used in prayer. That name will resonate deeply in your heart and reflect God's relationship to you and your personal relationship with God. Ask for the grace to discover the name for God that touches your heart most intimately unlocking your selflessness and neutralizing your self-centeredness.

You will know the right name because it has the power to unlock your trust, love and to stir your affections.

The following names may help you in your discovery:

Merciful Father, Loving Father, Almighty Father, Our Father, Father God, Loving Creator, Creator God, God of Love, My God, Holy God, Father of the Poor, God of All Mercy, God of All Compassion, Father of Jesus, Lord Jesus Christ, Lord Jesus, Christ Jesus, Dear Jesus, Adorable Jesus, Adorable Christ, Good Jesus, Jesus, Merciful Savior, Jesus My Savior, Son of God, Dearest Lord, My Lord, My Lord and My

God, Sacred Heart of Jesus, Lamb of God, Good Shepherd, Crucified Savior, Holy Spirit, Spirit of Jesus, Spirit of the Lord, Loving Spirit, Holy Spirit of God, Love of God, Divine Spirit, Creator Spirit, Creator God.

Write the name for God in your notebook when you discover it. From this point forward, use this name when you address God.

God delights when you use a personal name and speak directly from your heart.
A suggestion: Use this name to address God every time you naturally think of God throughout the day. For example, you may say in your heart before a meeting: "Lord Jesus, be with me now." Say it, and then just move on with your meeting.

Do not make this a tedious exercise, but one that feels natural and relaxed. You do not have to think long and hard about God.

The purpose of this spontaneous prayer is just a short, friendly reminder of God's presence and love for you. Use this name in all your True Heart exercises and prayers from this day forward.

DISCOVERING THE KEY PERSONS, EVENTS AND ISSUES THAT SHAPE YOUR SPIRITUAL HISTORY

This exercise will help you "see" your life history in light of the opposing values of selflessness and self-centeredness. God is with you. Be Not Afraid!

Each of us has persons, issues and life events that shape our life story, our history. These persons, life events and issues are linked to the spiritual plotlines in our life story, leading towards or away from God—towards selflessness or self-centeredness.

We are conscious of some of these persons, issues and events but others are buried deep in our memory. Because these significant elements often evade our conscious awareness, we need to rely on God's grace to reveal them. We ask for grace to understand those things that, in negative and positive ways, most strongly shape us.

Today we seek God's grace to awaken to our *affective memories*. That is, we want to recall the persons, life events or issues, and *feel* the emotional weight, and the heart-value they have in our history. Seek insight into the closest, most intimate circle of people and events in your life story—parents, family, friends, and important events. Try to be attentive to the feeling these memories evoke.

For one life event, I might feel fear (something that has the power to generate the anxiety I know as fear). For another life event, my predominant feeling might be anger (someone or something that hurt me or a loved one).

For one person, I might feel mostly love (someone who has cared deeply for me). For another person, I might feel anger (someone who hurt me in some way). For one issue, my predominant feeling might be grief (the loss of a loved one or an opportunity that grieves my heart). For another issue, my experience might be gratitude or hope (an issue that has positively transformed my life for the better).

Pray that God enlighten your mind and heart to know each person, issue or life event and the *single, predominant* feeling (fear, anger, grief or self-centeredness—gratitude, hope, love or selflessness) each inspires. Take some time today to write below the three in both categories that most readily come to heart.

As you become aware of each, pause briefly and write down the name of the person, or the issue or life event that comes to memory. Next to each of these, write a single word for the most predominant *feeling* that arises in your heart. A word of caution here: do not succumb to the temptation to analyze or judge the feelings as they arise. Let the Holy Spirit guide you. Be Not Afraid! THREE PERSONS/LIFE

THREE PERSONS/EVENTS/ISSUES THAT GENERATE GRATITUDE, HOPE, LOVE & SELFLESSNESS

Persons/Life Events/Issues	*Gratitude/Hope/Love/Selflessness*
1.	1.
2.	2.
3.	3.

THREE PERSONS/LIFE EVENTS/ISSUES THAT GENERATE FEAR, ANGER, GRIEF & SELF-CENTEREDNESS

Persons/Life Events/Issues	*Fear/Anger/Grief /Self-Centeredness*
1.	1.
2.	2.
3.	3.

Sacred Story Institute © 2019

WHAT TOUCHES MY HEART AND BRINGS ME TO TEARS?

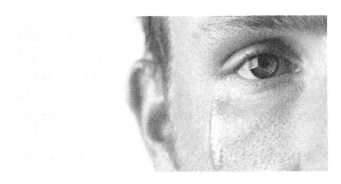 

For this exercise, pray for the grace to remember the movie, song or novel (story) that has the power to bring you to tears.

Use your personal name for God to be graced to remember the turn of phrase, the lyric, the dialogue, the word spoken, the melody, the image that has touched your heart so profoundly that your only response were tears.

What causes us to weep holds significance in our history, and informs our life story. Pray to remember and feel what moves you to tears.

The Gospels record that Jesus wept twice. He wept over Jerusalem, for failing to recognize that the time of its deliverance was at hand (Lk 19: 41-44). And He wept for His good friend Lazarus, "see how he loved him" (Jn 11: 33-36).

Both instances reveal Jesus' deep longing for humanity's reconciliation and peace. It is Christ's desire to bring freedom from death's grip—freedom from the death that resulted from humanity's disobedience and self-centeredness. Jesus' weeping expresses the deepest longings of His selfless heart. His tears reveal His mission in life, a mission He received from the Father, to save those He loves.
Tears reveal many of the deepest longings of our own hearts, too. They are a window to the heart and soul.

Ask God for the grace to remember and understand what brings you to tears, what breaks your heart or expresses your heart's longings for healing and peace.

Sit apart in a quiet place. Find a comfortable position that permits you to be alert. Breathe deeply for a few minutes, mindful that God's love sustains your very life. Using your personal name for God to ask for enlightenment in your memory and imagination so that you can remember and understand what brings you to tears, and why.

How is your life-mission—your story—revealed in your tears?

What movie, song or novel (story) moved you to tears and what can God help you understand about your life from those artworks?

Before your prayer period ends, write down what caused your tears. Record why it caused your tears if it is clear to you. Reflect further on what this might possibly reveal to you about your selfless True Heart.

DECALOGUE EXAMINATION OF CONSCIENCE
THE LAWS OF "RIGHT RELATIONSHIPS"

Gebel Mousa - The "Mountain of Moses"

In this exercise, review the Decalogue known as the Ten Commandments, in order to help you to better understand your life story and the gift of healing, balance and selflessness that God desires for you.

Use your personal name for God and pray that your imagination be illumined so that the *most important* issues in the Commandments, those that illuminate your history in both its selflessness and self-centeredness, will come into your mind and heart.

Pray to "see" what you have *never* seen before. Pray to see your life as God sees your life.

Read these words and hold them to you as you prepare for a reflection on these "laws of right-relationship."[5]

---

[5] "The Commandments were given to the Chosen People in a Covenant that was sealed with a blood sacrifice. The Church reflects that the power of the animal sacrifice sealing the Covenant receives its power from Christ's blood, which it foreshadows. The Commandments, as *gift,* are a foundation for God's work to repair our broken self-centered human nature, to forgive us, and reopen the

For this exercise, you will reflect on the Commandments to enhance your understanding of their richness and wisdom. The exercise will help to clarify how each Commandment carries its own responsibilities and boundaries for *you*. These *Decrees*—a synonym for *Commandments*— will ignite your imagination so you may be able to hear them differently now than ever before.

The ten decrees serve as a reminder to us when we have forgotten to *remember and know the truth* about God, humanity and ourselves. They are a *gift* to guide our way home so our thoughts, words and deeds bring selflessness and life, not self-centeredness and death.

Before concluding your prayer period today, use your notebook to record where in your life you have missed the mark in living the Decree you reflected on. Be specific, honest and courageous. Ask for the grace of integrity and openness to embrace the truth of your own experience.

A helpful format to follow as you reflect on each Decree is this one: Identify the Decree (and the sub-themes in the Decrees) as mild, moderate, or strong depending on the challenge this specific Decree presents to you.

For example, in this format, you might write:

"6th—moderate, especially regarding (put your issue in this parenthesis);"
"4th—mild regarding (put the person here);"
"7th/10th—strong regarding (place the event here)."

Use codes, if you prefer, to safeguard confidentiality. By protecting confidentiality, you can be fully honest without worrying about hurting someone should your journal get read in the future by someone other than you.

Note: The purpose of this exercise is to simply identify your challenges with the Commandments. With Christ by your side, explore this exercise with curiosity and detachment, without self-blame. God sees beyond any patterns of sin and failure you have or think you have. God knows *you* for who you are. God loves you.

God is the Divine Physician who desires to help you honestly see your life as it is so that He can bring forgiveness, healing, freedom selflessness and peace into you.

---

way to eternity through selfless thoughts, words and deeds: the work of Christ's death and resurrection. It is no wonder then that laws enshrining the Commandments' truths have transformed stories of self-centeredness and injustice to stories of selflessness and justice for countless millions of people in the last three millennia."

Before concluding your prayer period, use a journal to record where in your life you have missed the mark in living the Decrees you reflected on. Be specific, honest and courageous. Ask for the grace of integrity and openness to embrace the truth of your own experience.

First Decree: I am the Lord your God, you shall have no strange gods before me

Decalogue Parchment by Jekuthiel Sofer 1768

Ask yourself some sacred questions:

Is God the center of my life?

Have I displaced God with my studies, technologies, or concern for wealth and pleasure?

Does the worship and honor of God take shape in my weekly religious practices?

Do I pray often?

Do I turn to God for forgiveness often?

Have I resorted to relying on superstition, the occult or astrology in place of asking for God's assistance?

As you feel moved, write brief answers here or in your journal.

If you see that you are unfaithful to this decree, how can you institute change in your life right now? Be inspired! Be a True Heart! Be Selfless!

Second Decree: You shall not take the Name of the Lord your God in vain

Decalogue Parchment by Jekuthiel Sofer 1768

Ask yourself some sacred questions:

Do I casually take God's name in vain?

Do I have a habit of swearing in jest or in anger?

Do I use God's name to damn other people?

Do I nurse hatred of God in my heart?

Do I harbor anger towards God for the difficult things in my life or in the world?

Do I revere God in my heart?

As you feel moved, write brief answers here or in your journal.

If you see that you are unfaithful to this decree, how can you institute change in your life right now? Be inspired! Be a True Heart! Be Selfless!

Third Decree: Remember to keep holy the Sabbath day

Decalogue Parchment by Jekuthiel Sofer 1768

Ask yourself some life-changing questions:
Do I make every effort to prepare myself for the Sunday Liturgy?
Do I make every effort to attend the Sunday Liturgy?
Do I allow social or sporting events to displace or limit my attendance at the Sunday Liturgy?
Do I limit unnecessary servile work on Sunday?
Is Sunday a true day of spiritual rest and refreshment?

As you feel moved, write brief answers here or in your journal.

If you see that you are unfaithful to this decree, how can you institute change in your life right now?
Be inspired! Be a True Heart! Be Selfless!

Fourth Decree: Honor your father and mother

Decalogue Parchment by Jekuthiel Sofer 1768

Ask yourself some key family questions:
Do I give proper reverence to my mom and dad for the gift of life?
Do I thank them?
Do I spend time with them?
Do I strive to forgive the shortcomings of my parents?
Do I hold anger or grudges against them in my heart?
Do I try to respond to them with love and charity?
Do I attend to them in their sufferings and weaknesses?
Am I patient with their infirmity as they age?

As you feel moved, write brief answers here or in your journal.

If you see that you are unfaithful to this decree, how can you institute change in your life right now? Be inspired! Be a True Heart! Be Selfless!

Fifth Decree: You shall not kill

Decalogue Parchment by Jekuthiel Sofer 1768

Ask yourself critical life questions:

Do I strive to overcome the prejudices I have against individuals or groups?

Do I resist acting on my prejudices so as not to harm persons with my words or deeds?

Do I act with cruelty toward others?

Do I risk my life or the lives of others by using legal or illegal drugs?

Do I risk my life or the lives of others by driving recklessly or intoxicated?

Do I strive in words and deeds to promote the value of life from conception to natural death?

Have I ever helped someone terminate a pregnancy or end his/her own life?

Do I strive to do everything I can to uphold the value of each person?

Do I harbor satisfaction in my heart at the death of those people whom I consider evil?

Do I vote for politicians/civil servants because of their positions to protect and promote abortion, euthanasia, capital punishment or pre-emptive war?

Do I mourn the loss of all human life, no matter the cause of death?

As you feel moved, write brief answers here or in your journal.

If you see that you are unfaithful to this decree, how can you institute change in your life right now? Be inspired! Be a True Heart! Be Selfless!

Sixth Decree: You shall not commit adultery.
Ninth Decree: You shall not covet your neighbor's spouse

Decalogue Parchment by Jekuthiel Sofer 1768

Ask yourself some critical relationship questions:

By how I live now, how will I protect my potential future covenant relationship with my spouse and uphold its sacredness?

By how I live now, how will I uphold my covenant by never engaging in any sexual activity with someone other than my spouse?

By how I live now, how will I protect my imagination from pornography's capacity to distort my image of women or men?

How will I strive to cultivate purity of heart as a sign of God's own single-heartedness?

How will I reverence sexual intercourse first and foremost as a gift of love to create a human life destined for an eternity with God?

As you feel moved, write answers in your journal. Write one or two sentences on what you would like the biography of your life to say regarding the sacredness with which you *live out the gift* of your human sexuality.[6]

---

[6] For challenges with unwanted sexual behaviors like sexting, masturbation and pornography, visit RECLAiM at www.ReclaimSexualHealth.com They are a Catholic web-based, inexpensive and anonymous program that use the latest in brain science to help people of all ages overcome unwanted sexual habits and find peace, hope and true relationships: "Mending Minds-Saving Souls-Healing Hearts."

Seventh Decree: You shall not steal.
Tenth Decree: You shall not covet your neighbor's goods.

Decalogue Parchment by Jekuthiel Sofer 1768

Ask yourself some important character questions:
Do I cheat to get ahead?
Do I take things that do not belong to me?
Do I keep things I have borrowed?
Do I vandalize or harm property or goods that do not belong to me?
Do I envy those who have more than I do?
Do I live with envy of those who have more than I do?
Do I respect the limited resources of the earth as a divine inheritance to benefit all people?
Do I give my old items and some money to the poor?

As you feel moved, write very brief answers here or in your journal.

If you see that you are unfaithful to these decrees, how can you institute change in your life right now? Be inspired! Be a True Heart! Be Selfless!

THE SEVEN CAPITAL VICES

Two valuable spiritual analytic trainings form the core of this exercise. They focus on our vices and addictions, offering you the potential for great enlightenment about both selflessness and self-centeredness. If we seek medical advice for pain, the doctor asks us where we hurt. Christ, the Divine Physician, asks us about our vices and addictions to discover where we are hurting, and our unsuccessful attempts to anesthetize our hurt—"self" centered therapies that ultimately don't help us.

The Gospel calls vices and addictions "sin" because they manifest habits that erode our true human nature and our faith, hope and love and are...well...self-centered. The doctor calls them destructive because they ruin our lives and relationships—our selflessness, joy and peace.

In the series of training exercises, you'll pay attention to your vices (Pride, Gluttony, Lust, Sloth, Envy, Avarice, & Anger). They are sometimes called capital sins (from *caput*, the Latin word for *head*) because they are root habits or vices that lead to our problems of self-centeredness. All of us are subject to vices that have the ability to hook us mildly, moderately or strongly.

As you work with this exercise, you will gradually identify your capital sins/vices. As you do this work, ask Christ, the Divine Physician, to help you understand their **source** and **context** in *your* life history. If you can honestly identify addictions and vices in your life, you are on a path to selflessness. If you pray to Christ, the Divine Physician, *to wake you up* to the *connections* between them in your life story, you can rejoice because your healing—the healing that leads to selfless freedom--will now begin.

Remember: Christ came to save self-centered sinners, not the righteous. *True Heart* is *about allowing Christ to help us identify* where we need His healing graces to overcome our self-centeredness. This is the great gift He wants to give to us. Be not afraid. Christ knows you are working with him to minimize self-centeredness and maximize selflessness.

So, use your personal name for God to pray with words from your heart that will enable you to see what you have not seen before *and* to see connections between aspects of your life story.

At the end of each prayer period mark down in your notebook all the capital vices that trap you and to which you are susceptible. Be brief in your writing, but specific. List how the capital sins/vices of Pride and Greed ensnare you and how intensely (mildly, moderately or strongly) they ensnare you in self-centeredness.

Ask for the grace of deeper understanding, and with Christ, observe your life with compassionate curiosity, and with objectivity. God sees beyond any vices you have or think you have. God knows you for who you are and loves you.

After reflecting on each vice, write in your journal briefly and specifically: list the capital sins/vices that ensnare you and how intensely (mildly, moderately or strongly) they ensnare you in self-centered behavior.

THE
SEVEN
CAPITAL
VICES

Allegory of Virtue and Vice – Lorenzo Lotto (1505)

PRIDE

Image by Dahlig

Image by Procrust

Pride, or Vanity, is an unrestrained and improper appreciation of our own worth. This is listed first because it is widely considered the most serious of the seven sins. A more modern word for pride is narcissism. This pride, this narcissism, was Adam and Eve's sinful fall into the serpent's temptation "to be like gods." Adam and Eve displaced God, the Creator, and made themselves the "center" of the world—self-centered. Their action led to the loss of paradise and to a world of sickness, self-centeredness and death.

Pride often leads to the committing of other capital sins. It is manifest in our lives as vanity and narcissism about our appearance, intelligence, status, wealth, cliques, connections, power, successes and all the other things that we use to stand apart from others and from God.

HUMILITY works against pride by removing one's ego and boastfulness, therefore allowing the attitude of selfless service.

In your journal, write very briefly one or two ways you see at this point in your life how pride (narcissism) manifests making you self-centered. How can you counter it with humility?

PRIDE

Engraving by Pieter Bruegel

Pride is an unrestrained and improper appreciation of our own worth. This is listed first because it is widely considered the most serious of the seven sins. A more modern word for pride is narcissism. This pride, this narcissism, was Adam and Eve's sinful fall into the serpent's temptation "to be like gods." Adam and Eve displaced God, the Creator, and made themselves the "center" of the world—self-centered. Their action led to the loss of paradise and to a world of sickness, self-centeredness and death.

Pride often leads to the committing of other capital sins. It is manifest in our lives as vanity and narcissism about our appearance, intelligence, status, wealth, cliques, connections, power, successes and all the other things that we use to stand apart from others and from God.

HUMILITY works against pride by removing one's ego and boastfulness, therefore allowing the attitude of selfless service.

In your journal, write very briefly one or two ways you see at this point in your life how pride (narcissism) manifests making you self-centered. How can you counter it with humility?

GREED

Image by Procrust

Image by Dahlig

Greed is also known as avarice or covetousness. It is the immoderate desire for earthly goods and power. It is a sin of excess. Yet the object of our greed need not be evil. The problem lies in the way a person regards or desires an object, making it a god and investing it with false value.

Money can be that object as greed for money can inspire sinful actions such as hoarding, theft, fraud, environmental waste, cheating or lying.

CHARITY or love works against greed by putting the desire to help others above storing up treasure for one's self.

In your journal, write very briefly one or two ways you see at this point in your life how greed manifests making your self-centered. Write one way you can mobilize charity to become more selfless.

GREED

Engraving by Pieter Bruegel

Greed is also known as avarice or covetousness. It is the immoderate desire for earthly goods and power. It is a sin of excess. Yet the object of our greed need not be evil. The problem lies in the way a person regards or desires an object, making it a god and investing it with false value.

Money can be that object as greed for money can inspire sinful actions such as hoarding, theft, fraud, environmental waste, cheating or lying.

CHARITY or love works against greed by putting the desire to help others above storing up treasure for one's self.

In your journal, write very briefly one or two ways you see at this point in your life how greed manifests making your self-centered. Write one way you can mobilize charity to become more selfless.

GLUTTONY

Image by Dahlig

Image by Procrust

Gluttony comes from the Latin word meaning to gulp down or swallow. It is the sin of over-indulgence and usually refers to over-consumption of food and drink. Gluttony can manifest in eating too soon, too expensively, or eating too much.

St. Alphonsus Liguori explained that feeling pleasure in eating is not wrong. Because food tastes good, we are delighted by this gift. It is not right, however, to eat with self-centered pleasure as the only motive and to forget food's function in sustaining vitality and health.

TEMPERANCE works against gluttony by implanting the desire to be healthy, therefore making one fit to serve others

In your journal, briefly write one way you see at this point in your life how gluttony manifests in your life as self-centeredness. Write one way you can employ temperance to become more selfless.

GLUTTONY

Engraving by Pieter Bruegel

Gluttony comes from the Latin word meaning to gulp down or swallow. It is the sin of over-indulgence and usually refers to over-consumption of food and drink. Gluttony can manifest in eating too soon, too expensively, or eating too much.

St. Alphonsus Liguori explained that feeling pleasure in eating is not wrong. Because food tastes good, we are delighted by this gift. It is not right, however, to eat with self-centered pleasure as the only motive and to forget food's function in sustaining vitality and health.

TEMPERANCE works against gluttony by implanting the desire to be healthy, therefore making one fit to serve others

In your journal, briefly write one way you see at this point in your life how gluttony manifests in your life as self-centeredness. Write one way you can employ temperance to become more selfless.

LUST

Image by Procrust

Image by Dahlia

The sin of lust refers to self-centered desires of a sexual nature. Sexuality is a gift from God and pure in itself. However, lust refers to the impure thoughts and actions that misuse that gift. Lust deviates from God's law and sexuality's sacred purpose of allowing woman and man to participate in God's creative nature—God's selflessness. Lust includes actions like sex outside marriage, adultery, rape, pornography and auto-erotic behaviors.

CHASTITY or Self-control works against lust by controlling passion and leveraging that energy for the good of others

In your journal, write briefly one way you see at this point in your life how lust manifests as self-centeredness. Write one example of how you can leverage a chaste attitude to become more selfless in your desires.

LUST

Engraving by Pieter Bruegel

The sin of lust refers to self-centered desires of a sexual nature. Sexuality is a gift from God and pure in itself. However, lust refers to the impure thoughts and actions that misuse that gift. Lust deviates from God's law and sexuality's sacred purpose of allowing woman and man to participate in God's creative nature—God's selflessness. Lust includes actions like sex outside marriage, adultery, rape, pornography and auto-erotic behaviors.

CHASTITY or Self-control works against lust by controlling passion and leveraging that energy for the good of others

In your journal, write briefly one way you see at this point in your life how lust manifests as self-centeredness. Write one example of how you can leverage a chaste attitude to become more selfless in your desires.

SLOTH

Image by Dahlig

Image by Procrust

Sloth is often described simply as the sin of laziness. However, while this is part of sloth's character, its true face is *spiritual* laziness. So the sin of sloth means being lazy and lax about living the Faith and practicing virtue. Paraphrasing The Catholic Encyclopedia, sloth means aversion to labor or exertion— *to spiritual training.* As a capital or deadly vice, St. Thomas Aquinas calls it sadness in the face of some spiritual good that one has to achieve. In other words, a slothful person is bothered by the effort to sustain one's friendship with God. In this sense, sloth is directly opposed to charity.

DILIGENCE or Zeal works against slothfulness by placing the best interest of others above the life of ease and relaxation.

In your journal, write briefly one way you see at this point in your life how sloth manifests in your life making you self-centered. Write one key way you can employ diligence to become more selfless.

SLOTH

Engraving by Pieter Bruegel

Sloth is often described simply as the sin of laziness. However, while this is part of sloth's character, its true face is *spiritual* laziness. So the sin of sloth means being lazy and lax about living the Faith and practicing virtue. Paraphrasing The Catholic Encyclopedia, sloth means aversion to labor or exertion—*to spiritual training.*

As a capital or deadly vice, St. Thomas Aquinas calls it sadness in the face of some spiritual good that one has to achieve. In other words, a slothful person is bothered by the effort to sustain one's friendship with God. In this sense, sloth is directly opposed to charity.

DILIGENCE or Zeal works against slothfulness by placing the best interest of others above the life of ease and relaxation.

In your journal, write briefly one way you see at this point in your life how sloth manifests in your life making you self-centered. Write one key way you can employ diligence to become more selfless.

ENVY

Image by Procrust

Image by Dahlig

The sin of envy or jealousy is more than just someone wanting what others have. Sinful envy leads us to emotions or feelings of upset at another's good fortune or blessings. The law of love naturally leads us to rejoice in the good luck of one's neighbor but envy opposes love. Envy is named among the capital sins because of the other sins to which it leads.

KINDNESS works against envy by placing the desire to help others above the need to supersede them

After reading about envy briefly write in your journal how it ensnares you and how intensely (mildly, moderately or strongly in self-centered behavior. Identify one main act of kindness you can use to counter it.

ENVY

Engraving by Pieter Bruegel

The sin of envy or jealousy is more than just someone wanting what others have. Sinful envy leads us to emotions or feelings of upset at another's good fortune or blessings. The law of love naturally leads us to rejoice in the good luck of one's neighbor but envy opposes love. Envy is named among the capital sins because of the other sins to which it leads.

KINDNESS works against envy by placing the desire to help others above the need to supersede them

After reading about envy briefly write in your journal how it ensnares you and how intensely (mildly, moderately or strongly in self-centered behavior. Identify one main act of kindness you can use to counter it.

WRATH

Image by Dahlig

Image by Procrust

Wrath or Anger may be described as excessive and powerful feelings of hatred and resentment. These feelings can manifest as a passionate denial of truths expressed by others. Anger can also manifest in the form of denying truths about one's own life and impatience with the procedure of law. Anger is manifest too, in the desire to seek revenge outside of the workings of the justice system.

Anger, in essence, is wishing to do evil or harm to others. The transgressions borne of vengeance are among the most serious, including assault, murder, and in extreme cases, genocide and other crimes against humanity. Anger is the only sin not necessarily associated with selfishness or self-interest, although one can be angry for selfish reasons, such as jealousy.

PATIENCE works against wrath by taking time to understand the needs and desires of others before acting or speaking.

In your journal, write briefly one way you see at this point in your life how anger undermines your True Heart and manifests as self-centeredness. Describe in your journal one main way you can practice patience in the face of those situations that stir up the most anger in you.

WRATH

Engraving by Pieter Bruegel

Wrath or Anger may be described as excessive and powerful feelings of hatred and resentment. These feelings can manifest as a passionate denial of truths expressed by others. Anger can also manifest in the form of denying truths about one's own life and impatience with the procedure of law. Anger is manifest too, in the desire to seek revenge outside of the workings of the justice system.

Anger, in essence, is wishing to do evil or harm to others. The transgressions borne of vengeance are among the most serious, including assault, murder, and in extreme cases, genocide and other crimes against humanity. Anger is the only sin not necessarily associated with selfishness or self-interest, although one can be angry for selfish reasons, such as jealousy.

PATIENCE works against wrath by taking time to understand the needs and desires of others before acting or speaking.

In your journal, write briefly one way you see at this point in your life how anger undermines your True Heart and manifests as self-centeredness. Describe in your journal one main way you can practice patience in the face of those situations that stir up the most anger in you.

The word *addiction* is used in many contexts. Common usage of the term has evolved to include psychological dependence. In this context, the term goes beyond drug addiction and substance abuse problems to reflect behaviors that are not generally recognized by the medical community as addictive problems such as compulsive overeating or hoarding.

When the term *addiction* is applied to compulsions that are not substance-related, such as problem gambling and internet or gaming addiction, it describes a recurring compulsion one engages in despite the activity's harmful consequences to one's individual physical, mental, social or spiritual health.[7]

Other forms of addiction could be money addictions, work addiction, exercise addiction, habitual overeating, habitual shopping, sex addiction, computer addiction, e-mail addiction, pornography addiction, and television addiction.

The medical doctor Gabor Maté sums up addiction's profile: "Addiction is any repeated behavior, substance-related or not, in which a person feels compelled to persist, regardless of its negative impact on his life and the lives of others. Addiction involves:

a. Compulsive engagement with a behavior, or a preoccupation with it.
b. Impaired control over the behavior.
c. Persistence or relapse despite evidence of harm.
d. Dissatisfaction, irritability, or intense craving when the object—be it a drug, activity, or other goals—is not immediately available."[8]

In your journal, write down the one hope you have regarding your life and addictions and one fear you have regarding your life and addictions. We all have addictions. They are manifestations of self-centeredness.

Based on the profile provided by Mate, reflect on any addictions you find yourself living with at this point in your life. Don't judge yourself.

Jesus the Divine Physician is by your side as you write. He is present to you to help you discover anything that can be identified to help you be more of the selfless True Heart you desire. Be not afraid! Be selfless in confronting the self-centeredness of addictive patterns![9]

---

[7] "Compulsion, impaired control, persistence, irritability, relapse, and craving—these are all the hallmarks of addiction—any addiction." Gabor Maté, *In the Realm of Hungry Ghosts: Close Encounters with Addiction* (Berkeley: North Atlantic Books, 2010), 136-7.

[8] Gabor Maté, *In the Realm of Hungry Ghosts: Close Encounters with Addiction* (Berkeley: North Atlantic Books, 2010), 136-7.

[9] For challenges with unwanted sexual behaviors like sexting, masturbation and pornography, visit RECLAiM at www.ReclaimSexualHealth.com They are a Catholic, web-based, inexpensive and anonymous program that use the latest in brain science to help people of all ages overcome unwanted sexual habits and find peace, hope and true relationships: "Mending Minds-Saving Souls-Healing Hearts."

Ignatius was addicted to gambling and possibly to sex. Everyone has addictions (whether mild moderate or strong) to one or more things. Our addictions reveal valuable analytic information about the sources of our self-centeredness and how we seek to escape the pain it causes. All this information is worth bringing to the Divine Physician.

Today sit apart in your quiet place. Find a comfortable position that permits you to be alert. Breathe deeply for a few minutes, mindful that God's love sustains your very life.

Use your personal name for God as you ask God to enlighten your memory and imagination so that you can see any addictions you have. Are you addicted to anything?

Based on the profile provided by Gabor Mate from Day Four, write down in your journal any addictions you find yourself living with at this point in your life.

As you do this training, don't judge yourself. Jesus the Divine Physician is by your side as you write. Be not afraid.

Be brief and specific. Identify each addiction by name and frequency: **S**eldom, **O**ften, or **C**onstantly. For example, you might write:

Internet Gaming—S;
Exercise—O;
Pornography—O;
Food/Purging—C.
Texting/Sexting—C

Seeking to become selfless involves many joys and many adaptations inside us. Hold this material about addictions near your heart as you move forward with your True Heart journey to selflessness. And always, be kind and patient with yourself as is the Divine Physician.

For this exercise, combine the spiritual diagnostics on vices and addictions into a single training exercise by praying for the grace to honestly recognize the vices and addictions manifesting self-centeredness that erode your freedom and compromise your True Heart.

To begin this training session, you can sit in your standard manner of private prayer then, during your training session, review what you wrote in your notebook and ask Christ, the Divine Physician, in very personal words, to help you discover the *connections* between the vices and addictions.

For example, you may notice that when you are angry, you might move toward one or other addictive behavior. Or when you are envious, you might be drawn to other addictive behaviors, and so on for the other vices.

The grace you are asking for today is the *inspiration* to *understand* the vices and addictions in and of themselves, and then to identify the *connections* between them as they manifest in your life story. When, through grace, you begin to wake up to the links between the thoughts, words and deeds of your life story, you will find your True Heart waiting to help you.

Record in your journal any discoveries you make between the vices and addictions that God reveals to you. Thank God for the courage to honestly see yourself as you are.

Thank God for the grace to wake up to live in greater freedom and selflessness. And always, be patient and kind to yourself as is Christ the Divine Physician who longs for your selfless freedom.

DISCOVERING LINKS BETWEEN YOUR VICES, THE COMMANDMENTS, ADDICTIONS & LIFE EVENTS

Review the vices and commandments (I've provided them here), then fill in the analytic chart on the next page. It is a powerful exercise that lets you see the connections between many dimensions of your life story in order to more fully discern your True Heart—to resist self-centeredness and embrace selflessness. Provide *at least three elements* for each of the statements.

VICES

Pride, Envy, Gluttony, Lust, Sloth, Greed, Wrath

COMMANDMENTS

First:	I am the Lord your God, you shall have no strange gods before Me.
Second:	You shall not take the name of the Lord your God in vain.
Third:	Remember to keep holy the Sabbath day.
Fourth:	Honor your father and mother.
Fifth:	You shall not kill.
Sixth:	You shall not commit adultery.
Seventh:	You shall not steal.
Eighth:	You shall not bear false witness against your neighbor.
Ninth:	You shall not covet your neighbor's spouse.
Tenth:	You shall not covet your neighbor's goods.

Sacred Story Institute © 2019

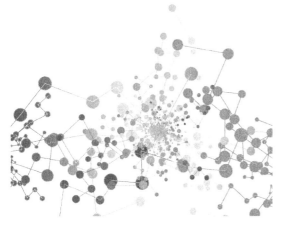

As you contemplate the analytic chart, pray for help from the Divine Physician so that you can be completely forthright about *obvious* links between Commandments, vices, addictions and persons or events. Be selfless in confronting self-centeredness! Draw lines linking the connections of what you write down in the different categories *that are clear to you.*

FIVE COMMANDMENTS I AM MOST CHALLENGED IN LIVING	FIVE VICES THAT ENSNARE ME	FIVE ADDICTIONS I LIVE WITH	FIVE PERSONS/EVENTS THAT CAUSE FEAR, ANGER, OR GRIEF

COMPREHENSIVE PERSONAL ANALYTIC CHART FOR ALL THE AUDIT EXERCISES

I fill in the diagnostic chart, with the goal to write at least two items in each category.

Pray over the results and ask God what are the most important insights for our own personal and spiritual growth.

A COMMANDMENT THAT CHALLENGES ME	
VICES THAT ENSNARE ME	
ADDICTIONS I LIVE WITH	
PERSONS/EVENTS THAT GENERATE FEAR, ANGER OR GRIEF	
PERSONS/EVENTS THAT GENERATE FAITH, HOPE OR LOVE	
STORY LINES IN BOOKS, MOVIES. THAT ALWAYS BRING ME TO TEARS	
WHAT ALWAYS MAKES ME ANGRY	
WHAT ALWAYS MAKES ME GRATEFUL AND MORE SELFLESS	
WHAT ALWAYS MAKES ME FEARFUL AND MORE SELF-CENTERED	

Sacred Story Institute © 2019

Contemplate the next personal analytic chart. In it you can see how sin impacted the life of St. Ignatius, especially links in his original (root), core (trunk), and manifest (fruit) sins. You'll also see questions for you to answer in your journal.

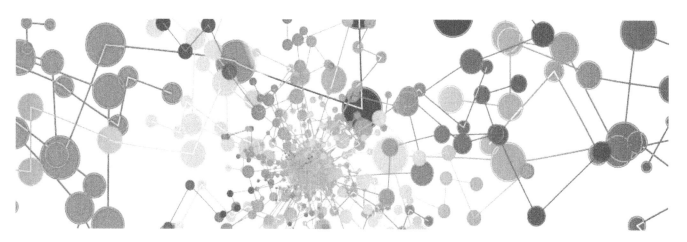

VISIBLE SINS

The Fruits & Ornamentation

(Ignatius' addictive gambling, reactive anger, and sexual self-indulgence)

*How do you manifest Fear, Anger, moral weaknesses, vices,
addictions, and sinful habits that are the most visible to you?*

CORE SINS

The Trunk & Superstructure

(Ignatius' arrogance, blinded conscience, and self-centeredness)

*How do disobedience and self-centeredness, along
with their related fear, anger, and grief, form the trunk or
superstructure of your daily life, feeding on originating sins and events?*

ORIGINAL SINS

The Roots & Foundation

(Original Sin and concupiscence that wounded Ignatius' heart and soul; distinctive family/clan sin and/or early life-events that wounded him spiritually, psychologically and physically)

*How do ancient, originating events that rooted the patterns of disobedience
and self-centeredness along with its Fear, Anger, Grief manifest in your life?*

MY PERSONAL VISIBLE, CORE AND ROOT SIN CHART

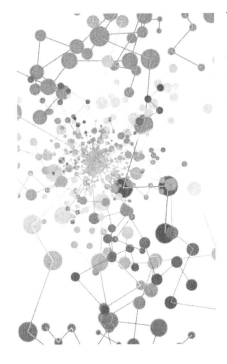

THIS short exercise helps us again to see the difference in our lives between selflessness and self-centeredness. To help with this exercise, feel free to contemplate the elements from the personal analytic charts you filled in earlier. Pray for the grace to see more clearly how sin and self-centeredness have impacted you at the roots, trunk and fruit of your life.

For each of the blank spaces on the next chart, write those elements (at least one each) that you believe are present in your life as:

Original Sins → Root
Core Sins → Trunk
Manifest Sins → Fruit

If you are finding any of this difficult, you can turn not only to prayer for help—prayers that give your voice the ear of the Divine Physician using your personal name for God—but you can also, if you feel it is appropriate, talk about all of this with your companion or mentor.

MY MANIFEST SINS—THE FRUIT FROM MY TREE

Example: I am constantly envious of other's talents

MY CORE SINS—THE TRUNK OF MY TREE

Example: My envy is linked to my desire to always want to be the best—the center of attention.

MY ORIGINAL SINS—THE ROOTS OF MY TREE

Example: I always felt growing up that my older siblings were praised for their talents and that
I was never paid attention to and this wounded my pride making me self-centered.

THE WHOLE-LIFE CONFESSION

Reconciliation Windows, St. John's Church Tralee, Ireland

The Whole-Life Confession culminates the first thirteen weeks of *Forty Weeks* and also the sixth week of *True Heart*. It is best utilized if there has been advance preparation like in the two mentioned books.

You can use it as a stand-alone exercise on a retreat or in combination with one or multiple of the Spiritual Audits in the previous chapter. However, you use it in your pastoral work, do allow some spiritual preparation, silence and prayer to precede this exercise. The more preparation you give, the more spiritual power the Whole-Life Confession (WLC) will have for those you invite into its graces.

In this edition of *True Heart Practices*, we have, like the main book, separated the WLC into four parts: Introduction and Letter to Jesus in three parts. Again, be creative in how you incorporate these sections of the WLC in your ministry or retreat exercises. This should be a prayerful exercise and one that does not induce anxiety because it is packed into too short of a time span.

It might even be a fruitful exercise for an RCIA program, marriage preparation or some other fixed program you have for spiritual formation. In those cases, you might allow weeks of preparation for the writing of the WLC and bringing it to a sacramental setting like Confession or some other spiritual exercise if you are from a different Christian tradition.

INTRODUCTION

Mining your life history is like going on a treasure hunt, pulling together the many diverse elements of your life story. Think of is as spiritual archeology on your past life. While the long process of piecing your story together will happen throughout the rest of your life—both by your careful attention and by the grace of God—it entered a new phase of your life in this exercise of a Whole-Life Confession.

And now, everything you have done up to this point will take on greater meaning for you. Because this exercise brings a great deal of your past together to prepare your Whole-Life Confession. As you move through the exercises, refer to some of what you wrote in in previous exercises and realize the tremendous spiritual effort you have accomplished. You have seen into your core being and are noticing great differences between selflessness and self-centeredness. Now your "seeing" will take a sacramental form in your Whole-Life Confession.

Reconciliation Windows, St John's Church, Tralee, Ireland

✠ A Whole-Life Confession is the opportunity of reconciliation for all the interconnected patterns of selflessness and self-centeredness and of grace, sin and difficulties across *your whole life.* The Confession helps you ask for God's help to see the big picture of your life—your story—with Christ by your side as your Merciful Divine Physician, forgiver and healer.

As St. John Paul II said in the Catechism: *This reconciliation with God leads to other reconciliations which repair the other breaches caused by sin. The forgiven penitent is reconciled with himself in his inmost being, where he regains his innermost truth. He is reconciled with his brethren whom he has in some way offended and wounded. He is reconciled with the Church. He is reconciled with all creation.*[10]

In this way, your Whole Life Confession is a letter to Christ based on your spiritual diagnosis achieved prayerful training. You will now be able to confess current issues and past issues that have been overlooked. As you do this, you are telling Christ the chronic *patterns* of sin and weaknesses that your prayer and reflection, with the help of God's grace, have shown you.

With all this in mind, look at your life story with Christ the Divine Physician beside you. Address Him directly and acknowledge why you need Him as your Savior. This *could* be the very first time you have reviewed your life, seen clearly why you cannot save yourself, and directly asked Jesus to be your Savior.   What a profound grace to know you cannot save yourself and to ask Christ for this tremendous gift!

There is no greater gift you give to Christ than your sinfulness and weaknesses as you ask for His healing love, mercy and forgiveness. By doing so, you take seriously the gift of His life, passion, death and resurrection. In this whole process, you will show that you are not afraid to look at your life from Christ's perspective, too. As you tell Jesus you need His cross to be healed you are thanking him for suffering and dying for *you* so that you can be renewed in Him.

✠ What follows are a few suggestions to help you prepare for this simple, holy and graced letter-- this statement of your need for Christ. It is a confession of your patterns of sin from a lack of selflessness and an indulgence in self-centeredness, as well as a request for forgiveness, healing and hope.

Read these suggestions today and let them work in your heart as you begin to write notes down or pieces of your Letter to Jesus.

You will have the rest of the week to write the full Letter.

1.   *One thousand words or less—*

---

[10]   *Catechism of the Catholic Church (CCC) 1469--John Paul II, RP 31, 5.*

Write a letter to Christ that is *no more* than 1000 words. <u>I repeat: write *no more* than 1000 words</u>. It is best to write long-hand so that you are connected heart and mind to your text. If you want a visual of 1000 words, it would be the amount of text from the start of this exercise through #4 below. And that is the maximum you are to write! Why? Because it is important to focus only on what is essential and not let yourself be overwhelmed thinking you have to write a book.

2. *Personal words that are heartfelt—*

Early on you identified the name for God that touches your heart. For this exercise, find the name for Christ that speaks to your heart. Perhaps it is Christ Jesus, Lord and Savior or My Lord. In this lesson, you will speak directly to Christ Jesus. You are speaking to the One who won your victory and who came into the world to save you.

Speak to Jesus in the first person like this: "Christ Jesus, please forgive my sin of _____."
"Jesus I remember_____."
"Lord I suffered_____."
"Christ please heal me of my addiction to_____."
"Christ Jesus please heal my anxiety about _____."
Write the confessional story—your history—directly from your heart to the heart of Jesus.

3. *Strive for honesty—*

Strive earnestly for courage and honesty in your letter. The letter is for you to read in a Whole-Life Confession (or how your leader suggests you present it). You need not impress anyone. Be honest about the forgiveness you need to extend to yourself and to others. *Write from your True Heart.*

4. *You are not climbing Mount Everest—*

Pray for the grace not to turn this simple, graced letter/confession opportunity into a huge, exhausting task. You are not climbing a mountain. You are having a conversation with Christ about your life. Hear Him say to you:

Come to me, all you who labor and are burdened, and I will give you rest. Take my yoke upon you and learn from me, for I am meek and humble of heart; and you will find rest for your selves. For my yoke is easy and my burden light. Matthew 11: 28-29

5. *Pray for Patience and Compassion—*

Being a True Heart will take the rest of your life. It takes a lifetime for Christ's work of healing and forgiveness to transform your heart and soul. There is no finish line or final enlightenment you can reach on this earth. You will always need healing and at deeper levels. You will constantly grow in love, selflessness and humility until the day you pass from this earth. You will not be finished until the day the Divine Physician sits you down at His Eternal Banquet. Pray to practice patience in your journey.

But as for the seed that fell on rich soil, they are the ones who, when they have heard the word, embrace it with a generous and good heart, and bear fruit through perseverance. Luke 8:15

6. *Set the scene in your heart's imagination—*

If you have any difficulty doing this Letter, imagine that you have been given the opportunity to be alone with Christ when He is walking from one town to another. He says to you: "I will have 15-minutes with you, dear one, just with you alone before I must turn my attention to those others." See the road and the other followers walking up ahead of you but notice that no one else can hear you—just Christ Jesus.

When you start writing your letter, write as if you are speaking to Christ personally He knows why you want to speak with Him and is ready to hear you. See him look you in the eyes just before you begin talking about your life.

Hear him say, "Soon I will be lifted up on my cross. I will do this for you so that you can find forgiveness, healing and hope for the sins, weaknesses and suffering you experience in your life. As I conquer all death and sin—as I breathe my last breath—I will hold you and your life story in my heart. You will find victory and eternal life in me and one day you will be with me in paradise."

Reread these instructions throughout your spiritual preparation. Don't write anything yet—just hold all of this in your True Heart for now. Write your letter when your leader gives you the time to do it.

Reconciliation Windows, St. John's Church, Tralee, Ireland

Here is Part One (of three parts) of your actual letter, your confession, to Christ Jesus, the Divine Physician.

Write these two sections of our letter in the time provided for you.

✠ "Dear Jesus, I am so grateful for all the gifts you have given to me." (Spend some time writing from your heart why you are grateful. Use Jesus' name often and give *very particular* examples of why you are grateful).

Then move to:

✠ "Lord, I am profoundly aware of how some of my past experiences, life history, family, friends, work, school, neighbors are linked to areas where I find a lack of freedom in my life. These experiences have created embarrassing and/or discouraging habits and rooted patterns of sinfulness." (Now use the other exercises you've completed in preparation for this letter as a way of looking back over your life. Offer particular examples to Jesus that capture the links and patterns of self-centered sins, addictions, vices, and commandments that cause you to stumble).

If you cannot discern exact patterns yet, simply speak about these areas individually. If there are central people in your life story who are linked to these destructive patterns, mention them to Christ. If you are confused about some of the things you do, tell Jesus what they are and then ask for His help to better understand why you do what you do.

From your heart, ask Christ's grace to gain greater freedom from these patterns of sin and self-centeredness, habits and vices.

Reconciliation Windows, St. John's Church, Tralee, Ireland

Now, as part two (of three parts) of your letter to Christ Jesus write these two sections of your letter in when your leader invites you to.

✠ "Lord, there is one central pattern of sin and self-centeredness that causes me the most embarrassment, shame, confusion and discouragement." (Spend some time being very specific in your conversation with Jesus about this pattern of sin and self-centeredness in your life and why it is so difficult for you. Tell Jesus the particular circumstances in which you seem to fall under the spell of sin the most. Tell Jesus how you feel when you fail. If there are specific incidents of this pattern of failure that you have not confessed, tell them to the Lord, and ask for His healing and forgiveness).

Then move to:

✠ "Lord Jesus, I have come to realize that I cannot save myself and I ask for your compassion. I ask that you be my Savior. Rescue me and be with me all the rest of my days." (Spend some time speaking with Jesus, in very particular words, about why you have come to realize you cannot save yourself and why you need His grace—why you need Him to be your Savior).

Be boldly honest. Tell Him in very clear words why you know—because of x, y and z— you cannot save yourself.

Tell Him about any persons you cannot forgive and what they did to you. Tell Him why it is difficult for you to forgive them. Tell Jesus that with His grace you can desire to forgive them, and in time you will be able to forgive them and ask humbly but clearly for that grace.

Ask the Lord to keep His attention on the core issues in your life (name them) that constantly trip you up. Pray that you never tire in seeking His forgiveness and that you never lose hope in yourself or in Him. Ask in words from your heart for the Lord to be your Savior.

Reconciliation Windows, St. John's Church, Tralee, Ireland

Now, for the third part of your letter to Christ Jesus, write these two sections in the time provided to you.

✠ "Lord Jesus, I thank you that you have given me the courage to face any fears I had and to trust you with my life in this healing sacrament of your redeeming love." (As you near the end of your letter and confession, end with very personal words from your heart, thanking Jesus that He has heard your prayer and that He will always be your Savior).

Thank Jesus that He understands your life and ask that He continue to walk with you, give you grace, and be with you till the end of your days. Ask Jesus for the grace to serve Him more each day with everything you think, say and do.

Ask for the grace to work for fruit that will endure to eternity.

Then move to:

✠ End your letter by these words or words just like them, "Thank you, Jesus, for being my Savior." In this ending to your Letter, you will be asking for His continued grace as He transforms you into a *True Heart*.

Now you should have your Letter, *your* Confession, in your journal. Hold it close to your heart and bring it to the Sacrament of Reconciliation or the service provided by your leaders.

INTRODUCTION TO DISCERNMENT

Jesus Reads Isaiah, St. John's Church, Tralee Ireland

The Vatican *Synod on Young People, The Faith and Vocational Discernment* concluded in late October of 2018. Many years before this synod was planned, I had begun work on making Ignatius' discernment rules accessible to laity outside of a retreat context. Starting in the late 1980s, it was clear that the individualism and relativism of the times were distorting the language and true interpretation of Ignatius' Rules for the Discernment of Spirits. Having time-trusted guidelines for helping young adults make good discernments in light of Gospel faith and values is critical for our age.

In both the *Forty Weeks* and *True Heart* programs, the sections on discernment come as the final set of exercises. The logic in the arrangement was that individuals would need to have begun the daily practice of prayer to have the context for paying attention to spiritual states in order for discernment to be possible. You may want to present the earlier exercises for those you work with from *True Heart Practices* before you have individuals do these discernment exercises. However, it is not essential. I leave it to your own judgment to decide what is best.

For this leader's manual, I have chosen to include the following section from the book: *Sacred Story – An Ignatian Examen for the Third Millennium*, as an overview on authentic interpretation of discernment in a contemporary context. It gets into technical philosophical and theological concepts but should be accessible to the lay reader. Please read it over to better understand the selection of exercises we have included in *True Heart Practices.* It will give you a crash course on discernment in the current cultural moment to better help you guide those you are called to form in the Christian Faith.

And while it focuses attention on the practice of the Ignatian *Examen* discipline, it's also relevant for all those who have a daily, serious life of prayer and sacramental engagement. Again, we need to teach authentic principles of discernment to our young adults. You will be a better leader if you understand the core issues over language and interpretation that are the subject of much debate in and outside the Church.

Note: Those who do the discernment exercises should have completed the *"DISCOVERING THE NAME FOR GOD THAT UNLOCKS YOUR HEART"* exercise from the section on Spiritual Audits in Chapter 7.

First, a summary of this somewhat technical discussion of Ignatian Discernment has the following elements:

1. Not all "discernment" is Ignatian Discernment
2. Ignatian Discernment has clear rules and boundaries
3. Ignatian Discernment and the formation of one's conscience takes dedicated effort and work.
4. An authentic Ignatian Discernment will not be contrary to Scripture, Tradition or the Teaching Church
5. Authentic discernment is grounded in the received/revealed moral law of the Old and New Testament
6. Authentic discernment will not discover "novel" moral laws that are different from what has been revealed in the Ten Commandments
7. Ignatian discernment, like St. Ignatius, "thinks with the Church (*SPEX* 352)."
8. Authentic discernment will reveal the God of Surprises who has placed the truth in our hearts for us to daily discover anew

9. Being an "authentic" person of discernment does not entail following *instinctual desires* but *spiritual desires* rooted in your True Heart

A QUICK COURSE ON CLARIFYING & CONTEMPORIZING IGNATIUS' DISCERNMENT RULES

Introduction: Third Millennium Challenges to Authentic Christianity and Ignatian Spirituality

Mid-last century two Christian scholars separated by distance and discipline identified the same threat as humanity's gravest. C.S. Lewis and Josef Pieper wrote works identifying loss of the examined life, contemplative rest, and God-consciousness as eroding culture and destroying humankind. Lewis' Screwtape Letters sketch a plan for humanity's destruction by blinding persons' awareness of the present and the eternal. The goal is a world devoid of reflective contemplation. Pieper's, Leisure, the Basis of Culture, affirms that the very survival of Western society hinges on the re-establishment of contemplative rest (leisure) as the preeminent, foundational value of an enlightened and creative culture.

Each writer identifies the fundamental challenge confronting the person seeking a measure of self-reflection. For Pieper, the world of total work is annihilating all unstructured time thus rendering impossible the capacity for self-awareness to open human consciousness to "the-world-as-a-whole." Lewis sees a strategist's hand in this global, evolutionary trend toward darkened conscience. The world of noise and chaos will in the end silence every heavenly voice as well as human sensitivity to the inner stirrings of conscience.

Pieper sees the erosion of a contemplative, reflective space slipping away with such "monstrous momentum" that he wonders whether its loss and the hyperactivity filling the void has demonic origins. His solution is to reclaim a space for leisure that provides "contact with those superhuman life-giving forces that can send us renewed and alive again into the busy world of work."

A divine counter-strategy for nullifying the demonic forces that Lewis and Pieper unmask is found in the Psalmist's words: "Be still, and know that I am God." Jesus too affirms that "the Kingdom is among you."9 These Scriptural prescriptions speak to us but shouting much louder are the cultural, psychological and spiritual forces arrayed against human consciousness' awakening to the world as a whole. We are losing touch with the intimate presence of God in and among us.

These overpowering forces gain strength each day. We are in fact in the full bloom of what Thomas Merton described as violent hyper-activism. The threat while still gaining force is; primeval. Strategies to confront it are as ancient as the threat itself. God, working through both the Chosen People and the Church's saints has provided us countless spiritual resources to meet it head-on.

Christianity and the Ignatian Discernment Rules and the Ignatian Examen propose a narrow path to spiritual growth that is demanding yet effective. Because they are demanding, many can avoid following this path. Many others avoid it because they can't reconcile feelings and attitudes towards religious beliefs and practices in light of the pressures and biases of modern culture. The dominant culture has reshaped our expectations on what is obligatory, healthy, and personally beneficial for a Catholic Christian's spiritual journey. The individualism of the age encourages us to pick and choose whatever is appealing to our immediate desires. This further complicates faith commitment, prayer and discernment.

The Church in every age must find a way to make both our Faith and Christ relevant amidst the all-encompassing changes in global consciousness. The mission today, as in the past, requires developing effective and dynamic evangelization strategies while holding fast to the anchors of Scripture, Tradition and the Magisterium. Jesuits have achieved great success historically in this mission of dynamic fidelity.[11] The Society's mission in this regard is simplified by the incredible legacy of St. Ignatius' spirituality.

Many of the deepest fault lines running through both our contemporary globalized culture and Catholic Christianity merge in the challenges posed by praying St. Ignatius' Examen. It is remarkable that Ignatius' spiritual genius anticipates and embraces those fault-lines. An Examen method faithful to his vision can respond to them.

I chose eight commentators on the Examen to appraise its problems and possibilities for our day.[12] All eight are faithful to the unique form of Examen the Ignatian Paradigm frames.[13] Collectively the eight

---

[11] The Church continues to call on the Society to evangelize dynamically and faithfully. "All the same, while you try to recognize the signs of the presence and work of God in every part of the world, even beyond the confines of the visible Church, while you endeavour to build bridges of understanding and dialogue with those who do not belong to the Church or who have difficulty accepting its position and message, you must at the same time loyally fulfill the fundamental duty of the Church, of fully adhering to the word of God, and of the authority of the Magisterium to preserve the truth and the unity of the Catholic doctrine in its totality...As you well know because you have so often made the meditation "of the Two Standards" in the *Spiritual Exercises* under the guidance of St. Ignatius, our world is the stage of a battle between good and evil, with powerful negative forces at work...This is why I have asked you to renew your interest in the promotion and defense of the Catholic doctrine 'particularly in the neuralgic points   strongly attacked today by secular culture,'...The issues, constantly discussed and questioned today, of the salvation of Christ of all human beings, of sexual morality, the marriage and the family, must be deepened and illumined in the context of contemporary reality, but keeping the harmony with the Magisterium, which avoids creating confusion and bewilderment among the People of God." Jesuit Life and Mission Today: The Decrees & Accompanying Documents of the 31st—35th General Congregations of the Society of Jesus (St. Louis: Institute of Jesuit Sources, 2008), 823-4. Cited hereafter as, "Decrees." The General Congregation responded positively to this invitation: "The 35th General Congregation expresses its full adherence to the faith and the teaching of the Church, as they are presented to us in the intimate relationship that unites Scripture, Tradition, and the Magisterium. The 35th General Congregation calls all Jesuits to live with the great spirit of generosity that is at the center of our vocation: "to serve as a soldier of God beneath the banner of the Cross...and to serve the Lord alone and the Church his spouse under the Roman Pontiff, the Vicar of Christ on earth." Ibid., 729-30.

[12] An analysis of the eight commentators and their writings can be found at: http://sacredstory.net/resources/Examining The Examen/. The eight commentators and their writings are listed below: George Aschenbrenner, SJ "Consciousness Examen," *Review for Religious*, no. 31 (January 1972). "Consciousness Examen: Becoming God's Heart for the World," *Review for Religious* 47, no. 6 (Nov/Dec 1988). Cited hereafter as *Aschenbrenner Heart*. "A Check on Our Availability: The Examen," *Review For Religious* 39, no. 3 (May 1980) David

uncover issues Ignatius had not explicitly addressed. But the issues and effective responses to them are implicit in both in Ignatius' spirituality and the Ignatian Paradigm.

Previous Themes

Common themes surface in the writings these eight commentators detailing rationales, methods and challenges presented by the Ignatian Examen. For example, the Examen 's focus on sin must also be inclusive of God's grace and mercy. This integrated character of the Examen has been missing at times. The Ignatian Paradigm faithfully followed compels this integrated approach. An Examen faithful to the Ignatian model should incorporate the full paradigm beginning in gratitude and culminating in a heartfelt contrition that leads to service.[14]

The Examen must also function as a vehicle of discernment. This is evident in the analysis of Ignatius' progressive conversion as he learns discernment techniques while undergoing integrated spiritual growth. In the Examen, discernment operates on two levels: first, discernment is necessary to separate the Divine spontaneities from the demonic in all the discreet moments of daily living; second, discernment is necessary in commitment to the Examen's life-long purgation. The life-long journey encompasses the purgation of manifest and root sins. Spiritual, psychological and moral confusion can reign supreme as one seeks spiritual docility and indifference to hear God's will and stay the course in the here and now. The Examen and discernment become inseparable disciplines in one's spiritual journey."[15]

Five New Themes

Townsend, SJ, "The Examen and the Exercises: A Re-Appraisal," *The Way Supplement* 52 (Spring 1985): 54. "Finding God in a Busy Day," *Review for Religious* 50, no. 1 (January-February 1991). Cited hereafter as *Finding*. Joseph Tetlow, SJ "The Examen of Particulars," *Review for Religious* 56, no. 3 (May- June 1997). Cited hereafter as *Particulars*. "Examen: Persons in Relationship," *Review for Religious* (March-April 2002). Cited hereafter as *Persons*. "The Most Postmodern Prayer: American Jesuit Identity and the Examen of Conscience, 1920-1990," *Studies in the Spirituality of Jesuits* 26, no. 1 (January 1994): 49-50.

[13] Research for this project uncovered dozens of articles on the *Examen*. Not all could be classified as authentic to Ignatius and the *Ignatian Paradigm* I detailed in the first chapter of *Sacred Story: An Ignatian Examen for the Third Millennium*. All components of this *Ignatian Paradigm* should be present for any *Examen* that wants to be identified as Ignatian. Other *Examen* modalities have inspirations that emanate from Ignatius' vision but are not necessarily consistent with a practice of the *Examen* and its formulation in the *Exercises*.

[14] Mary Hugh Campbell captures this full movement succinctly: "[T]he first point is a prayer of gratitude for the goodness and forgiveness which are man's twofold debt. Louis du Pont has probed the familiar method in order to discover its marrow: the optimism which prescribed gratitude first, thus guarding against sadness; the realism of seeing that the memory is so unfaithful, the mind so darkened, and the will so loveless that there is deep need of prayer for light. The examination itself, the third point, is a sincere acknowledgment of good, where this is recognized; and in the admission of sin or failure there is counsel to do this in a spirit of the untranslatable *douceur*—that that gentleness which refrains from turning bitter reproaches against itself, but rather grieves over the injury to One who has poured himself out, as fountain and light, in such generous giving. After the expression of perfect sorrow, one is urged in a fifth point to efficacious resolution—so practical as to foresee and so circumvent future failure." Hugh Campbell, 779-780.
[15] *Ibid.*, 780.

Sacred Story method had to address five critical issues unique to our times. The five issues have roots in the Examens' structure and require analysis: (1) narcissism and individualism; (2) narrow moralism; (3) the interplay between sin and psychological compulsions; (4) the social dimensions of sin; and (5) modern secularizing trends and their impact on God-mindedness or God-consciousness.

Narcissism and Individualism

The words "narcissism" and "individualism" are not common to Ignatius' milieu. However, pride and vainglory certainly were. There is a long tradition in both ancient and contemporary literature warning about pride and vainglory's cancerous influence. Augustine's majestic Book Ten of the Confessions speaks to pride's control of his inmost thoughts.[16] Augustine's confession of pride mirrors Ignatius' "overpowering desire to gain renown." Diadochus of Photice writing in the 5th century pointedly notes that self-love and love of God are mutually exclusive.[17] Rodríguez too gives evidence that from early in the Society's history pride and vanity were corrosive to the Ignatian Examen.[18]

Individualism and narcissism were revealed as dominant cultural trends in the decade of the 1980s when the Examen commentators critiqued these "isms" as poisonous for spiritual growth. The social critic Christopher Lasch views individualism as a form of reactive narcissism linked to the overwhelming global problems of modern society.[19] He relates Genesis' thesis in contemporary

---

[16] "But. O Lord, you who alone rule without pride since you are the only true Lord and no other lord rules over you, there is a third kind of temptation which, I fear, has not passed from me. Can it ever pass from me in all this life? It is the desire to be feared or loved by other men, simply for the pleasure that it gives me, though in such pleasure there is no true joy. It means only a life of misery and despicable vainglory." As cited in: *Confessions*, 244.

[17] "No one who is in love with himself is capable of loving God. The man who loves God is the one who mortifies his self-love for the sake of the immeasurable blessings of divine love. If a person loves himself, he seeks his own glory...Once the love of God has released him from self-love, the flame of divine love never ceases to burn in his heart and he remains united to God by an irresistible longing. The Liturgy of the Hours, Divine Office Ordinary Time: Weeks 1-17, vol. 3 (New York: Catholic Book Publishing Co., 1975), 101-102.

[18] "But if a man goes on making his examen out of routine and for form's sake, without any true sorrow for his faults and any firm purposes of amendment, that is no examen, but a vain ceremony and a Christmas game. Hence it is the same evil propensities and the same bad habits and inclinations that a man brought from the world, he keeps after many years of religion. If he was proud, proud he is today...as self-willed, as greedy, as great lover of his own comforts." Rodríguez, 463. (The Jesuit historian, Michael Maher, suggests that a "Christmas game" likely refers to the very popular role-playing games commonplace in the Renaissance but especially during the Baroque period. These games included such parodies as a boy dressed up as a bishop. In this context, Maher suggests, Rodríguez's comment about the routine exercise of the *Examen* would be a game or a parody of the real event).

[19] "The awareness of the world as a dangerous and forbidding place, though it originates in a realistic awareness of the insecurity of contemporary social life, receives reinforcement from the narcissistic projection of aggressive impulses outward. The belief that society has no future, while it rests on a certain realism about the dangers ahead, also incorporates a narcissistic inability to identify with posterity or feel oneself part of a historical stream." As cited in:

categories: that personal sin expressed as narcissism facilitates the individual's retreat from the sphere of social concern and relationship. The predictable outcome, historically viewed, is the chaos the Christian tradition reliably identifies as wholesale evil in our world.

The American Psychiatric Association (APA) first listed narcissism as a personality disorder (NPD) in its fourth Diagnostic Statistics Manual (DSM IV) catalog in 1980. The APA estimates that only one percent of the general population and about fourteen percent of the clinical population has NPD as a serious pathology. Still in examining the nine characteristics of NPD indicative of the characterological disorder identified by the APA one can conclude that indeed most people manifest many of their traits—in thoughts, words and deeds—which can be deemed sinful.[20]

The APA is not in the business of identifying sin. They describe narcissism as a clinical disorder with purely psychological origins. As a "serious pathology," it accounts for a mere one percent of the population. Yet contemporary researchers have documented an explosion of narcissistic tendencies, especially among the younger generation.[21] The Christian tradition would view many of the behaviors and actions of a narcissistic personality as objectively sinful, e.g. "envy," "lacking empathy," or being "interpersonally exploitative."[22]

Christopher Lasch, *The Culture of Narcissism: American Life in an Age of Diminishing Expectations* (New York-London: W. W. Norton & Company, 1991), 51.

[20] "Diagnostic criteria for 301.81 Narcissistic Personality Disorder: A pervasive pattern of grandiosity (in fantasy or behavior), need for admiration, and lack of empathy, beginning by early adulthood and present in a variety of contexts, as indicated by five (or more) of the following: (1) has a grandiose sense of self- importance (e.g., exaggerates achievements and talents, expects to be recognized as superior without commensurate achievements); (2) is preoccupied with fantasies of unlimited success, power, brilliance, beauty, or ideal love; (3) believes that he or she is "special" and unique and can only be understood by, or should associate with, other special or high-status people (or institutions); (4) requires excessive admiration; (5) has a sense of entitlement, i.e., unreasonable expectations of especially favorable treatment or automatic compliance with his or her expectations; (6) is interpersonally exploitative, i.e., takes advantage of others to achieve his or her own ends; (7) lacks empathy: is unwilling to recognize or identify with the feelings and needs of others; (8) is often envious of others or believes that others are envious of him or her; (9) shows arrogant, haughty behaviors or attitudes." As cited in: The American Psychiatric Association, *Diagnostic and Statistical Manual of Mental Disorders: DSM-IV-RT* (Arlington, VA: American Psychiatric Association, 2007), 717.

[21] Those who work with high school or college students are aware of the discussions about the problem of entitlement and individualism. For some excellent research on the issues see the books by Jean Twenge, PhD., Christian Smith, PhD., and David Kinnaman: [Twenge, Jean M., Keith Campbell. *The Narcissism Epidemic: Living in the Age of Entitlement.* New York: Free Press, 2010.] [Smith, Christian. *Lost in Transition: The Dark Side of Emerging Adulthood.* Oxford, Oxford University Press, 2011.] [Kinnaman, David. *You Lost Me: Why Young Christians Are Leaving Church and Rethinking Faith.* Grand Rapids, MI: Baker Books, 2011.]

[22] The Church's position on the sinfulness of these actions can be tempered by the degree to which any objectively sinful actions were committed with "full consent of the will." The APA is only concerned with narcissism in its most extreme manifestation where it becomes a debilitating psychological "pathology." The Church is concerned with narcissism in all its forms. As a spiritual disorder it is sinful for it blocks a person's openness to grace and conversion and concern for others.

Ignatius' vainglory would be noted by Ecclesiastes' Teacher, Augustine, Diadochus, Lasch, and even the APA. Many of Ignatius' personality traits are visible in the APA's categories. Pride and narcissism are similar with equivalent personal, spiritual, psychological and social consequences. What may be new and worth noting is the clinical use of narcissism to describe this ancient spiritual malady first documented in the Book of Genesis (Gen 3:1-7).

A modern bias favoring scientific categories over their moral counterparts might explain the new terminology. Or perhaps science is just now recognizing this ancient defect. Whatever the reason, narcissism appears to be the word of the moment for defining the root sin that tore through Ignatius' early life.

The word narcissism has a greater wince factor than either pride or self-love. The later have positive connotations denoting self-esteem and personal self-worth necessary for proper human flourishing. And in an age of public obsession with celebrity, the word vanity is more virtue than vice. But to invite someone to examine her or his narcissist tendencies carries a clinical and moral gravitas that provokes serious self-reflection, even shame.

Pride was Ignatius' Achilles' heel. Pride is the vice linked in tradition to Original Sin more than the other six vices. The advantages semantics can provide to induce self-reflection need to be seized. Consequently, the word "narcissism" is used in Sacred Story to help people better understand the cancerous aspects of egoistic pride.

Narcissism is the principal element of the Examen targets. Individuals must identify it in their thoughts, words and deeds to advance spiritually. Life as Sacred Story begins when narcissism can be targeted and neutralized by God's grace.

Narrow Moralism

Narrow moralism is an undue, exclusive and non-integrated focus on moral acts. The Examen, especially the PE with its marking system, can prove detrimental to spiritual growth by creating obsessive anxieties as each new instance of some sin is cataloged and marked. This is especially true in scrupulous persons like Ignatius himself. A narrow focus prevents one from gaining a holistic view of one's life and history. When this happens, spiritual growth is limited.[23] The Examen has been a damaging exercise for some by fostering neurotic, obsessive/compulsive behaviors.

---

[23] Sin in English's paradigm is both Original and personal and both forms of sin have to be acknowledged and resisted by the examinee. Original sin for English has an evolutionary dimension, accruing power since the first sin of Adam. It is also traceable in the very structure of one's family. English affirms with theorists that the first five years of existence fix much of a person's responses to life. Each individual has the responsibility to sort through the *movements across one's being* and determine what is biological, psychological, and spiritual. Thus, English urges each individual to seek knowledge of her history, for in the spiritual realm of this history, she can discover where sin and love have made their home. In this regard, each individual is accountable for the presence of both sin and love as driving forces of

To prevent an Examen from devolving into a narrow moralistic exercise does not mean eliminating from the Examen's purview the Commandments and the moral code they embody. Ignatius had no such qualms, either in his practice of the Examen or in his public ministry.[24] Still, narrowly focusing on an action by extricating it from both a specific context and a wider life-story effectively prevents access to the higher perspective necessary to see the sin and/or a behavior's root cause, which are the major goals of the PE.[25] Access to the interconnected life-patterns and narratives to which sin, addiction, vices and grace are tethered is central to the Examen's function. The spiritual and psychological data needed for effective discernment is eliminated without them.

The philosopher Charles Taylor highlights narrow moralism in another context that invites reflection and comment. By framing the call to holiness reductively, with an exclusive focus on moral conduct, a belief system forms that views human effort alone as sufficient for benevolence, happiness, and human flourishing. The need for God and God's grace to reform lives is displaced; a major contributor modern secularism.[26]

With the widespread belief that persons can both confront and master their darker impulses and attain happiness unaided by grace, two additional challenges are presented for Sacred Story Examen. The first is expanding the meaning of discipleship the Ignatian Examen invites beyond the narrow righteousness achievable solely by human effort (Mt 5:20). And the second is to ensure the method is faithful to the Ignatian model, i.e., that it identifies the full demands of the Commandments. True Heart invites the constant petitioning of God's grace to open one's eyes and heart to see and feel the effects of God's mercy, in light of one's sinfulness, narcissism and addictive vice.

Both an awareness of sin's corrosive effects plus a felt understanding of the role God's saving grace plays in light of personal sinfulness must be experienced. This is necessary to convince one that she

---

the personality. John English, *Discernment and the Examen* (Guelph, Ontario: by Ignatius Jesuit Centre of Guelph, 1979), 48. Cited hereafter as, "English."

[24] The list of commandments in the *GE* encompasses all traditional moral categories. Also, Ignatius was direct in his denunciations of the kinds of immorality that he himself engaged in while a solider (Loyola, 28, 31). He also publicly challenged gambling, one of his former addictions, and lax sexuality like the practice of clergy taking concubines, of which his priest-brother in Azpeitia was guilty (Loyola 62).

[25] One assumes that Ignatius must have had a more integrated holistic focus to achieve such balanced and continuous spiritual growth. "Laynez said in 1547 that Ignatius had 'so much care of his conscience that each day he compared week with week, month with month, day with day, seeking daily to advance.' In the case of a person as faithful and fervent as he was, it is difficult to think that continuous increase in merit was the only development which took place in his interior life." de Guibert, 39-40.

[26] "As we move from the Cambridge Platonists through Tillotson to Locke and the eighteenth century, apologetics, and indeed, much preaching, is less and less concerned with sin as a condition we need to be rescued from through some transformation of our being, and more and more with sin as wrong behavior which we can be persuaded, trained, or disciplined to turn our backs on. This concern with a morality of correct conduct has been observed by many historians of the period. Religion is narrowed to moralism." As cited in: Charles Taylor, *a Secular Age* (Cambridge, MA: The Belknap Press of Harvard University Press, 2007), 225. Cited hereafter as "Taylor."

cannot achieve Gospel benevolence and righteousness unaided.[27] Such experiences can further shatter the "dignity" of the self-sufficient, buffered identity.[28] In addition, they open the self-enclosed to the transformative power of the personal God.

Taylor identifies another cultural issue an authentic Ignatian Examen method must address. It is related to the narrow moralism just discussed. He traces in secularism's rise during the Enlightenment a strong negative bias against orthodox Christianity. At times the anger devolves into hatred.[29] The modern expression of this anger may well influence attitudes toward the ascesis the Examen requires. This would include striving to master vice and reign in disordered passions that is part and parcel of the Examens' discipline.

A Christian discipline too passionate and enthusiastic in seeking holiness is highly suspect in an age that values a detached and rational intellectualism.[30] Religious practices that aspire for a more transcendent moral order beyond mere human flourishing are seen as proposing goals that deny some the right to happiness.[31] The suspicion of a Christianity that demands perfection and moral zeal over and above what a polite, enlightened society deems appropriate has subtly evolved in our age. It is in part embodied in those whose passion for tolerance and inclusion stands in opposition to those who reproach anything that falls short of tradition's moral codes and Commandments. This skirmish between the "tolerant" and the "intolerant" is found as often inside of religious confessions as it is between a specific confession and society's humanists and secularists.

A way forward must be found that fosters the quest for the transcendent moral and spiritual values that the Ignatian Examen demands. It needs to confront and disarm both the rigid ideologies of the "intolerant" and the "tolerant." The call to conversion must invite the tolerant beyond the fear and anger they believe the Commandments and the received Tradition demand, which leads at times to

---

[27] "The disengaged, disciplined agent, capable of remaking the self, who has discovered and thus released in himself the awesome power of control, is obviously one of the crucial supports of modern exclusive humanism." *Ibid.*, 257.

[28] *Ibid.*, 264. Ignatius' correspondence typically closed with the phrase, "poor in goodness." Surely Ignatius did not see himself capable of benevolence unaided by God's saving love. One might see in his iconic expression an experience to both desire and emulate, i.e., the experience of a sinner rescued and humbled by God's mercy.

[29] "Hume distinguishes the genuine virtues (which are qualities useful to others and to oneself) from the 'monkish virtues' ('celibacy, fasting, penance, mortification, self-denial, humility, silence, solitude') which contribute nothing to, even detract from human welfare. These are rejected by 'men of sense', because they serve no purpose; neither advancing one's fortune, nor render one more valuable to society, neither entertain others nor bring self-enjoyment. 'The gloomy, hare-brained enthusiast, after his death, may have a place on the calendar; but will scarcely ever be admitted, when alive, into intimacy and society, except by those who are as delirious and dismal as himself." Taylor, 263.

[30] Friedrich Schleiermacher enshrined this class of detached intellectuals as religion's "cultured despisers."

[31] Taylor, 262

their outright rejection and denunciation of them. For the intolerant, it means going beyond a rigid and narrow application of the moral code that fosters scrupulosity, zealotry and fanaticism.

An authentic Ignatian Examen invites practitioners to honestly identify the moral dimension of their life narrative according to the normative standards of Tradition. Its methods avoid promoting the Pelagianistic, obsessive worries, reactive anger and the monocular vision a narrow moralism fosters. The method promoted Sacred Story is a merciful discipline leading to genuine and integrated human flourishing. It is geared to benefit the practitioner no matter his or her stance toward authoritative tradition.[32]

The means for achieving this balancing act in Sacred Story is a process fully engaging Ignatius' "sourcing" method that impels one to search for the root causes of sin and dysfunction. It is these "unexamined" core sins and wounds, and the anger, anxiety and grief linked to them, that can generate most of the unreasoned, reactive ideologies that short-circuit any conversion process.

The sourcing method of Sacred Story and True Heart is supported by other Ignatian-inspired disciplines. Sacred Story has a narrative introduction and "Rules of Engagement" incorporating wisdom from the Introductory Observations of the Spiritual Exercises. The Rules of Engagement challenge the reactive ideologies of both right and left, while the narrative addresses potential biases before one engages the discipline.

Clarifying that the Examen is rooted in the Church's tradition and not simply a legalistic obligation imposed by an outside authority is emphasized. The narrative avoids any impression that its goal is the counting of moral peccadilloes. Doing so holds the interest of the religious skeptic who might not affirm traditional moral categories. It also helps mitigate the anxieties of the conscientious traditionalist who may tend toward scrupulosity. Consequently, the Sacred Story Examen can help diffuse tensions and fears associated with both poles along the "narrow moralism" continuum.

One final issue surfaced directly in Aschenbrenner's work and more obliquely in Campbell 's writing that Sacred Story's discernment method addresses. Both wrote their articles on the Examen at the height of the Cultural Revolution in the late 60s and early 70s. It is the period of history Taylor defines as the "Age of Authenticity." It is characterized by a revolution in changing attitudes and sexual mores.[33] The meaning of language shifts in this epoch. Words like "genuine," "freedom" and "authenticity" are appropriated to define the evolving ethic of free sexual expression and spiritual-

---

[32] The Examen must not be a discipline that lacks mercy, nor can it be simply an exercise in mercy without discipline. The Examen needs both discipline and mercy to be effective.

[33] Taylor, 485.

seeking common to our contemporary culture. This new consciousness imprisons many traditional Christian, and specifically Catholic sexual teachings, in a cage of narrow moralism.[34]

Culture attributes positive virtues or at least a stance of 'non-judgment' to a liberated expression of instinctual desires. Ignatius himself rejected the free expression of his instinctual desires as antithetical to his truest human nature. For contemporary individuals, an evolving sense of human self-experience easily compromises the "genuineness" Campbell ascribes to the Examen as an ascesis or "discipline of authenticity."[35]

So too are Aschenbrenner's insights faithful to Ignatian discernment principles distinguishing between two spontaneities; one Divine and one inspired by the enemy of human nature.[36] The dominant culture encourages that desires remain undifferentiated viz. spiritual and moral categories of right and wrong. Those faithful to Ignatius' discernment methods must demand such differentiation, or risk stripping the spirituality of its power to change lives.

A call to discern desires grounded in Ignatian principles and a testing of their authenticity in light of these same Ignatian principles can, in today's milieu, lead to serious charges of intolerance. Hence one is adrift with an ever-evolving description of human nature that can't be easily measured against the definition of desolation Ignatius defines in his Rules as coming from human nature's enemy. The dominant culture also censures measuring the truth or authenticity of desires and/or actions against the Decalogue and the laws of the Church that anchor the Exercises considerations on sin, SpEx [42].

One is subject to reproaches of 'narrow moralism' in favoring the received (moral) Tradition as guide and norm for living in a milieu where 'freedom' and 'authenticity' have been so wedded to expressions of instinctual desire, viz., Freud. The positive value generally ascribed to the expression of instinctual desires in today's Western cultures challenges the belief that the moral ascesis the PE fosters is necessary, or even more negatively, whether it promotes spiritual and psychological damage.

What Ignatius suggests in his Rules and tangentially Campbell and Aschenbrenner as well, is that the genuine Divine inspirations of God lead one to reject definitions of the self-inspired by the "enemy of human nature." One is instead to labor under the banner of grace and allow God to heal one's authentic human nature hidden by sin, wounds narcissism and psychic dysfunction.

---

[34] "Indeed, precisely the soft relativism that seems to accompany the ethic of authenticity: let each person do their own thing, and we shouldn't criticise each other's "values"; this is predicated on a firm ethical base, indeed, demanded by it. One shouldn't criticise others' values, because they have a right to live their own life as you do. The sin which is not tolerated is intolerance." *Ibid.*, 484.

[35] Hugh Campbell, 777.

[36] Aschenbrenner, 14; 19-20.

Ignatius discovers an instinct of purity and selfless service during his conversion. The new man God revealed is antithetical to the old man who freely indulged in instinctual desires that defined his first thirty years. The fantasies and desires of the old man are rooted in a pre-purgative imagination. The release from instinctual compulsions, sins and addictions, the shattering of his pride, and his humble, obedient service to Christ and the Church are his new benchmarks for defining true freedom and authentic human nature.

The challenges presented by these contemporary readings of "narrow moralism" in light of the Age of Authenticity are not easily solved.[37] Additionally, the Church is confronted today with pressures in advancing a morality consonant with Ignatius' own instinct of purity, weakened as it is by sexual scandals. But more importantly, we live in an age where pleasure and physical intimacy are equally or more highly valued than procreation as end goal and ultimate significance of genital sexual expression.

Nonetheless, four small steps are taken in Sacred Story to address these challenges. First, the Sacred Story Examen incorporates, as did Ignatius' original Examen, considerations of the Commandments and teachings of the Church in its discernment method. Second, it re-appropriates the language of "genuineness," "freedom" and "authenticity" for those unique Divine inspirations that Ignatius himself discovered as the genuine expression of his human nature. Third, it invites the direct, personal encounter with Christ as the individual to whom one conforms oneself. This, so that the graced encounter that transforms one's emotional, intellectual, and spiritual horizon is not a law or an institution, but the Person who embodies true human nature. This direct, personal encounter with Christ is a signature element of the Spiritual Exercises and of all Ignatian Spirituality.

And finally, Sacred Story defines the positive and negative boundaries of Ignatian discernment. For Ignatius, authentic consolation is always consonant with the Decalogue and received Tradition while attractions to and indulging in pleasures Ignatius describes as "low and earthly," are both a temptation and one of the principle signs denoting spiritual desolation.[38] The spontaneity inviting surrender to such passions—passions that symbolize a core value of the Age of Authenticity—constituted the first serious temptation Ignatius experienced after his conversion and frame the Truth Paradigm.[39]

---

[37] "The fateful feature of roman-clericalism, which erects such a barrier between the Church and contemporary society, is not its animating spirituality; our world is if anything drowned in exalted images of sexual fulfillment and needs to hear about paths of renunciation. The deviation was to make this take on sexuality mandatory for everyone, through a moralistic code which made a certain kind of purity a base condition for relating to God through the sacraments. What Vatican rule-makers and secular ideologies unite in not being able to see, is that there are more ways of being a Catholic Christian than either have yet imagined...But as long as this monolithic image dominates the scene, the Christian message as vehicled by the Catholic Church will not be easy to hear in wide zones of the Age of Authenticity." Taylor 504.

[38] See, *The Boundaries of Ignatian Discernment* below.

[39] Loyola, 17-18.

These four small measures incorporated in Sacred Story help those living in the shifting paradigms of contemporary culture. It is addressed both to those who, for whatever reasons, have strong feelings and/or prejudices against an external authority or those who cling to laws as their sole security and identity. The disciplines of Sacred Story invite individuals to set aside prejudices. It demands that they open their hearts to an experience of integrated conversion like Ignatius'.

The Matrix of Sin and Psychological Compulsions

The description of Ignatius' conversion experience highlights the matrix of sins and vices he manifested and confessed. It also identified probable psychological influences that at least in part likely contributed to them and/or acted as their fuel. The study identified as well the integrated spiritual and psychological growth the Autobiography documents.

Ignatius' spiritual and psychological maturity is manifested by the mastery of sinful behaviors and addictions after the Loyola recuperation. It deepens with the identification of, and commitment to eradicate the root sin of pride in the struggle with scruples during his harrowing at Manresa. It is also manifest in his balanced calm after an intense period of dangerous, neurotic mood swings that characterized his spiritual torments.

Ignatius' struggle at Manresa was a battle with both the sinful and psychological root issues—deep-seated concupiscence—necessary to achieve integrated healing. Using both classical theological formulations and modern psychological categories the Powerless Paradigm is elemental purgation.[40] The Spiritual Exercises that Ignatius was living facilitated this integrated, spiritual-psychological healing.[41]

Many Examen commentators discuss the importance of identifying the interplay between sin and the psychological defenses. It is essential to identify the life events and traumas that can act as sin's

---

[40] "Consequently, when one who has received the sacrament turns to prayer and embarks on the way of purification, the person does not do so in order that sins may be forgiven (for they are already forgiven) but in order that he or she may be liberated from the shackles of concupiscence–that is to say, from the inclination towards evil, the inordinate affections, the uncontrollable appetites, the craving, the clinging, the attachments and all those debilitating tendencies that we moderns call compulsive addictions, infantile fixations and ungovernable drives. In short, the path of purification is a path of liberation." William Johnston, *Mystical Theology: The Science of Love* (London: Harper Collins *Religious*, 1995), 194.

[41] The early history of the *Exercises* indicates that they were especially successful with those who were in some way dissatisfied with their lives. Ignatius himself indirectly, but successfully, healed certain types of affective instability, neuroses and psychological disturbances through the Exercises. We have already mentioned commentators who emphasize the psychotherapeutic usefulness of the *Exercises*." Egan, 159.

source and accomplice.[42] The examinee must source sin's origins and its evolutionary character in his/her family. Cognizant of theorists who trace life's fixed patterns, for good or ill, to the first five years of life, we are invited to examine, "across our being," issues that might be spiritual,[43] biological or psychological.[44] The biological and psychological play their part but sin finds it habitation in the spiritual. In this, what is sinful must be examined and resisted.

The Examen practitioner must see the familial roots of Original Sin and learn the difference between "sin, my sin, and sin in me." In order for purgation to promote transformation, an Examen practitioner must discern his complicity in the sinful compulsions, neuroticism, addictions, and negative self-image he experiences. Taken together, these form the 'dark night of the senses' typical for the common person. Using psychological challenges to scapegoat sin is not satisfactory. A person must accept responsibility for working against sin that manifests as psychological complexes. Individuals must confront the shame, embarrassment, and humiliation that admitting sin requires. Rationalizations and defenses can act as impenetrable armor preventing the awakening of one's conscience.[45]

---

[42] For a discussion of childhood stresses that can damage the personality, leading to habitual sinful and psychological complexes, see: Allers: Rudolf Allers, *Practical Psychology in Character Development* (New York: Sheed and Ward, 1934; repr., Fort Collins, CO: RC Books, 2002).4-101. (page references are to the reprint edition). Cited hereafter as "Allers PPCD." [Allers broke early with Freud and became a close collaborator of both Victor Frankel and Alfred Adler. Allers, a mentor to both the young Hans Urs von Balthasar and Edith Stein, was armed with doctoral degrees in medicine, psychiatry and philosophy. He published works in psychiatry, philosophy, theology, linguistics and physiology. He was uniquely attuned to the interplay between the spiritual, intellectual, and psychological components of the personality and developed a psychology sensitive to the best in the Christian tradition. His last teaching posts were at The Catholic University of America and Georgetown University. Most of Allers' works, and a large collection of his personal papers and conference notes, are available at Georgetown University's Lauinger Library].

[43] Such deprivation leads to stress and biochemical deficiencies that make forming intimate relationships difficult. All of which increase propensities to addictive substances and behaviors. Gabor Maté, *In the Realm of Hungry Ghosts: Close Encounters with Addiction* (Berkeley: North Atlantic Books, 2010), 197-210. Cited hereafter as: *Maté*.

[44] Maté, 390. See also these sections: "How the Addictive Brain Develops" and "The Addiction Process and the Addictive Personality (Maté's methods to deactivate maladaptive habits and addictions in order to establish emotional balance will be examined later, along with the awareness exercises of Michael Brown's *Presence Process*. Insights from both authors are used to highlight inherent aspects of Ignatius' methods in order to create a holistic updating of the vital *Examen* consciousness techniques and discernment principles).

[45] "(4). The neurotic need for power: Domination over others craved for its own sake; Devotion to a cause, duty, responsibility, though playing some part, not the driving force; Essential disrespect for others, their individuality, their dignity, their feelings, the only concern being their subordination; Great differences as to degree of destructive elements involved; Indiscriminate adoration of strength and contempt for weakness; Dread of uncontrollable situations; Dread of helplessness. (6). The neurotic need for social recognition or prestige: All things—inanimate objects, money, persons, one's own qualities, activities, and feelings—evaluated only according to their prestige value; Self-evaluation entirely dependent on nature of public acceptance; Differences as to use of traditional or rebellious ways of inciting envy or admiration; Dread of losing caste ("humiliation"), whether through external circumstances or through factors from within. (7). The neurotic need for personal admiration: Inflated image of self (narcissism); Need to be admired not for what one possesses or presents in public eye but for the imagined self; Self-evaluation dependent on living up to this image and on admiration of it by others; Dread of losing admiration ("humiliation"). (8). The neurotic ambition for personal achievement: Need to surpass others not through what one presents or is but through one's activities; Self-evaluation dependent on being the very best—lover, sportsman, writer, worker—particularly in one's own mind, recognition by others being vital too, however, and its absence resented; Admixture of destructive tendencies (toward the defeat of others) never lacking but varying in intensity; Relentless driving of self to greater achievements, though with pervasive anxiety; Dread of failure ("humiliation"). Trends 6, 7 and 8 have in common a more or less open competitive drive toward absolute superiority over others. But though these trends overlap and may be combined, they may lead a

Recidivism in the Examen's practice should be noted. The recidivist might simply blame her constant failures on psychological problems or neuroticism. Thus, she is not responsible for her behaviors. One might conclude that this particular problem emerges most often when a deep, integrated exploration of sin and its spiritual and psychological roots have been avoided.

One easily affirms that the matrix of sin, combined with what our commentators define as sinful, psychological compulsion, has characterized every individual's spiritual struggles since time immemorial. It is a cosmic struggle that has evolutionary dimensions:

> Sin, we begin to see, is more than a violation of a law. In the Byzantine liturgy, before receiving the Eucharist both the priest and people pray together for forgiveness of all sin, deliberate and inherited. Sin is anything that prevents God from being God in our life. It is as much the brokenness of our ancestors that we have inherited as our own willfulness. It is the "sin of the world" or a sharing in original sin. We open ourselves to the cancerous, cosmic influences of sin by being born into this world. And to this inherited evil we add our own deliberate sin. Our whole being shudders at the fragmentation. We feel caught in a prison of darkness and yet we see a delicate ray of light leading us out through the crack of metanoia, a conversion to the Lord.[46]

Ignatius indirectly addresses the distinctively psychological, familial and developmental elements of the spiritual journey. His compendium in the Exercises of Rules for dealing with scruples and the psychological insights woven into the Rules for discernment are easily interpreted as a response to his acute awareness of the psychological dimension of integrated spiritual growth necessary for authentic wholeness and holiness. One can make the case that for Ignatius' day a psychological method of sorts is encapsulated in the rules for scruples.[47] The Sacred Story Examen provides a technique that takes the spiritual and psychological elements of the personality into account. The method allows for personal responsibility in the face of sin. It also provides strategies for helping examinees access and disarm the psychological stresses and cross-pressures that can fuel sinful patterns and passions.[48]

---

separate existence. The need for personal admiration, for instance, may go with a disregard of social prestige. (10). The neurotic need for perfection and unassailability: relentless driving for perfection; Ruminations and self-recriminations regarding possible flaws; Feelings of superiority over others because of being perfect; Dread of finding flaws within self or of making mistakes; Dread of criticism or reproaches." Karen Horney, MD, *Self Analysis* (New York: W. W. Norton & Company, Inc., 1994), 53-56. Cited hereafter as: "Horney."

[46] George A. Maloney, SJ, *Alone with the Alone* (Notre Dame, ID: Ave Maria Press, 1982), 46.

[47] *SpEx* [345-351]. Read also how Ignatius dealt with Favre's scruples and sexual temptations: José Ignacio Tellechea Idígoras, *Ignatius of Loyola: The Pilgrim Saint*, trans. Cornelius Michael Buckley, SJ (Chicago: Loyola University Press, 1994), 310-11. Cited hereafter as, "Idígoras." There are many other accounts that reveal Ignatius' keen understanding of the complexities of the human personality. He was able to bring a person to integrated, spiritual growth. Unaided by modern psychological disciplines, he was cognizant of the psychological dimension of human nature and the emotional stresses of the spiritual journey.

[48] All our commentators call for this integrated approach. They are aware that Ignatius' spirituality compels such integrated "sourcing" but none offer specific plans to achieve it.

An integrated approach that encompasses both the spiritual and psychological dimensions of human experience is important for everyone. Perhaps it is especially imperative for those whose principal experience in life is being sinned against. For Original Sin that is generational and familial generates significant static in the form of fear, anger, and grief. Early memories of innocence betrayed and trusts broken make the project of self-examination and discussions of sin radioactive. They block the process of reflection, acceptance, and forgiveness that the Ignatian Examen encourages.[49]

Sinful passions and habits whose roots in early developmental experiences might be repressed or forgotten, pose unique challenges. Maté, Allers, Horney, Idígoras and Meissner focus on the shaping influence of early life experiences. Of the Examen commentators reviewed, English takes the presence of early childhood traumas seriously and is the most helpful in providing constructive ways of approaching these early childhood wounds. He understands that the memory can provide access to life's significant events, and be a channel for graces and healing.[50]

Sacred Story provides a method for accessing memories and experiences that have interrupted or injured one's spiritual and psychological maturation. It does it in much the same way that the PE is used to "source" those sins and vices that are the origin of many others. Today, Ignatius would consciously seek the source events— both spiritual and psychological—that form the basis of his narcissism and the manifest sins disguising it. He has already done this for us by sourcing his root sins in the tripartite shield of "riches, honors, and pride." It is from these "three steps" Ignatius says that "the evil one leads to all other vices." These are Satan's signature in the meditation on the Two Standards SpEx [140-142].[51]

A Return to Childhood Innocence

---

[49] "It is important to remember that some people are deeply wounded because they have been sinned against. Ignatius does not consider this aspect of sin in the *Exercises*. Rather, he sets up exercises to help those who have truly sinned." *Spiritual Freedom*, John English, SJ, *Spiritual Freedom* (Chicago: Loyola University Press, 1995), 55. Cited hereafter as "Spiritual Freedom."

[50] "Our memory retains all the events and responses to our life. These include those events that are immediately present to us and those that were unconscious or forgotten. Events are relegated to the unconscious for a number of reasons. Some are repressed…. Other events, both positive and negative, are not repressed, but only forgotten. These events are significant for our life with God and other human beings. There are simple ways of remembering these experiences. For example, we can begin with our earliest recollection and move forward to the significant events in each year of our lives, or we can begin with the present and move back to our early years. Once we have done this we can reflect on these events and appreciate them. We are in a position to grasp their meaning in our lives, and then go forward with new energy and determination." *Ibid.*, 263.

[51] Ignatius grew up in a family culture immersed in "all other vices." Surely, then, he would not have second-guessed the *riches, honors and pride* that sourced them. Ignatius had to backtrack from those manifest sins to their roots before he could gain a complete picture of how the "enemy of human nature" helped him evolve, from infancy, to become the dissolute and vainglorious soldier of Pamplona. Thus, Ignatius' growth and illumination was progressive, from identifying and "controlling" his most manifest sins, to his graced discovery of the root ride underlying his disordered history.

In the Exercises, the "Consideration of Different States of Life" immediately precedes the meditation on the Two Standards.[52] In his "Consideration," it is telling that Ignatius recaps previous exercises of the Christ child's spiritual and moral development: 1) from his foster father and his mother he learns to observe the Commandments and the life of obedience, and; 2) from his eternal Father, he learns the life of evangelical perfection.

The juxtaposition of these exercises and their summary in the Consideration's introduction with the Two Standards reveals more clearly Ignatius' comments in the Autobiography intimating a return to his own childhood to learn aright what it means to be man. He learns this not from a surrogate for his father Beltrán, nor his brother Martín García. He learns it from God who "treated him as a schoolteacher treats a child...because he was thick and dull of brain."[53]

The meditation on the "Standard of Satan" reveals the negative spiritual influences that work directly on the human subject. In the modern-day application of the Ignatian Rules, it is common to perceive such influences flowing directly from spiritual powers but also through the history of family, clan and nation. Ignatius affirms that the Standard of Satan was dominant, king, in his first thirty years of life.[54]

Yet his conversion amply demonstrates that malformation of spirit and/or psyche and lack of love or proper example of Christian living early in life is trumped by God's grace working cooperatively with the individual who submits to graced conversion. Simplicity, obedience and innocence of heart transform a heart divided by pride, addictive passions and disobedience.

Ignatius' story also reveals that to begin afresh one must work with grace and the Spirit's illuminations. One does this not only to identify the roots of one's maladaptive behaviors but also to allow them to be uprooted so a new life can take hold. Using Ignatius' own story and adding what we know of human psychological development, the search for root causes should include those formative

---

[52] "The example which Christ our Lord gave of the first state of life, which is that of observing the Commandments, has already been considered in meditating on His obedience to His parents. The example of the second state, which is that of evangelical perfection, has also been considered, when He remained in the temple and left His foster father and His Mother to devote himself exclusively to the service of His eternal Father. While continuing to contemplate His life, let us begin to investigate and ask in what kind of life or what state His Divine Majesty wishes to make use of us. Therefore, as some introduction to this, in the next exercise, let us consider the intention of Christ, our Lord, and on the other hand that of the enemy of our human nature. Let us also see how we ought to prepare ourselves to arrive at perfection in whatever state or way of life God our Lord may grant us to choose." *SpEx* [135]; Puhl, 59.

[53] Ignatius Loyola, *A Pilgrim's Journey*, trans. Joseph N. Tylenda, SJ (Wilmington: Michael Glazier, Inc, 1985), 37. Cited hereafter as "Tylenda."

[54] Catholic doctrine declares: "the whole of human history is marked by the original fault freely committed by our first parents" (CCC 390). It is natural to view the transmission of sin, as a general evolutionary force, coming through those first parents. But we need to expand this view, and attune to the evolution of spiritual corruption, as a general force throughout time, but also *mutating* in specific ways because of the unique choices, personalities and histories of individual, cultures, nationalities, clans and families. Clearly Ignatius' *family* sins and traumas cast long shadows over his life.

events and life situations—both suffered and committed—that fashion desires and lifestyles eroding childhood innocence.[55]

Spiritual and emotional backtracking is absolutely essential for spiritual insight and growth. It is congruent with Ignatius' own strategy in searching out every source blocking the free activity of grace, especially ones that are the "cause of many others." A diagram that reveals Ignatius' progressive enlightenment on the nature of sin in his life, as well as the element of psychological/family history, is used in Sacred Story:

SACRED STORY INTEGRATION AND AWARENESS TEMPLATE

MANIFEST SINS
THE FRUIT OR ORNAMENTATION

(Ignatius' addictive gambling, reactive anger and sexual self-indulgence) Manifest Fear, Anger, and Grief, moral weaknesses, vices, addictions, and sinful habits that are the most visible to you.

CORE SINS
THE TRUNK OR SUPERSTRUCTURE

(Ignatius' arrogance, blinded conscience and narcissism)
Disobedience and Narcissism, along with its Fear, Anger, and Grief, that Forms the Trunk or Superstructure of Your Daily Life, Feeding on Originating Sins and Events

ORIGINAL SINS
THE ROOTS OR FOUNDATION

(Original sin and concupiscence that wounded your heart and soul; distinctive family/clan sin and/or early life-events that wounded you spiritually, psychologically and physically)
Ancient, Originating Events that Rooted the Patterns of Disobedience and Narcissism along with its Fear, Anger, Grief

---

[55] The beginning of this process should begin like Ignatius', i.e., a clear-eyed examination of those habits and vices—thoughts, words and deeds—contravening the Commandments and The Standard of Christ.

Sacred Story's Examens methodology provides tactics for moving in both directions along this continuum, from root to branch and branches to root. This gradual awakening is necessary in order to facilitate an integrated "reading" of one's life, much in the same way Ignatius appears to have done during his own awakening.

A Broken Heart as a Paradigm for Lost Innocence

The dogma of Original Sin is abstract and difficult for most people to grasp easily. New categories and paradigms for describing the effects of sin 's evolutionary impact on the human family are helpful. Original Sin can be better understood if identified not only by a constitution weakened by Original Sin, what the Tradition has described as concupiscence but also of a heart broken by a world of sin.[56]

Simply put sin breaks relationship with God, the self, others and creation. And broken relationships break hearts. Broken hearts, in turn, manifest in the loss of faith, hope and love, all principal characteristics of spiritual desolation. A broken heart and crushed spirit—cut off from faith, hope and love—hence from meaningful relationship, seeks anesthesia for its pain and sorrow in pleasure, material acquisition, addictions and reactive violence as Maté documents. The reality of a wounded, broken heart as a symbol of sin's impact makes the dogma of Original Sin immediate, personal, and heartfelt. Accordingly, the image and language of a broken heart are used throughout Sacred Story to illumine sin's impact.

The Social Dimensions of Sin

Ignatian mysticism has been depicted as a mysticism of service. The purgation that the Examen facilitates leads to a union with God that expresses itself in labor for the Kingdom on behalf of Christ and his Gospel. Sin and dysfunction block a person's freedom and availability for this service.[57]

Sin's impact, therefore, is not only an inner reality but also social. It is social not just because sin hinders availability for service. Sin is social because it also harms those in one's "life-world;" the milieu in which one makes her way in the world.[58] The socialization of sin in the Ignatian Examen also includes the fractured relationship between the human person and creation. After all, Ignatius' mysticism is about finding God in all things.

An individualized understanding of sin as a principal focus of the Examen's ascesis is shortsighted. For sin is both personal and social. We have come to understand that engaging our Catholic, Christian faith entails an integrated responsibility to advance justice on all fronts. Ascetical disciplines like the

---

[56] Augustine speaks of sin as a wounding of the heart: "For in my wounded heart I saw your splendor and it dazzled me." Saint Augustine, *Confessions*, trans. R. S. Pine-Coffin (London: Penguin, 1961), 249.

[57] Aschenbrenner had this insight. It is why he wrote his further reflection on the Examen as a verification of our availability. It is also the basis of Hugh Campbell's reflections on the PE as the touchstone of a genuine apostolic spirituality.

[58] *Particulars*, 238.

Examen are suspect if practitioners are led into a privatized spirituality disconnected from the world's suffering and pain. Sacred Story highlights the Examen's innate dynamic as a discipline both personal and social.

A fully realized Examen enables and encourages one to see the links between thoughts, words and deeds in one's own life, with the persons in one's social milieu, and to the situation of the poor and the environment. A fully realized Examen emphasizes the interconnected dimension of creation and the personal responsibility each possesses for either adding to Church, community and society's problems, or becoming part of the solution. Expanding our view of the Examen's social dimensions—a view of creation's interconnectedness—is rooted in the Ignatian Contemplatio; SpEx [235, 236]. Ignatian spirituality reveals a mysticism of God's in-dwelling and laboring in all creatures and elements, both on earth and in the heavens. After all, Ignatius' mysticism is about finding God in all things.[59] We remember that Ignatius' early conversion at Loyola opens him to the beauty of a starry night.

Praying the Examen invites God into our lives to reveal our sinfulness, addictions and dysfunction. In so doing, God heals us, and opens our hearts to loving service, allowing us to see the world around us both in its beauty and in its suffering. The Examen leads to interior freedom for our self-donation in service to the Kingdom.

Pierre Teilhard de Chardin expands on Ignatius' themes of cosmic mysticism in reflections on sin in the world. Teilhard discerns even in the face of evil as a destructive and atomizing force, an inevitable and intensifying understanding of the person's inherent unity with others and all creation:

> Every new war, embarked upon by the nations for the purpose of detaching themselves from one another, merely results in their being bound and mingled together in a more inextricable knot. The more we seek to thrust each other away, the more do we interpenetrate....Moreover, being each exposed at the core of their being to the countless spiritual influences emanating from the thought, the will and the passions of all their fellow-creatures, they find themselves constantly subjected in spirit to an enforced rule of resonance...—there is only one way the tide can flow: the way of ever increasing unification.[60]

Teilhard's mysticism compels us to see that even the most cancerous aspect of Original Sin signified by the violence that isolates and separates people from each other will as it increases, conspire to force individuals and societies to confront their very dependence and interconnectedness.

---

[59] "Do I have a God-centered, sacramental reverence for the earth? Do I see the cosmos as 'a body of God'? As a steward and co-creator of the planet, do I express gratitude for the beauty of God's creation and work responsibly with others to preserve it?" Joan L. Roccasalvo, CSJ, *Prayer for Finding God in All Things* (St. Louis: Institute of Jesuit Sources, 2005), 21.

[60] Teilhard de Chardin, *The Future of Man* (Glasgow: William Collins & Son Co. Ltd, 1959), 132-33.

Joseph Ratzinger acknowledges that Teilhard's Ignatian-influenced mysticism shows clearly that man and cosmos "belong to each other" and will "become one through their 'complexification' in the larger entity of the love, that...steps beyond and encompasses bios."[61] Using Teilhard's template, he reveals how it "renders comprehensible" St. Paul's vision of all things being one in Christ Jesus.[62] It reflects Paul's image of Christ as the firstborn of creation (Col. 1:15-22).

This understanding of the interconnectedness of human networks in both sin and grace naturally expands to the Examen's focus on the natural world. We now understand environmental ecosystems are vital to our survival. Degradation of ecosystems is increasingly viewed by the Church as "sin" that violates the commandment of love because of the human threat they occasion. Individual and cultural expressions of narcissism and pride manifested as excessive consumption need to be linked to such exploitation that affects people and ecosystems.[63] They are "sin" because they threaten and destroy life.

This does not necessarily mean I examen during prayer how I am or am not working directly with or on behalf of the poor or fragile ecosystems. But it does mean examining greed, waste, indulgence, overconsumption, and selfish "use of creatures" in my life. It also means inviting graced insight helping me see how my choices and lifestyle lack freedom, and these are connected to my addictions and sin. I need to awaken to how my choices and lifestyle might have destructive consequences not just for "me" but also for all God's creation.

This holistic world-view creates a greater sense of urgency in the use and practice of the Examen. But it also directly challenges those who facilely disconnect personal lifestyle choices and consumption habits—narcissisms and addictions of all kinds—from their impact on the earth and humanity. The "individual" conversion process facilitated by the Ignatian Examen as a life-prayer however it may have been understood in the past is not a monadic exercise focusing ultimately on "my sin," "my personhood," or "my life-story" as an isolated instance of the creation/redemption work of Christ. Understanding it in this narrow sense violates its purpose and makes it irrelevant to the Gospel's, the Church's, and the Society of Jesus' mission of universal reconciliation. The personal responsibility of

---

[61] Joseph Ratzinger, *Introduction to Christianity* (New York: The Seabury Press, 1968), 178-179. Cited hereafter as: "Ratzinger."

[62] As an "I," man is indeed an end but the whole tendency of his being and of his own existence shows him also to be a creation belonging to a "super-I" that does not blot him out but encompasses him; only such an association can bring out the form of the future of man, in which humanity will achieve complete fulfillment of itself...From here onwards faith in Christ will see the beginning of a movement in which dismembered humanity is gathered together more and more into the being of one single Adam, one single body – the man to come. It will see in him the movement to that future of man in which he is completely "socialized," incorporated in one single being, but in such a way that the separate individual is not extinguished but brought completely to himself. *Ibid.*, 178-9.

[63] "Destruction of the environment harms the good of creation given to man by God the Creator as something indispensable for his life and his development...We need to realize therefore that there can be grave sin against the natural environment, one which weighs heavily on our consciences and which calls for grave responsibility toward God the Creator." Pope John Paul II, "Zamosc Homily," speech delivered to Polish Congregation, June 12, 1999, Zamosc, Poland.

one's labor in the practice of the Examen must instead be framed as collaborative effort joined with God's grace, reconciling one with God, the self, others, and creation.[64]

Sacred Story facilitates this higher perspective and the communal dimension it signifies by inviting us to labor in awakening to our sin, addiction and dysfunction. It invites one to accept responsibility for his or her share of sin's devastation in our lives and in our larger social universe. It allows Christ to heal us and transform the way we labor in our own Sacred Story with his own in the work of universal reconciliation.[65] Personal transformation is an intrinsically social act, and Ignatius' Examen is at its core an exercise in communal prayer.

Secularization and Its Impact on God-Consciousness

Most Examen commentators are aware of the difficulties secular culture presents to persons seeking to cultivate critical self-awareness. Aschenbrenner hints that undefined pressures make it difficult for persons to achieve the daylong attentiveness the Examen invites. Townsend highlights the materialistic bent of modern society that erodes one's awareness that "all is gift," the fundamental gratitude so central to Christianity, and expressly highlighted in Ignatian spirituality.[66] English decries the market culture's "drive to success" as an embodiment of anti-Christ, fostering self-indulgence so cancerous to the spiritual life.[67] Tetlow sees modernity's false freedom as individualism and narcissism, turning a person from both an honest assessment of his life and from others in his life-world, and ultimately, from God.[68]

These pressures and challenges act to constrict one's heart and imagination making it difficult not only to desire engaging the Ignatian Examen (what can it do for me?) but also continuing its practice once it starts to take bites out of our time and our egos. Any self-discipline poses challenges. What usually motivates action however is a compelling belief, personally experienced, that makes a discipline worthwhile. We must possess a frame of reference that gives value to engaging a practice like the

---

[64] "In this global world marked by such profound changes, we now want to deepen our understanding of the call to serve faith and promote justice, and dialogue with culture and other religions in the light of the apostolic mandate to establish right relationships with God, with one another, and with creation...We are sent on mission by the Father, as were Ignatius and the first companions at La Storta, together with Christ, risen and glorified but still carrying the cross, as he labors in a world yet to experience the fullness of his reconciliation. In a world torn by violence, strife and division, we then are called with others to become instruments of God, who "in Christ reconciled the world to himself, not counting their trespasses." Decrees, 27.

[65] "Only the light of divine Revelation clarifies the reality of sin and particularly of sin committed at mankind's origin. Without the knowledge Revelation gives of God we cannot recognize sin clearly and are tempted to explain it as merely a developmental flaw, a psychological weakness, a mistake, or the necessary consequence of an inadequate social structure, etc." CCC, 87.

[66] *Finding*, 48-50.

[67] English, 13.

[68] *Persons*, 119.

Examen and staying the course once a commitment is made. Certainly, Ignatius had compelling reasons to stay the course that addresses some of the threats modernity's secularism is defined as posing to 'God-mindedness'; reasons an effective and enduring practice of the Examen requires.

The discipline and ascetical effort Ignatius invested daily and hourly to achieve docility and the spiritual indifference the Examen cultivates is manifest in the First Principle and Foundation. His insights draw on the energy generated by both his passionate belief in and desire to be united with the Trinity in the eternal Kingdom of the saints and blessed. For Ignatius, these transcendent and eternal goals are the purpose and end of human striving. We see evidence of this in both his letters and the Constitutions' General Examen. In these sources, we hear Ignatius address the theme of the Christian life in light of this "eternal" horizon.[69]

It may be true that Christians today affirm an afterlife as part of the creedal inheritance of their faith. Yet the concept that the journey of life is but a step to an eternity with God in the Kingdom of the righteous—an operative and vital belief capable of shaping attitudes and values for daily living—has lost ground. Replacing it are more powerful market-driven, self-help forms of Christian spirituality that compel us to focus on instantaneous success.

Taylor offers an explanation for this loss of transcendence in modern culture and specifically in Christianity. Very few act on the belief that that actions in the here-and-now link to an eternal and transcendent realm. The consciousness of life events grounded in "higher time" has given way to viewing events in "vertical time- slices." The assorted unrelated incidents of daily living cohere only in one-dimensional perspectives of "profane time."[70]

---

[69] "We must never lose sight of the fact that we are pilgrims until we reach it (our heavenly country), and we must not let our affections tarry in the hostelries and the lands through which we pass, lest we forget our destination and lose our love of our last end. And the better to attain it, our eternal Father has given us the use and service of creatures….One can thus spend an entire lifetime seeking to pass these few days of our pilgrimage in the midst of honors, wealth, and self-satisfactions, without a thought of that which must be the cause of inestimable and unending riches, honor, prosperity, and satisfaction in our heavenly fatherland. Truly, that saying of the prophet applies to such men: "And they set at nought the desirable land." Or if they did have regard for it, they would do as much to live happily in it as they do to live contentedly in the pilgrimage in which God has placed us all on the way to that land. Letter to Anthony Enriquez: Rome; March 26, 1554 in: Young, 332-333. "I have a very great desire indeed, if I may say so, to see a true and intense love of God grow in you, my relatives and friends, so that you will bend all your efforts to the praise and service of God…It is none of my business to condemn a man who in this life lies awake with plans for adding to his buildings, his income, his estate in the hope of leaving behind him a great name and reputation. But neither can I praise him, for, according to St. Paul, we ought to use the things of this world as though we used them not, and own them as though we owned them not, because the fashion of this world passes and in a moment is gone (1 Cor. 7:29-31). God grant that it may be so." Letter of Ignatius to his brother, Martin Garcia De Onaz: Paris June 1532 in Young, 7-8. "For our profession requires that we be prepared and very much ready for whatever is enjoined upon us in our Lord and at whatsoever time, without asking for or expecting any reward in this present and transitory life, but hoping always for that life which lasts for eternity, through God's supreme mercy." *Constitutions*, 41.

[70] "Now the move to what I am calling "secularity" is obviously related to this radically purged time-consciousness. It comes when associations are placed firmly and wholly in homogeneous, profane time, whether or not the higher time is negated altogether, or other associations are still admitted to exist in it. Such I want to argue is the case with the public sphere, and therein lies its new and (close to) unprecedented nature." Taylor, 196.

His narrative on the migration of human consciousness from belief in a "demon-haunted world" requiring the holy powers of saints, angels, and miracles, through "disenchantment" and, finally, "excarnation," is multi-dimensional. One of his so-called "modern social imaginaries" facilitating this migration deserves comment. Along with a flattened time-consciousness, comes the "innovation" to conceptualize the business of daily life as exclusively intra-human. All aspects of daily commerce, labor, and exchange can be "disengaged" from any reference to God.

This hermeneutic allows human imagination to unchain itself not only from God-consciousness but all meaning-making that relies on God as source and end. This imagination revolution opens the way for exclusive humanism and atheism. For the non-believer, this "disengaged" stance is associated with rationality and freedom from the confining and odious aspects of religiosity. It grants dignity, meaning, and prestige to its adherents. This disengaged stance once confined to cultural élites is now the principal hermeneutic for whole societies in the world today.[71]

The majority of religious believers easily adopt this temporal/secular world-view. We can all consciously or unconsciously operate on its terms in the business of daily life. To varying degrees, all of us are "buffered" from both the transcendent and the world of "higher time." It is not that Christians do not believe in God or an afterlife. Rather, what generates passion, energy, interest, and meaning is skewed in favor of the visible, material world, not the Kingdom-to-come.[72] In this anthropocentric shift, persons easily lose sight of the relational dimension of faith. What is lost is the awareness that intercommunion with the Divine is not only possible but also transformative in this life.[73]

Sacred Story's method does not rely on denunciations of materialism and hyper-activism, at least not as a first strategy. It can't because these realities are consciously or unconsciously operating as principal meaning-makers for engaged Christians. Contemporary formulations of the Christian kerygma have unwittingly led many to associate more work, more donations of time or money, more

---

[71] "What is clear, however, is the present condition of belief and unbelief can't be described purely in terms of élite culture. One of the important events of the twentieth century is that the nova (of unbelief) has come to involve whole societies. It has become the "super-nova." Taylor, 412.

[72] An example of this is the prevalence in the Evangelical Christian world of preachers focusing on the Gospel of wealth and success. In my own work with Catholic executives, I have often been asked what take home value a particular retreat experience would give them. In both instances, the Christian message is understood in material and quantifiable categories. This sort of materialism (distinguished from "consumerist" and "materialistic") can also manifest in many Christian justice movements. The concept of faith is framed more or less exclusively as action for justice. Here, the challenge is an exclusive focus on the second of the two great Commandments. See Edward Vacek, SJ, "Religious Life and the Eclipse of Love for God" Review for Religious, 57 #2 (March-April 1998), 118-37.

[73] "Body, heart, emotion, history; all these make sense only in the context of (6) the belief that the highest being is a personal being, not just in the sense of possessing agency, but also in that of being capable of communion." Taylor, 278. And in relation to the "anthropomorphic shift": "Alongside this, I spoke of the lesser importance of grace in this scheme, the eclipse of mystery, and the foreshortening of the earlier views of the eventual human transformation at the hands of God, evoked by the patristic notion of 'theiosis.'" Taylor, 290.

social engagement, more action on behalf of justice—more investment of effort in the material realm—as the signature of the modern apostle.

Sacred Story follows the advice of Ignatius and uses through-the- day awareness disciplines and the Examen periods of contemplative rest to attune our hearts to both God and "higher time." This is what Pieper and Lewis invite: step into the contemplative stream where the present touches the eternal, the place where the personal God can be encountered and the place where the world as a whole can be glimpsed. Sacred Story is framed as a consciousness-altering activity that grants its practitioners a higher perspective by offering disciplines that ground them firmly in this "present-eternal" realm of the God who is yesterday, today and forever.

With this grounding comes the ability to discern what is and is not of value. In this way, our judgments are not based on the limited, rationalistic assertions of a "buffered identity." They are rooted in a heart and mind that by grace have become attuned and vulnerable to all of creation and to the Presence—the One who is the Way, the Truth, and the Life—who invites us to produce fruit that endures to eternal life (Jn. 14:6; 6:27; 15:5).

Scripture provides multiple stories valuing the contemplative pause, possibly the most familiar is Martha and Mary (Lk. 10:42). Jean-Pierre de Caussade highlights the value of contemplative rest in defining the "present moment" as a "sacrament."[74] Buddhists call it mindfulness. In our age, Eckhart Tolle[75] and Michael Brown use techniques of a consciousness grounding in the present to achieve breakthroughs in perspective.[76]

Ignatius, by his hourly Examen, anchored his heart and consciousness in the present moment. In so doing he seemed always to know his final end, his final home. But more than just awareness of eternity, Ignatius gained wisdom grounded in a holy and holistic awareness of the material, political, human and spiritual worlds. His genius and holistic perspective compelled the Russian mystic and hermeticist Valentin Tomberg to see Ignatius' spirituality as the perfect melding of intellectuality and spirituality, a conjoining that holds faith and knowledge in balance.[77] Ignatius embodies The Fool of the twenty-first Arcanum in that "he succeeded in attaining to the wisdom of perfect equilibrium

---

[74] Jean-Pierre De Caussade, SJ, *The Sacrament of the Present Moment*, trans. Kitty Muggeridge (San Francisco: HarperCollins, 1982). See also De Caussade's: *A Treatise on Prayer from the Heart*, trans. Robert M. McKeon (St. Louis: Institute of Jesuit Sources, 1998), 103-124.

[75] Eckhart Tolle, *The Power of Now* (Vancouver: Namaste Publishing, 2004). See also: Andrew Ryder, "The Sacrament of Now," *The Way* 2 (April 2007); and Tolle's, *A New Earth*, (New York: Dutton, 2005).

[76] Brown's method accomplishes this much more systematically and effectively than Tolle, and does so in ways quite synchronous with Ignatius' *Examen*. Michael Brown, *The Presence Process: A Healing Journey into Present Moment Awareness* (Vancouver: Namaste Publishing, 2005). Cited hereafter as "Brown."

[77] [Valentin Tomberg], *Meditations on the Tarot: a Journey into Christian Heremeticism* (Shaftesbury Dorset, England: Element, 1991), 615. Cited hereafter as "Meditations."

between the world of the mystical revelations and the world of human task and actions:" as a fool, he is a "man placed as an intermediary between two worlds—the divine world and the human world."[78] This "practical mysticism" of Ignatian spirituality, specifically the Examen, joins the transcendent and eternal with the immanent world of action. Ignatius' spirituality has in the past been defined this way: as "contemplation in action."[79] Tomberg suggests it has an even more universal reach, encompassing Eastern religious modalities.[80] It is, he says, a spirituality that unites the consciousness of the Divine with that of the human, transforming the "schizophrenia of two consciousnesses not in harmony with one another—into wisdom."[81]

The Examen, more than any other spiritual discipline anchored Ignatius' heart and mind in this present/eternal realm where he encountered the mystery of God in his daily faith journey. It can still serve this purpose, and must, especially in our catastrophic loss of Kairos—of transcendence—and the suffering and boredom it creates in our time-flattened Chronos.[82]

Sacred Story vitalizes innate aspects of Ignatius' Examen. Especially those that correspond to the deep hungers people in our age have for religious transcendence. Its method responds to those moderns whose only alternative for transcendence has been secular presence awareness techniques or the mindfulness principles of Eastern spiritual disciplines. Remarkably, Ignatius' spirituality and his Examen encompass all these techniques and disciplines. Sacred Story invites the awakening to higher consciousness a less "buffered" experience of the Divine promises. It facilitates an escape from the malaise of immanence where the sheer force of a time-flattened, disenchanted world blocks our path to religious transcendence.[83] Sacred Story opens a path to this mystical discipline of gratitude,

---

[78] *Ibid.*, 616.

[79] Joseph F. Conwell, SJ, *Contemplation in Action* (Spokane: Gonzaga University Press, 1957).

[80] Ignatius' spirituality embodies an "impressive prefiguring" of the characteristics the future Buddha-Avatar will possess: "He will bring human beings themselves to attain to the illuminating experience of revelation, of a kind that it will not be he who will win authority, but rather He who is "the true light that enlightens every man coming into the world" (John 1:9) – Jesus Christ, the Word made flesh, who is the way, the truth and the life. The mission of the Buddha-Avatar to come will therefore not be the foundation of a new religion, but rather that of bringing human beings to the first-hand experience of the source of all revelation ever received from above by mankind, as also of all essential truth ever conceived of by mankind. It will not be novelty to which he will aspire, but rather the conscious certainty of eternal truth." Meditations, 614-15.

[81] *Ibid.*, 616.

[82] Chardin, too, recognized the malaise of modernity as an enervating boredom. Thomas King's reference to Teilhard de Chardin's last years is instructive: "Among the people whom Teilhard knew, there were many weary of life with little motive for living. He believed this number would increase as humanity became more reflective; people were losing the will to live." Thomas M. King, S.J. "Teilhard de Chardin's Devotion to the Sacred Heart," *National Jesuit News*, May-June 2005, p. 8.

[83] Taylor, 308-10.

discernment, reconciliation, and Christian decision- making. The goal is an ongoing pledge "to labor for fruit that endures to eternity."

The Need for Discernment

Those engaging in a daily prayer life and the Ignatian *Examen* practice will regularly experience blockages to integrated growth that are spiritual, psychological and emotional. This will be true even as they awaken to avenues for integrated progress. Ignatius encountered the same types of blockages and opportunities on his conversion journey.

A process of conversion facilitated by an effective and strategic sacramental, prayer and *Examen* practice is always accompanied by the push and pull of consolations and desolations. As Ignatius' progressive conversion illuminates, these two spontaneities indicate paths to positive growth or blockages to integrated growth.

It is essential for those engaging a daily faith practice and an *Ignatian Examen* to understand basic discernment principles. If the *True Heart* practitioner awakens to the consolations and desolations of conversion without a roadmap, they will be lost. The feelings and choices that are inspired by experiences of consolation and desolation can lead one to mistake the light for the dark, the dark for the light, and a counterfeit identity as authentic.

Adapting Ignatius' Classic "Rules" for Sacred Story and True Heart

The *Spiritual Exercises* are the usual forum for discerning major vocational choices. Major vocational choices are usually single acts that oftentimes alter the fundamental course of our lives. Ignatius intended the *Examen* to be used by those who never engaged the full *Exercises*. It too requires discernment methods. The focus of a daily *Examen's* discernment is not a vocational state per se but the thoughts, words, and deeds of one's life, whatever one's chosen vocation. Its strategic purpose is to examine whether those thoughts, words, and deeds express quest and tendency towards God and the Kingdom, or towards the enemy of human nature and his realm.[84]

We want to contemporize Ignatius' *Rules* to make them accessible for a self-guided process. The inspiration for updating the *Rules* comes from Ignatius' progressive conversion as detailed in his

---

[84] "…an act and art of choosing which, the more profoundly they are exercised, the more they become in reality the act and art of 'allowing' oneself to be chosen. This ultimately is what discernment is all about; allowing oneself to be taken by God, allowing Him to act through oneself in every event of history. Thus for Ignatius union is always a quest and a tendency, never a definitive state." Javier Melloni, SJ, *The Exercises of St Ignatius Loyola in the Western Tradition*, trans. Michael Ivens, SJ, (Leominster, England: Gracewing, 2000), 50. Cited hereafter as, "Melloni"

Autobiography.[85] The very crises caused by his faith commitment are the tools God uses to illuminate discernment principles and allow him to negotiate the crises.

We create a new paradigm for expressing Ignatius' *Rules* and facilitates discernment encompassing holistic, integrated growth that is both spiritual and psychological. The *Rules* anticipate the relativism that disconnects human desire and action from Christian norms of right and wrong. Our goal is to help people reflect on desires and choices in light of Ignatius' definitions of consolation and desolation, and in light of the Divinely crafted human nature, both those spontaneities seek to influence and inspire.

The Boundaries of Ignatian Discernment

The *Autobiography* reveals that Ignatius discovers the First and Second Week *Rules* organically and progressively as his purgation unfolds. Some distinguish between Ignatius' "first" conversion at Loyola and his "second" conversion at Manresa, implicitly supporting the idea of Ignatius' organic, progressive conversion and congruent development of the *Rules* with this two-tiered conversion.[86]

The temptations Ignatius confronted early in his conversion process— temptations distinctive to those discussed in his First Week discernment principles—unfold in the purgation of his more manifest sins and vices. He was still lured by the pleasure of instinctual satisfactions that characterized his life up to this point. What Ignatius describes in his *Autobiography* are First Week temptations and consolations typical of the purgative stage of spiritual growth.

 The temptations unique to Second Week principles are those temptations that Ignatius encountered deeper in his conversion journey. The scruples crisis fed the good or holy illusion of his rigorous confession habit. Ignatius had gained mastery over the manifest sins of his former life. Evil had to insinuate itself in a more subtle and nuanced way—under the guise of "good"— one that hooked into his root sin of narcissism and pride. It is this root struggle with pride (manifest in his scruples, obsessive confessional practice and its successful resolution) that forms the *Powerless Paradigm* and the signature elements of the Particular Examen (*PE*).

The *Rules* of Week One and Two are inspired and originate during the very purgative process that gives birth to Ignatius' unique habit of general and particular examen. For our purposes, we reimagine

---

[85] Michael Buckley's seminal essay on Ignatius' discernment *Rules* analyzes their origins and says they can be sought in "his unfolding *Autobiography*" more than any place else. *Rules*, 26. Michael J. Buckley, "The Structure of the Rules for Discernment of Spirits," *The Way Supplement*, no. 20 (Autumn): 28. Cited hereafter cited as "Rules."

[86] Ignatius supports when he states in the Introductory Observations that Weeks One and Two of the *Rules* align with the purgative and illuminative stages of spiritual growth. *SpEx* [10]. Ignatius Loyola, *The Spiritual Exercises of St. Ignatius*, ed. Louis J. Puhl, SJ (Chicago: Loyola University Press, 1951), 4. Cited hereafter as, "Puhl". Egan, Harvey D., SJ. *The Spiritual Exercises and the Ignatian Mystical Horizon*.(St Louis, MO: The Institute of Jesuit Sources, 1976), 21.

the *Rules* with the dynamic fidelity characteristic of St. Ignatius. A first step in framing the *Rules* for a self-guided process is helping users understand discernment's boundaries.

Discernment is difficult and Ignatius gifts the Church with clear discernment boundaries. One of those boundaries is a benchmark for spiritual consolation. The other is a benchmark for spiritual desolation. Together they furnish practitioners with two clear signposts for their progressive conversion journey. *First Benchmark:*

A Definition of Consolation: *Inclinations, Inspirations and Choices that:*
1. *Enflame the heart with love for God,*
2. *Increase docility and humility and,*
3. *Align the heart to truths proposed by the Scripture, Tradition and the Magisterium.*

The foundation for the first benchmark comes in a congruent reading of Ignatius' definitions of regular consolation and consolation without previous cause; consolación sin causa (CSC/CSCP) *SpEx* [332.2].[87] There are diverse readings of what Ignatius means by CSC; its purpose, frequency and signature characteristics. Ignatian scholars have debated the differences.[88]

What is CSC? Ignatius says that it "belongs solely to the Creator to come into a soul, to leave it, to act upon it, to draw it wholly to the love of His Divine Majesty," *SpEx* [330.2]. This "quality" of activity by God and the "type" of effects it produces in the soul are congruent with Ignatius' preliminary definition of consolation in Week One:

> I call it consolation when an interior movement is aroused in the soul, by which it is enflamed with love of its Creator and Lord, and as a consequence, can love no creature on the face of the earth for its own sake, but only in the Creator of them all. *SpEx* [316.3].

A consolation of this type is "prompted (sine causa) in a person by some influence beyond his or her affectivity and awareness."[89] The heart "enflamed" is paradigmatic of all consolation. It is the direct consequence of the Holy Spirit's most profound actions in the human subject moving one toward selfless charity. Consolation of this type can only come from God: "The CSCP (CSC) therefore, sums up that Father-initiated 'flight from self-love, self-will, and self-interest' [Ex 18]…and corresponds to the exercitant's basic dynamic for fulfillment…arising from a gratuitous and purely disinterested love…The

---

[87] Different commentators use the longer or shorter Latin abbreviation for "consolation without previous cause." Thus, CSC and CSCP are both accepted as an abbreviation for "consolation without previous cause." Likewise, "sin causa" and "sine cause" are Spanish and Latin forms of the same phrase.

[88] It is valuable to identify aspects of CSC that are generally accepted and juxtapose them with Ignatius' progressive conversion detailed in the *Autobiography*. Toner, Jules J., SJ. *A Commentary on Saint Ignatius' Rules for the Discernment of Spirits*. St. Louis, MO: Institute of Jesuit Sources, 1982, 291-313.

[89] *Ibid.*, 99.

CSCP is emphatically Christocentric."[90] The role of Spirit, Father and Son in the impact of CSCP is a Trinitarian grace unique to Ignatius' mysticism.[91]

There is a third dimension to CSC apart from being "enflamed" with love for God and led toward selfless charity. This third element is its "ecclesial" context, a dimension that is both a quality and a confirmation of the consolation's character as "sin causa".[92] Such consolations never contradict received Tradition. Ignatius' letter to Dominican sister Theresa Rejadell is the clearest example to confirm this characteristic of CSC.[93]

Consolation without previous cause is a graced encounter that draws one wholly to God, and to selfless love, without contradicting the truth of received Tradition. It can be conceived as the grace of fundamental conversion that reorients one in the direction of the Divine. In this Ignatian context, CSC provides "illumination" but not in the sense of private revelations. Instead, it facilitates a wisdom revealing one's authentic personality before God; one's sins, yes, plus the evidence of things in one's life that are opposed to God.[94] Most importantly, one's authentic self is revealed in light of God's fundamental and all-embracing love for God's creature.

This form of consolation is what Ignatius receives while recuperating at Loyola. It propels him into the desert of his first purgation of the senses, his First Week exercises, temptations, consolations, and insights into discernment in light of these desolations and consolations. The CSC is also evident in Ignatius' illumination at Manresa; his "great clarity of mind" enables him to "see" the wrong in his

---

[90] Egan, 36-37.

[91] "One cannot find any adequate cause for it in sensible experience. Rather, it is an experience of being grasped or elevated by the love of the Trinity. The truth is in the experience. Simply, I know I am taken over by the Trinity's love when this happens. Paul speaks about this in Romans when he says: 'This hope is not deceptive for the love of God has been poured into our hearts by the Holy Spirit himself and our spirits bear witness that we are children of God' (Rom. 8: 14-16). Such self-authenticated experiences of the unconditional love of God St. Ignatius calls "consolation without previous cause." John J. English, SJ, "The Mind and the Heart of Christ," *The Way* 23 (October 1983): 296.

[92] "Ignatius' transcendence is not without dogma, because the same Spirit who guides the exercitant's transcendence to Election also 'guides and governs our Holy Mother Church' (*Ex* 365). The CSCP, therefore, is intrinsically linked to established, historical, ecclesial norms which may be used to measure the CSCP's authenticity (*Ex* 170).). For Ignatius, even a vocation discovered not to be from God cannot be changed, if that choice is deemed immutable by the hierarchical Church (*Ex*. 172)." Egan, 64.

[18] "It remains for me to speak of how we ought to understand what we think is from our Lord and, understanding it, how we ought to use it for our advantage. For it frequently happens that our Lord moves and urges the soul to this or that activity. He begins by enlightening the soul; that is to say, by speaking interiorly to it without the din of words, lifting it up wholly to His divine love and ourselves to His meaning without any possibility of resistance on our part, even should he wish to resist. This thought of His which we take is *of necessity* (italics supplied) in conformity with the commandments, the precepts of the Church, and obedience to our superiors." Padberg et al., 22. See also Toner, 217.

[94] Ignatius affirms that shedding tears for one's sins, in light of God's love and mercy, is spiritual consolation, *SpEx* [316.3].

scrupulous habit so destructive of his spiritual goals and also to surrender "control" of his life entirely to God.

The trials at Manresa, followed by his illumination and "great clarity of mind" vis-a-vis the compulsive confession habit, constitute Ignatius' more integrated "second" conversion that led him to a deeper selflessness, docility to the Spirit, obedience, and his signature mystical graces.[95]

Consolation without cause is rightfully viewed as the fundamental reorienting grace of conversion. It is made possible by Christ's supreme sacrifice, a sacrifice that is visibly and invisibly, with deliberate intention and relentless love, repairing the damage to human nature wrought by Original Sin and the enemy of human nature (1 Cor. 15:25-28; 2 Cor. 5:16-20; Col. 1:15-20; Phil. 3:21).

The subject who receives it might not be aware of consolation as a reorienting grace, but consolation is operative nonetheless. It becomes more thematic as the subject's conversion deepens. It is operative because Christ wishes all to be saved.[96] Definitions of CSC and regular consolation are thus always one and the same: grace. The effects of those graces are progressive, deepening as one advances on the path of purgation, through illumination, to union.

The effects of consolation always enflame the heart with love for God, compel growth in selflessness and charity, and increase docility and obedience. And the obedience is to the Truth of the one whose Spirit and Presence confirms the faith of the Church (Mt. 16:17-19, 28:16-20; Jn. 20:19-23). It is not a rigid adherence to rules and norms or a blind conformism to the law of external authority. Instead, it is the harrowing and hallowed surrender in freedom of one's life to the One who is the Way, Truth, and Life.

The meeting between the soul and Christ denoted by the CSC has the effect of fostering a deeply integrated conversion like that of St. Ignatius. It initiates a new consciousness of life's possibilities that leads to an awareness of one's visible sins in light of these holy stirrings of grace. As one's conversion

---

[95] It has been disputed that CSC is a frequent and fundamental form of graced consolation that anchors all Ignatian discernment. The weight of evidence aligns with the argument toward the greater "frequency." Toner, 313. Rahner and Egan argue for the theory of greater frequency. See also: Lawrence Murphy, "Consolation," *The Way* 27 (Spring 1976) 38.

[96] Yet, it is possible to infer that Ignatius' explication of CSC in the Second Week Rules has less to do with the rarity of CSC as argued by Toner, than the *type* of temptation that is particularly destructive and deformative of its graces at this deeper and more integrated level of conversion; that conversion typified more by the purgation of the "spirit" than of the "senses." It is at this more critical stage of conversion and purgation that the enemy of human nature insinuates itself and "hides" behind the deeply entrenched vices of the intellect and spirit, like Ignatius' narcissism masked by his scruples. Here the "enemy" can mimic "an angel of light" and subtly lead one astray through "seemingly good" and even holy thoughts, just when one is on the cusp of a "fundamental" surrender of control of one's life to God in the purgative process, or during a vital "election" of a way of life. Hence, we have Ignatius' warning to be particularly wary during certain critical stages of spiritual development and election. See: Hugo Rahner, Hubert Becher, Hans Wolter, Josef Stierli, Adolf Haas, Heinrich Bacht, Lambert Classen and Karl Rahner, *Ignatius of Loyola: His Personality and Spiritual Heritage 116-1956*, ed. Friedrich Wulf (St. Louis: Institute of Jesuit Sources, 1977), 291.

deepens, the touch of God penetrates to the roots that fuel those sins and the intellectual and psychological defense structures that support those roots.

The further one moves towards God, the more one can accomplish for Christ's work of universal reconciliation. At these critical points of conversion, there is more reason for the enemy of human nature to do everything possible to disrupt a life that is oriented to the glory of the Divine Majesty.

In summary, the signature characteristics one uses to determine the authenticity of genuine spiritual consolation are these: genuine consolation will always open and enflame the heart with love for God; it will increase one's docility of spirit and one's humility; and the inclinations and choices inspired by authentic consolation will not contravene Scripture, the received Tradition or the Teaching Church. For the Spirit of God, which inspires each of them, is not divided or contradictory.[97]

Second Benchmark:

A Signature Definition of Desolation: "Inclination to Things Low and Earthly"

1. *Defines Appetites Dissimilar to Scripture, the Received Tradition, and the Teaching Church.*

St. Paul in his letter to the Colossians encourages his listeners to "put to death" those actions and aspects of self that are opposed to Christ.[98] St. Ignatius defines these Pauline attributes of the "old self" more succinctly as "inclinations to things low and earthly."[99] The Age of Authenticity celebrates and elevates such instinctual desires as benchmarks of human freedom and expressions of individuality.

This would include not just sensuality but also lusts for material gain and comforts that far exceed the basic necessities of life. Inclinations and appetites that contravene Scripture, received Tradition and the Teaching Church (STTC) are, according to the measures used by Ignatius, indicators of spiritual

---

[97] Rahner states that Ignatius did not expect life in the Church to "be without pain or conflict." Nor can one simply "deduce" from doctrines how one is to make decisions. Otherwise he says: "Ignatius' Rules for an Election, which put the individual on his own before God, would make no sense and have no area where they could be applied." Neither is an election "anti-ecclesial for the "charismatic element" that informs election and conversion "belongs to the nature of the Church." Ibid., 293.

[98] *Put to death, then, the parts of you that are earthly: immorality, impurity, passion, evil desire, and the greed that is idolatry. Because of these the wrath of God is coming (upon the disobedient). By these you too once conducted yourselves, when you lived in that way. But now you must put them all away: anger, fury, malice, slander, and obscene language out of your mouths. Stop lying to one another, since you have taken off the old self with its practices and have put on the new self, which is being renewed, for knowledge, in the image of its creator.* Col. 3: 5-10.

[99] *SpEx* [317.4]

desolation.[100] Ignatius provides guidelines for those trying to navigate the radically individualistic waters of human desire in our contemporary world.

St. Ignatius calls Satan "the enemy of human nature." Ignatius' distinctive use of the spiritual signatures of the enemy human nature in his *Rules* and his definitions of desolation as "darkness of soul, turmoil of spirit, inclination to what is low and earthly," signifies an understanding of human nature that is consonant with STTC upon which his *Examination of Conscience* in the *Spiritual Exercises* is based.[101]

Ignatius' own struggles with "things low and earthly" prior to his conversion—addictions to gambling, undiscriminating sexual behavior and a violent temper—are in part what ground his graced insights into the meaning of spiritual desolation and dysfunction. And together, Ignatius' strategic identification of inclinations and actions contravening the three pillars of the Church (STTC) as symptoms of desolation, create significant dissonance in an age of quieted conscience.

Ignatius' *Rules* link spiritual desolation with actions based on instinctual desires and pleasures that contravene STTC norms of truth.[102] Ignatius says that desolation is "entirely opposite" consolation and that the "thoughts that spring from consolation are the opposite of those that spring from desolation" *SpEx* [317.4]. If consolation's thoughts lead to inclinations supporting STTC, then desolation's inspirations lead one in entirely the opposite direction.

Linking desolation's "low and earthly" inclinations to the objective norms of Gospel and Ecclesial-sanctioned righteousness guarantees through the ages the reliability of Ignatius' *Rules* for Christian decision-making. Shifting the ground-rules based on the objective rightness or wrongness of moral inclinations and actions according to individual whim or the relativism and individualism of any given age compromises Ignatian discernment as a system: it dissolves and renders it useless.

---

[100] *SpEx* [42]. As such, both St. Paul and Ignatius' benchmark of human nature appears to conform less with those who propose an evolving ethic of human nature and align instead with formulations of human nature and natural law like those put forth in papal encyclicals like *Veritatis Splendor*, (Boston: Pauline Books and Media, 1993). [Especially: *VS*: §32, 34, 38, 42, 46, 48, 50, 53, 55, 64, and §84-94 on the role of faith in Christ in relation to freedom, truth, and the good].

[101] Catholic moralists can support culture's drift in this direction. They do this by positing an evolving view of human nature, the malleability of which is especially evident in the area of human self-experience and self-identity. Richard Gula is a good representative of this school of thought. See: Richard M. Gula, SS, *Reason Informed by Faith* (New York: Paulist Press, 1989), 228.

[102] St. Ignatius is a strategist. He made his mark on Christian spirituality, and spiritual discernment, because of his attention to the *particular* details of his pre and post-conversion life. His introduction to the nuance of sin in its various guises came at Montserrat from the guides compiled by Abbot Garcia Cisneros. The *particular* details of sin and conversion are so critical to Ignatius that he walks away from his early ministry in Salamanca when the Inquisition forbids him from making distinctions between mortal and venial sin. *Obras Completas de San Ignacio De Loyola: Edicion Manual*, ed. Iparraguirre, SJ, Ignacio (Madrid: Biblioteca De Autores Christianos, 1952), 76. Cited hereafter as "Obras."

Greed, materialism, anger, sexual lust and all inclinations to things "low and earthly" are things Ignatius defines as enemies of true human nature. For discernment to be effective and strategic as Ignatius intended, all such inclinations must be examined as indicators of inordinate attachments, and signs of one whose interior spiritual freedom is compromised.

Helping individuals accurately identify inclinations and behaviors that fail to align with STTC and revealing them as *indicators of spiritual desolation* will lead the willing to probe much more deeply into their emotional, spiritual, personal and psychological history for the roots of those inclinations. Because a chief goal of Ignatian discernment is to identify "inordinate attachments" so that one can gain the freedom to more fully engage their new life in Christ and like Ignatius himself, allow God to draw out their *True Heart*.

Applying Insights on Ignatian Discernment Rules to Sacred Story

Purgation is the school in which Ignatius learned to discern the various spirits. Our new reading of his principles employs the *Rules* as they develop organically in the *Autobiography* through his progressive purgation to illumination. The *Rules,* called "Guidelines" in *True Heart*, retain their basic structure as Ignatius wrote them. Cast in a semi-narrative format, they complement *True Heart's* narrative of Ignatius' spiritual and psychological development condensed from his *Autobiography*. Detailed here are attributes that are unique to the *Rules* (Guidelines) and their application to *True Heart*: spiritual and psychological maturity, authenticity, inspiration, desolation and consolation as lifestyles, heart and mind illumination to new consciousness.

Spiritual and Psychological Maturity: Spiritual and psychological aspects of growth are incorporated into the language of *True Heart* Guidelines. The language fosters the more integrated approach to self-awakening and spiritual development vital for an effective *Examen*. The framework of two "Weeks" has been replaced with two "foundations," to distinguish the progressive dimension of spiritual/psychological maturity denoted by Ignatius' spiritual growth from Loyola to Manresa—from purgation to illumination. In the daily practice of *True Heart*, one moves from understanding manifest sinfulness to discovering the more subtle and nuanced dimensions of sin and temptation at the root of one's personality. This process of spiritual growth is a life-long task.

The language of fear and anxiety Ignatius employs in the *Rules* to convey the actions and marks of the "enemy," are expanded to capture the psychological aspects such fear triggers during the purgation process. This helps to mine the more therapeutic aspects of Ignatius' wisdom. The words "panic," "menacing fear" and "dread" are incorporated to help practitioners better identify the states of desolation that can actually have both spiritual and psychological manifestations.[103]

---

[103] Blending spiritual and psychological insights into Ignatius' spiritual system is not new. In the last century, Hugo Rahner identified aspects of Ignatius' prayer methods that are useful for their therapeutic benefits. Hugo Rahner, *Ignatius the Theologian*, trans. Michael Barry (New York: Herder and Herder, 1968), 181-213.

Authenticity: The word "authenticity" has been inserted into the *True Heart* language of "human nature." This is done to address: (1) the complications arising from surrender to the instinctual pleasures that the "Age of Authenticity" defines as normative for human flourishing and (2) the fluidity of gender and human self-identity typical of a relativistic age. Authenticity is used to denote only those aspects of consolation that according to Ignatius' norms, spring from a source clearly distinguishable as Divine and as validated by the congruence between consolation without previous cause (CSC)- by Scripture, Tradition and the Teaching Church (STTC).

Inspiration: Today the words "consolation" and "desolation," do not readily reveal the meanings Ignatius wanted to convey. Consolation and desolation actually denote "inspirations" coming from either divine or demonic sources. What people consider the "spontaneous," the "authentic," the "real" etc. can actually spring from either a divine or a demonic source. The new *Rules* define such spontaneities as "inspirations," i.e., as people actually register them. *True Heart* uses the language of "inspiration" (Divine-Inspirer, counter-inspirer; divine inspiration, counter inspiration) to render Ignatius' wisdom of two spontaneities more accessible and intuitive to those in today's culture using a self-guided process of discernment.

Desolation and Consolation as "Lifestyles:" Desolation and consolation as depicted in the *Exercises* are spiritual "states." They might also be considered lifestyles.[104] Consolation and desolation do not always align along the "pleasure-pain" axis. Life is not a collection of disconnected, isolated events; "time-slices" in Charles Taylor's illustration.[105] Life is a progressive 'story' whose purpose is a trajectory pointing toward the Divine or demonic. There is no static state in life. A person is either moving toward or away from God. People living by the "low and earthly" appetites defined as spiritual desolation have chosen a trajectory that shapes a life narrative or story. The same is true for those choosing to live by selfless love and faith.

Defining the 'states' of consolation and desolation as lifestyles is an effective way to personally apply Ignatius' insights of spiritual discernment. The *Examen's* commentators clearly delineate the challenges and pressures that the lifestyles of success and materialism pose in market-driven cultures. John English uses the biblical term "anti-Christ" to define these market forces contrary to Gospel

---

[104] "Men with their arms locked, singing bawdy songs on their way to the local whorehouse, are in desolation for Ignatius." Rules, 29.

[105] Taylor offers an explanation for a loss of transcendence in modern culture and specifically in Christianity. Very few act on the belief that that actions in the here-and-now link to an eternal and transcendent realm. The consciousness of life events grounded in "higher time" has given way to viewing events in "vertical time-slices." The assorted unrelated incidents of daily living cohere only in one-dimensional perspectives of "profane time." He writes: "Now the move to what I am calling "secularity" is obviously related to this radically purged time-consciousness. It comes when associations are placed firmly and wholly in homogeneous, profane time, whether or not the higher time is negated altogether, or other associations are still admitted to exist in it. Such I want to argue is the case with the public sphere, and therein lies its new and (close to) unprecedented nature." Charles Taylor, *a Secular Age* (Cambridge, MA: The Belknap Press of Harvard University Press, 2007), 225.

values.[106] Another Jesuit, Bernard Lonergan, prefers to identify individual and societal progress systematically undermined by false intellectual systems and ideologies as unconsciousness or a collective blindness, but the impact is identical.[107]

It is difficult to be objective about anti-Gospel lifestyles when one's culture is in decline. The influence of a dominant culture weighted against Gospel values can be intensified by similar self-selected sub-cultures. The combined effect clouds one's ability to gain objectivity or to discern effectively. Anti-Gospel sub-cultures can be economic, political, artistic, ethnic, intellectual, sexual, athletic, addiction-based, Internet/technological-based and so forth.

An individual cocoons in these cultures, allowing its definitions of happiness, success, the good, the beautiful, and the moral to isolate that individual from the data coming from deep in their heart or from any other source. This process of cocooning marks the impenetrable individualism of the age. For these reasons, consolation and desolation have been described more comprehensively as lifestyles so one can measure the arc of one's life—one's lifestyle—against the traditional categories Ignatius defined as originating in either the Divine or the demonic.

The standard definitions of consolation and desolation (as Divine Inspiration and counter inspirations) have been expanded to include a broader array of words than Ignatius used, such as "single-hearted" and "cynicism." The goal is for individuals to better identify embedded attitudes and tendencies, both positive and negative, linked to prevailing life narratives and/or lifestyles.

Heart and Mind—Illumination and Awakening to New Consciousness:

Ignatius awakened to new levels of consciousness as he sought the sources of the disorder in his life. The *Autobiography* recounts his initial awakening to "manifest" sins while recuperating at Loyola. The harrowing struggle with his scruples is resolved when Ignatius awakens "as if from a dream" to his damaging habit of confession and to pride—the core sin fueling it.

The *Examen's* commentators expect that the psychological dimension of sin be sourced. Ignatius would likely concur today. Along with the corruption caused by Original Sin, we can only surmise the

---

[106] John English, SJ, *Spiritual Freedom* (Chicago: Loyola University Press, 1995), 13. Cited hereafter as "Spiritual Freedom."

[107] "Decline has a still deeper level. Not only does it compromise and distort progress… But compromise and distortion discredit progress. Objectively absurd situations do not yield to treatment. Corrupt minds have a flair for picking the mistaken solution and insisting that it alone is intelligent, reasonable, good. Imperceptibly the corruption spreads from the harsh sphere of material advantage and power to the mass media, the stylish journals, the literary movements, the educational process, the reigning philosophies. A civilization in decline digs its own grave with a relentless consistency. It cannot be argued out of its self-destructive ways, for argument has a theoretical premise, theoretical premises are asked to conform to matters of fact and the facts in the situation produced by decline more and more are the absurdities that proceed from inattention, oversight, unreasonableness, and irresponsibility." Bernard Lonergan, *Method in Theology* (New York: The Seabury Press, 1971), 54-55.

"originating sins" of the Loyola clan. In his early life, experiences that in part shape his desire for riches, honor and pride, lead him to immoral, aggressive and addictive passions that characterize his first thirty years.

The discernment resources in *Sacred Story* and *True Heart* compels this three-level "sourcing"— visible disorders, hidden vices and pride, and the originating sins—that can lead to both the spiritual and psychological wounds fueling one's visible disorders. The goal is to help *engaged Christians* to form an integrated and holistic picture of their lives for effective spiritual growth.

A broken heart, lost innocence, dissolute passions and sinful pride result from events both inflicted and chosen. We first feel the afflictions of Original Sin through the evolutionary surge of corruption in family, culture and other life events that distort our human nature, our physical capacities and the innocence of our hearts. Once afflicted—infected might a better word—we end up cooperating, to one degree or another, with the sin and dysfunction that sickens body, mind, and heart. In the end, there is no one without guilt and no one without need for redemption.

An integrated picture of life can help one move beyond a narrow moralism to understand, along with our inherited concupiscence, the "original" events that may have helped one turn from God and make oneself a god.[108] To understand patterns, to retrace steps, to remember where one has been and how one got to be where one is or how one is deifying oneself and things over God, requires God's grace and enlightenment, but also an effective and strategic method of prayer like the Ignatian Examen.

The terms "enlightenment," "illumination," "lost innocence," "broken hearts," and "awakening," are used in *True Heart* to reinforce the sourcing and searching that await the engaged practitioner; a process that God's grace must support.[109] The new consciousness that *True Heart* holds forth as a reward is the awareness signified by a full and honest apprehension of one's life and the need for redemption in light of God's love. *True Heart* offers hope for integrated healing that leads to higher consciousness, both as positive inducement to begin the search, and to stay the course once engaged.

Additional Reflections on the Second Foundation Choices

Ignatius' Second Week *Exercises* are dominated by "rules" "meditations" and "considerations" that point toward life choices and the values to be sought in making those choices. Ignatius intended the purgative process of the First Week to initiate a dynamic during which one is asked to consider anew

---

[108] This is to deify what Rahner describes: "a finite reality, through the identification of my absolute worth that can only be related absolutely to God, with things that cannot be posited absolutely." Karl Rahner, *Spiritual Exercises: Prayer and Practice* (London: Sheed and Ward, 1966), 40.

[109] John Horn's work on the Ignatian *Exercises* and the *Examen* as a source of mystical healing is based on the mending of broken hearts by the power of God's love and mercy. In particular, see the section on discernment and the *Examen*, (117-126) in: John Horn, *Mystical Healing: The psychological and Spiritual Power of the Ignatian Spiritual Exercises* (New York: Crossroads, 1996).

the pattern of one's life and to further consider whether a "reform" of sorts is demanded by the spiritual and psychological growth that one experiences.

The discernment method developed for *True Heart* is conceived as a practical application of Ignatius' *Rules* for those who daily engage the purgative path of *True Heart*. The individuals are not discerning life choices but rather patterns of thoughts, words and deeds that express "quest and tendency" towards or away from God. Those who engage *True Heart* with serious intent, however, are liable to ponder life choices and decisions as the growth process stirs up new inspirations, similar to dynamics in the *Spiritual Exercises*.

Anticipating this, an additional reflection is added in the Guidelines stressing the developments leading one to ponder new directions in life, principally the particular tensions created by opposing "inspirations" at such times. This additional reflection draws on the *Rules* appropriate to Second Week dynamics in light of those who, during the course of serious spiritual growth that we hope *True Heart* promotes, are inspired to consider new lifestyles, career changes, or vocational commitments.

DISCERNMENT EXERCISES

We have taken the discernment exercises from *True Heart* and put them in this section to be used as single exercises for various pastoral settings. You may use them in a retreat setting, an evening discussion exercise on discernment, a class on decision making, etc.

Consequently, since they are a progressive set of Rules that build on the previous ones, you may choose to use them in the order you find them here over a matter of days, weeks or months (or in a retreat on discernment as exercises for that retreat).

No matter how you use them, we would be grateful for the wisdom you can offer us on "best practices" for these exercises in spiritual discernment.

DISCERNMENT
A YOUNG MAN'S STORY

Jesus Reads from Isaiah, St. John's Church, Tralee Ireland

Let me tell you a story. A college senior asked me if he could attend a five-day retreat. I asked him why he wanted to attend. He said a freshman girl asked him if he would be her first love. He wanted to make the retreat to decide whether he would accept her offer. Well, at least he was honest with me!

I could tell him what the Bible said about sex and marriage, or what the Catholic Church teaches or what Jesus says but that would not have held any weight with him. He was going to decide this on his own. But at least he was open to having God be part of the conversation. That is why he wanted to make a retreat.

Something very powerful happened to him on that five-day silent retreat. One afternoon he was having a cup of coffee and looking out the window of the retreat center. Sitting there he "remembered" when he lost his virginity as a sophomore in high school. Up to his senior year in college, this memory was really just a piece of data: "I saw my first Major League Baseball game, went to the Jersey Shore for vacation and lost my virginity." The memory had no feeling connected with it—no emotion at all.

While sitting, drinking a cup of coffee and looking out the window, the Spirit gave him access to what his heart actually *felt* when he lost his virginity. He described it this way: "When that happened to me, I was overcome with an incredible grief and sadness that something of great value was now lost and I would never get it back again."

He said the grief and sadness were about his loss of virginity, yes, but also about his loss of innocence. Why did his heart not allow him to "feel" at the time what he was actually feeling? Because we can hide what we truly feel *even from ourselves*. We can hide our True Heart. It might be because of shame or fear or some other powerful emotion but we can hide our *True Heart*.

This young man came on a retreat to make a decision. God responded to him by giving him access to his True Heart so he could make that decision. He knew now what he lost six years ago as a sophomore. At the end of the retreat, he told me: "She does not know what she is giving up and I won't be the one to take it from her." Knowing his True Heart helped him choose. And the choice he made was not because some outside authority forced his hand. The authentic choice he made was grounded on the inner authority of his True Heart.

So you see my friend, it is hard to be authentic—to be a True Heart—without spiritual training and the grace of God in the Holy Spirit! We must work to be a True Heart. But most importantly, let God work in us to help us be true to ourselves.

Each age presents new challenges to discovering our True Heart. Pope Francis has reflected on how the overconsumption of technology is robbing us of our identity—our True Heart. He says:

It has become countercultural to choose a lifestyle whose goals are even partly independent of technology, of its costs and its power to globalize and make us all the same. Technology tends to absorb everything into its ironclad logic, and those who are surrounded with technology "know full well that it moves forward in the final analysis neither for profit nor for the well-being of the human race", that "in the most radical sense of the term power is its motive – a lordship over all."[110] As a result…our capacity for making decisions, a more genuine freedom and the space for each one's alternative creativity are diminished.[111]

Reflection Questions:
--Can you recall the first time you acted in such a way as to "lose your innocence?
--What was the context of the choice?

--Do you recall feeling anything at the time akin to sadness and grief?

--Did you make any resolutions at the time in light of the experience?

--Would you characterize the experience as selfless or self-centered?

---

110 Romano Guardini, *Das Ende der Neuzeit*, 63-64 (*The End of the Modern World*, 56).
111 Laudato Si, 81.

DISCERNMENT
A YOUNG WOMAN'S STORY

Detail: Jesus reads from Isaiah, St. John's Church Tralee, Ireland

For a weekend retreat, I asked a senior to give a talk entitled, "God's Creative Love." Her task was to remember just one episode in her 20 years when she *knew for a fact* that God was real and that God's love was creative. I asked this senior to give the talk because she was very engaged in the practice of her faith and had been all the way through high school and college. I thought it would be an easy talk for her to do and a great talk for the retreatants.

Well she surprised me a week later when she came to my office and said could not "remember" a single event in her life where she "felt" God's love in any way. She really shocked me by saying this. How could someone so engaged in her faith not have any memory of God's love for her when she had a whole twenty-year history to pull from?

We spent a week going back and forth. She was asking God for insight to help her remember something. Nothing worked. A week before the retreat she shared with me a memory from when she was five years old. Her favorite person in the whole world died—her grandpa. She told me when her mom shared this sad news she went out into the backyard and started digging in the dirt. She remembered her heart saying: "God hates me because he killed grandpa and I hate God for killing him!" She had not consciously recalled this event for fifteen years!

As she sat in my office telling me the story, I could see the twenty-year-old talking to the five-year-old. The twenty-year-old said: "Grandpa was eighty-eight years old. Of course, God did not kill grandpa! He lived a full life and I was so grateful to have known him. The five-year-old in her "heard the news" about the death of grandpa with a new perspective. She was reaching across the years of her heart's memory to make peace with God and herself.

Within days, memories of "God's Creative Love" started pouring out of her. There were so many it became hard for us to choose which was the best memory to share. Her True Heart had actually registered many events of God's Creative Love, but buried anger and fear from the past was blocking those graced events.

I wonder if not for this retreat and having to do this talk, could she have gone on for many years walking through the practice of her faith, but with a True Heart completely buried in a five-year old's angry and fearful memories? I think the answer is, "YES!"

So you see my friend, it is hard to be authentic—to be a True Heart—without spiritual training and the grace of God in the Holy Spirit! We must work to be a True Heart. But most importantly, we need to allow God to work in us to help us be true to ourselves.

Each age presents new challenges to discovering our True Heart. Pope Francis has reflected on how the overconsumption of technology is robbing us of our identity—our True Heart. He says:

It has become countercultural to choose a lifestyle whose goals are even partly independent of technology, of its costs and its power to globalize and make us all the same. Technology tends to absorb everything into its ironclad logic, and those who are surrounded with technology "know full well that it moves forward in the final analysis neither for profit nor for the well-being of the human race", that "in the most radical sense of the term power is its motive – a lordship over all."[112] As a result...our capacity for making decisions, a more genuine freedom and the space for each one's alternative creativity are diminished.[113]

Reflection Questions:
--Can you recall discovering a strong emotion like anger or hate that you had suppressed?

--How long was the time from the event till you actually "felt" it for what it was?

--Do you remember who or what stirred the feelings inside of you?

--In hindsight, were the strong emotions justified in light of the event?

--Have you ever reassessed a situation like the young woman in the story?

--What was the situation and why did you reassess it?

---

[112] Romano Guardini, *Das Ende der Neuzeit*, 63-64 (*The End of the Modern World*, 56).
[113] Laudato Si, 81.

DISCERNMENT
CREATION STORY TOLD ANEW

Hubble Telescope "Deep Field" View of Our Universe

Read the following familiar story told in a new way and reflect on the questions.

In the beginning, God created the heavens and the earth. But God's greatest work was fashioning our human nature. In our beginning, the energy field that is our body and spirit was in complete harmony and we lived before God in complete selflessness. That perfect balance "created" by God is why we were immortal. Our human nature in this state of original innocence was completely oriented selflessly toward God.

Because God made us in in the Divine image, we had to be free to accept or reject God's gift of love and immortality. We had to be free to reject selflessness and become self-centered. The pure spiritual beings in the heavens God created, what Scripture names as the powers and principalities, were also free to accept or reject God's love—to be selfless or self-centered.

Some of those spiritual beings did reject God and then selfishly sought to destroy God's creation. The main way they could destroy God's creation was to corrupt the beings God made in God's likeness: to turn them from selflessness to self-centeredness. If corrupted, humans would be susceptible to selfishly destroying each other and even creation itself. St. Paul describes this ancient battle with these words:

Finally, draw your strength from the Lord and from his mighty power. Put on the armor of God so that you may be able to stand firm against the tactics of the devil. For our struggle is not with flesh and blood but with the principalities, with the powers, with the world rulers of this present darkness, with the evil spirits in the heavens. Therefore, put on the armor of God, that you may be able to resist on the evil day and, having done everything, to hold your ground. So stand fast with your loins girded in truth, clothed with righteousness as a breastplate, and your feet shod in readiness for the gospel of peace. In all circumstances, hold faith as a shield, to quench all [the] flaming arrows of the evil one. And take the helmet of salvation and the sword of the Spirit, which is the word of God. Eph 6:11-17.

The greatest tragedy since the beginning of time is that we rejected God's life and surrendered selfless freedom and peace for self-centered constraint and anxiety. At this pivot point, we broke the unified field between spirit and body and we not only lost our innocence but our immortality. From the point of corruption onwards to right now, spiritual discernment—including developing radar for selflessness and self-centeredness—is an essential discipline for us. I know you, like me and everyone we know, has felt original sin inside you. You know how easy it is to give in to self-centeredness and how challenging it can be to choose selflessness.

If we are to find our way home to our self-less True Heart, we must learn to master this spirit-body discipline of spiritual discernment.

Reflection Questions:
--What is the first instance I can remember being confronted with a choice between good and evil in the form of selflessness vs. self-centeredness?

--What was the context? What did the struggle feel like?

--What did I choose selflessness or self-centeredness?

--What were the consequences of my choice?

--Have you ever encountered the reality of evil in a spiritual form? If so, what was it like?

If you want, write a very short two-sentence reflection in your journal about this experience.

DISCERNMENT LESSON
INSPIRATIONS & COUNTER-INSPIRATIONS

Detail: Jesus reads from Isaiah, St. John's Church, Ireland

Because we have a human nature that can connect with good or evil spiritual energy, we want to learn how it reaches us. This exercise looks at three distinct sources of spiritual energy or "inspirations" that can guide our thoughts, words and deeds.

Saint Ignatius learned about these spiritual energy sources by careful attention to his affective states. That is why True Heart exercises invite you to tune out the electronic world so you can hear the spiritual world. Saint Ignatius learned Inspirations affecting your human nature (spirit-body) originate from three *different* sources:

1. Spiritual energy inspirations can originate from your own life-energy or spirit.

2. Spiritual energy inspirations can originate from a Divine source: the *Divine-Inspirer*.

3. Spiritual energy inspirations can originate from a demonic source, the *enemy of human nature*: the *counter-inspirer*.

There are three *sources* of spiritual energy inspiration, but only two spiritual energy *states*. St. Ignatius names the two spiritual energy states *consolation* and *desolation*.

The spiritual energy of consolation is when one *experiences*, to a lesser or greater degree, an *increase in faith, hope and love*. The spiritual energy of desolation is when one *experiences,* to a lesser or greater degree, *a loss of faith, hope and love.*

OUR QUICK REVIEW:

Sources of Inspiration
--Human nature as an energy source of spirit/body
--God as the *Divine-Inspirer*
--The enemy of human nature as the *counter-inspirer*

Types of Inspiration

Spiritual Energy of Consolation—increase of faith, hope, love and selflessness

Spiritual energy of Desolation—decrease of faith, hope, love and selflessness

Reflection Questions

Pray to the Divine-Inspirer to have your memory "energized." Use the name for God-the Divine-Inspirer—you discovered in the exercise for

Ask for the grace to remember one time that your radar picked up the spiritual energy of consolation where you experienced an increase of faith, hope, love and selflessness. What was the event/experience and what would you guess was the source? REMEMBER!

Next, pray to the Divine Inspirer to have your memory "energized" again. Ask for the grace to remember one time when your radar picked up the spiritual energy of desolation where you had a decrease in faith, hope, love and selflessness. What was the event/experience and what would you guess was the source? REMEMBER!

Briefly write one or two sentences in your True Heart Training Log about each memory that captures the experience and how you felt during these two different "energized states" and the source from which you think they originated.

For Example: "Today when I invited Greg to come on the weekend camping trip with our group he realized people care about him. Seeing him smile made me feel great and I knew I had done the right thing. His smile made me feel faith, hope and love."

For Example: "When Kimberly asked if she could come with our group to the game, I was not honest and told her we had no more room. Seeing her disappointment made me feel bad about my lack of honesty and what it did to her really decreased my faith, hope love and selflessness."

DISCERNMENT LESSON
YOU HAVE A RADAR FOR SELFLESS JOY

Detail: Jesus reads from Isaiah, St. John's Church, Ireland

First Benchmark Strategy for a True Heart's Spiritual Discernment

We can collaborate with spiritual entities that lead us to an immortality of happiness and selflessness or loneliness and self-centeredness. God has given us spiritual radar to help us follow the path to eternal selflessness and reject the path of eternal self-centeredness.

To help your awakening and initiation into the spiritual discernment of a True Heart, two benchmark guidelines will be beneficial in many life situations.

As I lead you in this work I want to speak a truth it has taken me a long time to accept: Divine inspiration, or consolation, does not always *feel good*. It is hard work sometimes. It feels like a struggle sometimes. That is okay.

Equally important is to realize that an unholy inspiration, or spiritual desolation, does not always *feel bad*. Temptation and evil can feel great. That is not okay. Because the "feel good" is only temporary before the darkness sets in.

We will explore this seeming paradox in a future reflection.

This first benchmark deals with energy-inspirations that come from the Creator of human nature. These, if followed, ultimately lead to eternal selfless joy.

Benchmark One: Authentic divine energy-inspirations called consolations will have specific features. Consolations will:

1) Increase your True Heart's love for God, family, and others

2) Increase the virtues of humility, self-generosity and selflessness

3) Not oppose the truths and teachings of Scripture, the Tradition and the teaching Church.

God's Direct Action—Consolation can be the consequence of the Divine Physician's Spirit working in you. This form of consolation helps strengthen your heart and soul, encouraging you to turn to God whenever you need spiritual and moral help. Consolation helps you to choose thoughts, words and deeds that express your authentic selfless human nature—your True Heart—made in the Divine image.

God's Action Though Your Human Nature—Consolation can also be the result of your Divinely-shaped human nature expressing itself through your daily life. God created your human nature as a gift in the Divine image and likeness. In spite of Original Sin's impact, cooperating with God's grace activates embedded life forces of your Divinely-shaped human nature. These strengths can help you heal not only spiritual but biochemical, physiological and emotional imbalances. They will energize you; and enable thoughts, words and deeds that express your authentic selfless human nature—your True Heart—made in the Divine image.

Reflection Questions

Pray to the Divine-Inspirer to have your memory "energized." Ask for the grace to remember one time that your love for God and/or other people was stirred in you. What was the context? Remember and briefly write the context and experience below or in your journal.

Example: "I remember on a first-year retreat we had a Mass that made me feel a part of not just my class, but something much bigger. That to me was a time I really felt God and really felt great about the whole world."

Then ask for the grace to remember one time that you were inspired to be more humble, selfless and giving of yourself to others. What as the context? Remember and briefly write the context and experience below or in your journal.

Example: "I remember when I won class president and my main opponent lost. I knew how I would feel if I had lost and I asked her to serve with me as my vice-president."

Ask for the grace to remember one time when you were inspired to follow the teachings of the Scriptures, Catholic Tradition or the Church that stirred your faith, hope and love. What was the context? Remember and briefly write the context and experience below or in your journal.

Example: "I read Tim Tebow's five reasons why not to have sex before marriage and really agreed with him. I decided that I would make it a goal for my life to deepen my faith and pray that I find someone worth spending my life with.

DISCERNMENT LESSON
YOU HAVE A RADAR FOR SELF-CENTERED LONELINESS

Detail: Jesus reads from Isaiah, St. John's Church, Ireland

Second Benchmark Strategy for a True Heart's Spiritual Discernment: We can collaborate with spiritual entities that can either lead us to an immortality of happiness and selflessness or one of loneliness and self-centeredness. God has given us spiritual radar to help us follow the path to eternal selflessness and reject the path of eternal self-centeredness.

This benchmark deals with counter energy-inspirations that come from the enemy of human nature. These, if followed, ultimately lead to eternal self-centered loneliness.

Benchmark Two: Authentic counter-inspirations called desolations will have specific features.

Desolations will:

1)   Increase self-centeredness, displacing God and others from your True Heart

2)   Decrease obedience and humility, and increase pride and self-satisfaction

3)   Arouse hungers and desires that, although they feel good but ultimately leave you empty, will typically contradict the truths and teachings proposed by the Scripture, Tradition, and the teaching Church.

The Enemy's Direct Action: The author of counter-inspirations is opposed to Christ and will lead you away from life and truth. Counter-inspirations will produce desires *that feel authentic* because they are linked to *fallen* human nature's physical lusts and spiritual pride. They are the familiar default drives of a broken heart and a sin-damaged human nature.

This form of desolation helps weaken your heart and soul, encouraging you to turn from God. Desolation helps you choose self-centered thoughts, words and deeds that are opposed to your Divinely-shaped human nature—your True Heart.

The Enemy's Action Though Your Sin-Damaged Human Nature: Desolation can also be the consequence of your own sin-damaged human nature. God created your human nature as a gift in the

Divine image and likeness. Yet, because of Original Sin's impact, not cooperating with God's grace erodes embedded life forces of your Divinely-shaped human nature, helping to undermine biochemical, physiological, emotional and spiritual balance; de-energizing you; and increasing thoughts, words and deeds that are in opposition to your authentic selfless human nature—your True Heart.

Reflection Questions

Pray to the Divine-Inspirer to have your memory "energized." Ask for the grace to remember one time when your love for God and/or other people was diminished in favor of more self-centered acts or inspirations. What was the context? Remember and briefly write the context and experience below or in your journal.

Example: "I remember on first-year retreat we had a Mass that made me feel left out because I was not chosen as part of the team to prepare it. I was angry about that and did not participate because of it.

Ask for the grace to remember one time that you were inspired to be less humble and giving of yourself to others. What as the context? Remember and briefly write the context and experience below or in your journal.

Example: "I remember when I got selected from a group of my peers for a coveted position. and someone I knew who was hoping to get selected was sidelined. I knew how I would feel if this happened and I was quietly pleased at their defeat. I could have asked them to share it with me (I actually thought about it) but decided against it."

Ask for the grace to remember one time when you were inspired by hungers and desires not follow the teachings of the Scriptures, Catholic Tradition or the Church. What was the context? Remember and briefly write the context and experience in your journal.

Example: "I read Tim Tebow's five reasons why he did not want to have sex before marriage and really liked it. But I did not want to be publicly ridiculed like him and chose not to follow his advice or talk about it to others."

DISCERNMENT LESSON
RADAR SIGNALS FROM EITHER THE DIVINE INSPIRER OR THE COUNTER-INSPIRER ACT AS HOMING BEACONS FOR YOUR TRUE HEART TO CAUSE THOUGHTS AND FEELINGS OF SELFLESS JOY OR SELF-CENTERED LONELINESS

Detail: Jesus reads from Isaiah, St. John's Church, Ireland

For your True Heart time, read and reflect on this training in discernment. Pay attention to your moods and *feel* the states of consolation and desolation in your True Heart. This process requires a *graced awakening*, so as you read this, please ask God using the name you discovered in Week 4 to give you "eyes to see" your story through the lens of these spiritual lessons. Be patient as you slowly learn this way of understanding your story.

You have learned already that there are three distinct sources influencing your thoughts, words, and deeds.

Both God and the enemy of human nature are aware of your strengths and weaknesses, wounded memories, your SELFLESS JOY and SELF-CENTERED LONELINESS, your hopes, dreams, and fears. God will build on your strengths, inflaming your holy desires, healing what is hurt and broken, and offering ETERNAL FRIENDSHIP to you.

The enemy of human nature seeks to silence your conscience and hide it in shadows. He will work to magnify your problems, diminish your holy desires and inspire a path that leads to hopeless, self-centered loneliness.

You can identify and distinguish Divine inspirations from counter inspirations by their *intellectual* and *affective* traits, or signature characteristics: *consolation and* desolation.

Reflection Questions

Pray to the Divine-Inspirer to have your memory "energized." Ask for the grace to remember one time that you are convinced you received a Divine inspiration that filled you with hope and deepened your love for God and strengthened your commitment to your Catholic faith. Remember. What was the context? Briefly describe the context and experience below or in your journal.

Example: "I remember during a hard time when I went to Sunday Mass and heard the Gospel story of Jesus healing people. I had a dream that night that everything would work out for the best. When I woke up I had chills because I knew God had helped me and I was not afraid anymore and realized how important my faith is to my life."

Pray to the Divine-Inspirer to have your memory "energized." Ask for the grace to remember one time that you are convinced you received a counter-inspiration that seemed right initially, but later diminished your love for God and weakened your commitment to your Catholic faith. Remember. What as the context? Briefly describe the context and experience below or in your journal.

Example: "I remember during a hard time I decided it would be best to miss Sunday Mass so I could go for a run and clear my head. It seemed like the right thing at the time, but later I realized it was a mistake because I did not feel better but more confused. It would have been better to go to Mass and let God help me instead of trying to do it all by myself." I went to confession for missing Mass on Sunday and learned a very valuable spiritual lesson.

DISCERNMENT LESSON
SPIRITUAL RADAR SIGNALS—WHEN FOLLOWED IN ONE DIRECTION OR ANOTHER CREATE ENERGY FIELDS OR "LIFESTYLES" THAT REVEAL WHICH "INSPIRER" YOU ARE FOLLOWING

Detail: Jesus reads from Isaiah, St. John's Church, Ireland

Remember there really is a Divine-Inspirer who is Lord of the Universe and a counter-inspirer who is the dark lord and the enemy of human nature. These are the real forces that are guiding hearts toward life or death.

For this training, we focus more sharply on identifying the ways in which these spiritual states manifest in our culture today as lifestyles. Throughout your life today, continue to pay attention to your affective moods to *feel* the states of consolation and desolation in your heart. Look for lifestyle attitudes or choices that bear the signature characteristics of consolation and desolation.

Individuals and groups can consciously or unconsciously live a life that is either aligned with life, selflessness and joy—Gospel Values and a True Heart *or* death, self-centeredness and sadness—a false heart not aligned with the Gospel. The book of Deuteronomy powerfully captures this reality. God placed before the people Israel two distinct choices:

I call heaven and earth today to witness against you: I have set before you life and death, the blessing and the curse. Choose life, then, that you and your descendants may live, by loving the LORD, your God, obeying his voice, and holding fast to him. For that will mean life for you, a long life for you to live on the land which the LORD swore to your ancestors, to Abraham, Isaac, and Jacob, to give to them (Dt. 30: 18-20).

If we have become insensitive to God's presence, our True Heart can be moving away from the Author of Life. We may not be aware of this because of a silenced conscience.

If you live in a culture or a sub-culture that is also insensitive to the Author of Life, you can be doubly challenged to find the path back to life—to a True Heart.

When you are sensitive to the Author of life, your *True Heart* is moving in the direction of producing fruit that endures to eternity. This will be correct even if you live in a culture that is insensitive to life's Author.

Christ promises: *Blessed are you when they insult you and persecute you and utter every kind of evil against you [falsely] because of me. Rejoice and be glad, for your reward will be great in heaven. Thus they persecuted the prophets who were before you* (Mt 5: 11-12).

What "Feels" Bad Might Actually Be Good & Vice-Versa

Things that feel bad can move us towards life and things that feel good can move us towards death.

We have to look not at what makes us feel good or feel bad, but the lifestyles and life-direction feelings move us towards.

Reflection Questions

Pray to the Divine-Inspirer to have your memory "energized." Think of a group you privately supported whose lifestyle was "Gospel-inspired" but it was not popular with the majority of your peers. Perhaps the lifestyle was linked to some hot-button social or moral issue like sex or marriage, abortion, the economy or politics.

What was the "lifestyle" that made them unpopular? Did you make your support known or keep quiet about it because of fear or majority group pressure?

Write briefly below or in your journal about one of this experience: why did you support the group and how did you act?

DISCERNMENT LESSON
SPIRITUAL RADAR SIGNALS
LEAD TO LIFESTYLES AND SUBCULTURES

Detail: Jesus reads from Isaiah, St. John's Church, Ireland

We can choose to align ourselves with sub-cultures that are counter to the life proposed by the Commandments, Scripture and the teaching Church—the life proposed by the very embodiment of human nature, Jesus Christ. It is difficult to be objective about anti-Gospel or "anti-Christ" lifestyles when we are immersed in these sub-cultures or peer groups.

For example, if you get involved with a group of peers that is using or abusing illegal or performance-enhancing drugs, it "sucks you in" and once you are sucked in, it is hard to fully see the damage it is doing to you. That is why we call it a "drug culture."

Or perhaps you get aligned with a group that uses texting to demean someone by hurting someone else to make you feel superior in your small circle of friends.

We can embed ourselves in these groups and allow definitions of happiness, success, the good, the moral and the beautiful to isolate us from the data coming from deep in our divinely inspired True Heart.

These anti-Gospel sub-cultures can be economic, political, artistic, ethnic, intellectual, sexual, athletic, addiction-based, and Web-based or just about anything else that a group endorses. The main challenge is that we can embed ourselves in these cultures, allowing their definitions of happiness, success, the good, the beautiful, and the moral to isolate us from the data coming from deep in our divinely inspired True Heart. Do you see this happening in your friendship groups at home, work or school?

So, *consolation* and *desolation* can be ascribed comprehensively as *lifestyles.* By thinking about them that way, we can measure the arc of our lives against the traditional categories of goodness the Church has defined.

Reflection Questions
Pray to the Divine-Inspirer to have your memory "energized." Think of one lifestyle the "majority" defends and one lifestyle the "majority" denounces. Examine each lifestyle in light of whether it aligns

or not with the Gospel, Jesus and the Church. Why do you think one is defended and the other denounced?

Example: Pope Francis has denounced gender ideologies saying that there was a war against marriage. He was both praised and ridiculed in the media for this position. He also called for every migrant who needed safety to be allowed in the countries of Europe. He was also praised and ridiculed for this position.

In light of what you have learned about spiritual discernment, write very brief observations below or in your journal about each instance of the rightness or wrongness of what is defended or denounced and what you have come to believe at this point in your True Heart journey.

Reflection Questions

What lifestyles do you engage in that you now realize are *spiritual consolation*?

Are you in lifestyles that you realize now are *spiritual desolation?*

How have you been courageous or fearful in defending what you think is right or wrong with your friends, colleagues or peers?

Here's how I think I've been courageous...(give examples to your companion)

Here's how I think I've been too scared to speak up...(give an example to your companion).

DISCERNMENT LESSON
COUNTER-INSPIRATION AS A LIFESTYLE

Detail: Jesus reads from Isaiah, St. John's Church, Ireland

Are you evolving under the counter inspirations opposed to true love? Are your thoughts, words and deeds self-centered and opposed to the Commandments, Scripture and the teaching Church?

The enemy of your human nature is able to hold you in the grip of self-centered false loves by deceit and deceitful appearances. How? What leads you away from God, from Love, appears pleasurable, and is presented as good, morally right, life-giving, fashionable, and enlightened. The false loves are like a drug for the interior pain we feel.

Reflection Exercise:
Pray to the Divine-Inspirer to have your memory "energized."

Map some of the influences in your life using the small chart below of two sub-cultures or peer groups where you spend most of your time each week: school culture, work environments, Internet, social groups and associations, exercise or athletic environments, groups aligned with arts and or entertainment, political parties, and the cultures of film, television and or gaming where you spend time.

Next to the two sub-cultures, write one sentence about what you believe is its signature characteristic regarding its overall influence on your lifestyle. Does it lead to selflessness or self-centeredness—to God and your faith or away?

If it is self-centered and leads away, write one sentence about how you could leave it or minimize its negative impact on you.

SUB-CULTURE OR PEER GROUP   KEY CHARACTERISTICS OF THE GROUP

Beloved,
do not trust every spirit
but test the spirits
to see whether they belong to God,
because many false prophets
have gone out into the world.
1 Jn 4: 1

DISCERNMENT LESSON
HOW TO RESPOND WHEN SIGNALS FROM THE DARKNESS
TRICK YOU TO TURN FROM THE LIGHT

Detail: Jesus reads from Isaiah, St. John's Church, Ireland

Diffusing Counter Inspirations

Ignatius offers four principles for how we ought to act when tempted by the counter inspirations of desolation. Here the first two:

1) When we are spiritually desolate--experiencing self-centeredness and a loss of faith, hope and love--we should NEVER change course away from the positive resolutions and decisions we reached while previously under the influence of the Divine inspiration of consolation. This means: True Hearts must be vigilant when tempted by an urgent or compelling impulse to act immediately.

If you are in an emergency situation, of course, you must act quickly, but Ignatius is talking here about the feeling of anxious urgency to reach a decision or engage an action that really needs more patience. For instance, you might know in your heart that you should wait another week to make a decision about something hugely important to you but you just impulsively decide. This may end up being a course change that you regret later.

2) During times of desolation, redouble efforts to open and orient your heart to God and act selflessly. Use prayer, examination of conscience, and perhaps some simple penance or fasting to seek God's grace (Mk 9:29).

Reflection Exercise:

Pray to the Divine-Inspirer to have your memory "energized." Remember a time when you were on a peaceful good course but then counter-inspirations upset you. The upset compelled you to make a hasty decision and looking back you can see you acted on fear, not peace. What was the context? Remember the anxiety you felt. Now remember a time when you were upset and turned to prayer and your spiritual disciplines for help and you found peace and calm. What was the context? Remember the relief you felt. Briefly write these memories below or in your journal.

DISCERNMENT LESSON THREE
SPIRITUAL RADAR SIGNALS
HOW GOD SUPPORTS YOU WHEN SIGNALS FROM THE
DARKNESS HAVE TRICKED YOU TO TURN FROM THE LIGHT

Detail: Jesus reads from Isaiah, St. John's Church, Ireland

Diffusing Counter Inspirations

You have studied Ignatius' first two principles for how we ought to act when tempted by the counter inspirations of desolation and here are the last two:

3) God provides the essential support and grace necessary to withstand these times of trial and purification.

The support you need will come from your natural abilities, assisted by Divine grace. You may feel completely overwhelmed by temptations or the darkness of spirit associated with disordered attractions and compulsive behaviors. Yet there is sufficient grace for salvation, even if the logic of the counter inspiration indicates otherwise! Jesus, the Divine Physician, is very close to you during these times of purification. Through trial and error, St. Ignatius learned that God is not absent.

When you do not feel the Spirit, consciously thank God, who in complete faithfulness, will embrace you. Thank God aloud and affirm God's salvific role in your True Heart.

4) Intentionally strive to cultivate patience and persevere in the religious practices of your faith when influenced by the desolation of counter-inspiration.

The Divine inspiration of consolation always returns but in the interim, we must use the divine means of prayer, penance, and self-examination and acts of selflessness to resist and gain the most from these times of trial. In this way, we can embrace desolation as an opportunity to deepen our maturing life with God.

Do Not Be Afraid!

Reflection Exercise:

Pray to the Divine-Inspirer to have your memory "energized." Remember!

What is the one experience or event that makes you question God's love for you? Say it aloud. Now hear the Lord say: "Nothing in the past or the future; no angel or demon; no height or depth; nothing in all of creation will ever separate you from my love in Christ Jesus." (Rom 8:38-39).

Write your experience and God's response in your journal.

Example: For me, the most powerful modern poem that captures this faithfulness of God is the Footprints Poem. You know it: It has the same wisdom Ignatius uses about trusting God during difficult times. God never leaves us!

DISCERNMENT LESSON
THE FIRST ATTACK STRATEGY OF THE COUNTER-INSPIRER
FEAR AND PANIC ATTACKS

Detail: Jesus reads from Isaiah, St. John's Church, Ireland

When you engage your faith practice daily, the enemy of human nature can employ three subtle and malicious lines of attack to discourage you. He will use the weaknesses and fears associated with your vices, your sinful appetites, your compulsive behaviors, your spiritual/psychological wounds, and your broken heart. This lesson we will consider the first of the three strategies:

1) Fear and panic attacks are strategically employed to block growth.

If you stay committed to the process of uprooting vices, sins, addictions and destructive habits from your life, you will often be attacked with waves of fear and panic. These may try to turn your attention away from the True Heart process.

Reflection Question:

Pray to the Divine-Inspirer to have your memory "energized." Remember! Think on the times when you were paralyzed by fear or panic attacks. They would be times too of self-centeredness. What were the "hooks" that triggered the terrible fear and how did self-centered behaviors manifest themselves? For example: was the "hook" your own perfectionism? Did you have a music recital or a huge game, a big test or a job interview or report to present that you prepared for quite well but as the time of performance got close, you started imagining everything that could go wrong, and before you knew it you felt paralyzed?

Remember an example like this in your experience and then look at it carefully—discern what "triggered" the panic? Did you, for instance, hear someone say something relatively harmless that you "heard" as a scary possibility? "You'll do great, just remember to focus before you act." This comment was innocuous but before you knew it your brain was seeing only all the bad possibilities?

Find your own memories of this kind of paralysis. Sit with the memories for a while. Let yourself understand the deep truth of the attack strategy. It happens to keep you off balance and away from your True Heart. Pray to "see" the wound or previous fears that initiated this pattern in your life. Briefly write your memory and what you've learning below or in your journal.

DISCERNMENT LESSON
THE SECOND ATTACK STRATEGY OF THE COUNTER-INSPIRER:
FALSE LOVES DISGUISED AS TRUE LOVES

Detail: Jesus reads from Isaiah, St. John's Church, Ireland

Consider the second of the three attack strategies used by our Enemy:

2) Self-Centeredness and false values masquerade as true love and authentic values.

The enemy can invade our thinking process to portray narcissism as authentic love and to make us see vices as positive values. "Drinking a lot is fine," we think, "in fact, it's great because it's a way I bond with my friends." Or: "I am better at _____ than just about everyone else—I'm the best—I've got it made."

Your heart can be easily fooled by false loves. All false loves—of drinking or pride or any other vice--are lusts masquerading as love. They are mirages for parched and anxious hearts hoping to quench their thirst. Instead of providing lasting peace, these illicit loves and illusions merely intensify self-centeredness, longings, and self-deception.

In all this, there is a seemingly infinite variety of deception and seductions. They are limited only by the numerous ways a heart can be broken. God will not sanction these lusts because they issue from a violated heart and lead to your heart's further violation. Once you act upon a false love or deceptive lust, you will most assuredly violate the hearts of others.

Remember: God is Love: the origin, the end, and the defender of the selfless human heart. While God is infinitely merciful with our struggles, God does not sanction anything that breaks your heart--destroys your own or another person's authentic human nature--or leads to your spiritual death. By not sanctioning false loves in you, God is actually doing you a great favor—protecting you! He does this by not enabling you—and hoping that you will one day, very soon, see through the self-centered deceptions and return fully to his Heart.

Sacred Story Institute © 2019

Reflection Exercise:

Pray to the Divine-Inspirer to have your memory "energized." Remember! Name your sins, addictions, and bad habits truthfully as self-centered, false lovers. In the light of grace, let one or more of them be revealed as neither true servants of the heart nor pathways to the Divine. Expose them! Focus on the main "false love" you need to see most clearly right now. Identify it and do the exercise below. When you are done, write a brief journal entry about what you learned today in this training.

Sacred Story Institute © 2019

DISCERNMENT LESSON
THE THIRD ATTACK STRATEGY OF THE COUNTER-INSPIRER
USE A HARDENED HEART TO DEFEND A BROKEN HEART

Detail: Jesus reads from Isaiah, St. John's Church, Ireland

This lesson we examine the third attack strategy used by the Enemy to obstruct our spiritual progress. Just as in the first two lines of attack, fear is the weapon used against you.

3) When you commit to uprooting sin, addictions, and vices from your body and soul, you will be assaulted by attacks directed at the spiritual and psychological wounds that make you most vulnerable.

The enemy of human nature can viciously attack you where past pain and wounds have left you most vulnerable. A wall, built with emotional and intellectual counter-inspirations, is erected around the injuries, darkening your conscience. The enemy's purpose in hardening your heart is to keep your emotional and intellectual defenses firmly in place; to keep your conscience dark and your true human nature hidden.

Perhaps you felt very hurt after your parents divorced or after your best friend moved away or being betrayed in a relationship or losing a job to someone else or... In response to the pain, you became more hardened in your judgments about the meaning of life, truth and beauty. Many normal things in life soon looked grim to you. You gradually stopped trusting people who love you. You started overreacting to people's ordinary, even loving intentions.

The enemy of human nature's chief goal is to permanently camouflage your heart. He loves it when you are wounded—this allows him to build walls in you. Jesus made reference to these forms of defensive structures. He said they keep people from believing in Him, even if He should rise from the dead (Lk 16:31), and they grieved Jesus because they harden hearts (Mk 3: 5).

Reflection Exercise:
Pray to the Divine-Inspirer to have your memory "energized." Remember! Think of one hard-hearted position you have taken that goes against the Gospel's and the Church's teachings of love. Remember all the intellectual arguments you make, internally or with others, that "justify" a position you know in your heart to be too extreme.

Bring your thoughts to Jesus in this exercise. See him sitting with you. Tell him what you believe and why you think yourself justified in holding it. What does Jesus, who is the truth and the model of human nature, say? What does he invite you to understand? Does he challenge you in any way? What do you say in return?

Write your experiences briefly in your journal.

Example: A college senior shared on a retreat how he had lost his virginity in high school. He was deeply in love with the girl and the event took place in his family home. He felt afterward that he betrayed his parent's trust (they were away). And very next day, the girl dumped him. She had simply "used" him for her own pleasure.

Since this was his first sexual relationship, his self-confidence suffered terribly. His heart was hardened twice—once over the shame of having betrayed his parent's trust and once over being "used." Both his relationship with his parents and women suffered. He shut his parents out of his life and started to "use" girls the way he had been used. But he felt justified because of the "hardness of his heart."

He only later realized how his heart had been broken by his own shame and by the pain of being used. It took six years to see how he was treating his parents and women and finally had the grace to change—to "see" what had happened.

DISCERNMENT LESSON SEVEN
SUMMARIZING YOUR INSIGHTS

Detail: Jesus reads from Isaiah, St. John's Church, Ireland

Take a few minutes to reflect on each of the unfinished statements below. In this conversation, you could say things like this:

"Just like St. Ignatius' Divine inspiration to reform his life was corrupted into a damaging habit of confessing old sins, I've realized that my divine inspiration is corrupted by:

"_____

_____."

"I know now that the counter-inspirer hurts me by manipulating my long-standing vulnerabilities which are:
"_____

_____.

"I understand that the Divine-Inspirer will always offer the graces and insights to lead me home. Here's how I've come to understand this:

"_____

_____."

As you work with God's grace to let your life be transformed into True Heart, never be discouraged by your failings, sins and weaknesses. The Divine Physician will never tire of forgiving you. Never tire of coming to Him for forgiveness. In this radical, loving trust, you encounter the unfathomable and unbounded mercy of God.

Reflection Exercise:
Pray to the Divine-Inspirer to have your memory "energized." Remember!

Write briefly below or in your journal as best as you can recall the one major lesson you learned from the previous eight strategies discussed in the last two weeks of True Heart.

Write a crucial insight you gained from meeting with your mentor.

Pray to be inspired and write briefly in your journal one or two lessons you "never want to forget!" Be brief but specific.

AUTOBIOGRAPHY EXERCISES

True Heart, A Way to Selflessness, concludes with two exercises inviting individuals to write a short autobiography about their life. The first exercise invites individuals to assess all their character weaknesses and write an autobiography as if they chose to give themselves over to a life of self-centeredness. The second exercise is just the opposite. It invites individuals to assess all their character strengths and write a short autobiography as if they chose to give themselves over to a life of selflessness.

The goal of the exercises is to have individuals take a good look and their strengths and weaknesses—their selfless and selfish tendencies—and to make future predictions on who they "could" become if one path is taken over another. It reminds one of the famous Robert Frost poem, The Road Not Taken, that concludes:

> Two roads diverged in a wood, and I—
> I took the one less traveled by,
> And that has made all the difference.

St. Ignatius' wisdom is also embedded in these exercises. The whole goal of the Ignatian Examen, what we call in Forty Weeks, Sacred Story Prayer, and here, True Heart Prayer, is to daily assess the tendencies and temptations toward selflessness and selfishness and to constantly set one's heart and mind on the true north—the TRUE HEART—of selflessness.

These exercises could be effectively used in many different settings. The two companion exercises might for the basis of a weekend or an overnight retreat for youth or young adults. They could be part of a Confirmation process. They could be used as a review of life in preparation for Sacramental Reconciliation.

You can also use them over multiple days or weeks, taking each section and having individuals take each segment on different days over weeks.

Consequently, you can use them as capstone exercises to many different pastoral initiatives with young adults. You might consider having individuals do a night vigil in the presence of the Blessed Sacrament in the evening and take one to two hours to do each of the autobiography sketches.

You might invite individuals to share their stories with each other and what they learned about themselves by projecting themselves into an imagined future once their life on earth was complete.

In days past, you could find images of saints, like St. Anthony and St. Francis of Assisi contemplating a skull. The spiritual meaning was to see the shortness of life and contemplate how I am living my life in the face of the eternity to come.

It is not easy to get young adults to think far into the future because a characteristic of youth is to have a sense of invulnerability. For the majority, two thirds or better of their lives lie ahead of them and that provides a buffer to considering ultimate realities.

These exercises can thus be powerful aids in helping young adults of all ages reflect on the meaning of their lives and the choices small and large that might put them on the sure path to happiness—to selflessness.

LISTENING TO MY STORY—SELFISHNESS

EXERCISE ONE

For this series of exercise spiritual exercises, you will be reviewing the patterns in your life of vain, self-centeredness. This is a holy exercise in spiritual growth that matches St. Ignatius' first week of his Spiritual Exercises. In the First Week, the one making a retreat seeks to understand the elements in his or her life that block the light of the Holy Spirit and render them less than free to follow the inspirations of God in their life.

To understand what takes away your spiritual freedom is to uncover your True Heart. Approach these exercises with great interest as you discover your life story in a wholly new way.

Reflection Exercise:
List your top three vices and addictions. Do an exercise where you try to find the links between them. Review the Ten Commandments, too. Write down the main patterns of self-centeredness you consider significant that you would like to avoid in your life.

Briefly review your last Confession. Write down the main pattern of self-centeredness that you want to confess that you consider significant and would like to avoid in your life.

Briefly review your life. Write down the three top patterns of self-centeredness that you consider significant that you want to avoid in your life.

LISTENING TO MY STORY—SELFISHNESS

EXERCISE TWO

Reflection Exercise:

Today, you are writing part one of a short autobiography of your life. You are looking to the future and imagining you have lived most of your life. You are writing a "future story" as if you had fully given yourself over to a life of self-centeredness. You are to write between two hundred and fifty to three hundred words; about one page of a double-spaced typed page of part one of your autobiography.

The themes you are covering in part one of your self-centered autobiography will deal with your education, your career(s), your wealth and your financial investments. Be very creative, bold and descriptive. Remember; you are writing as if you gave yourself over completely to a self-centered life.

LISTENING TO MY STORY—SELFISHNESS

EXERCISE THREE

Reflection Exercise:

Today, you are writing part two of a short autobiography of your life. You are looking to the future and imagining you have lived most of your life. You are writing a "future story" as if you had fully given yourself over to a life of self-centeredness. You are to write between two hundred and fifty to three hundred words; about one page of a double-spaced typed page for part two of your autobiography.

The themes you are covering in part two of your self-centered autobiography will deal with your status as married or single (if married, how many marriages?), your children if you had any, your friends and social circles and a description of your charitable giving. Be very creative, bold and descriptive. Remember; you are writing as if you gave yourself over completely to a self-centered life.

LISTENING TO MY STORY—SELFISHNESS

EXERCISE FOUR

Reflection Exercise:

Today, you are writing part three of a short autobiography of your life. You are looking to the future and imagining you have lived most of your life. You are writing a "future story" as if you had fully given yourself over to a life of self-centeredness. You are to write between two hundred and fifty to three hundred words; about one page of a double-spaced typed page for part three of your autobiography.

The themes you are covering in part two of your self-centered autobiography will deal with your faith practice, your political views/causes if any, the most notable events in your life, any awards you received and that for which you are most notorious. Be very creative, bold and descriptive. Remember; you are writing as if you gave yourself over completely to a self-centered life.

LISTENING TO MY STORY—SELFISHNESS

EXERCISE FIVE

FAITH PRACTICES TO AVOID A SELF-CENTERED LIFE

Reflection Exercise:

Briefly review all three parts of your self-centered autobiography. Write down the four main spiritual habits and/or practices you would have to incorporate into your regular regime in order for you not to give yourself over to a life of self-centeredness. Be brief but also say why these particular practices are important as spiritual preventative medicine to self-centeredness.

LISTENING TO MY STORY—SELFLESSNESS

EXERCISE ONE

For this exercise, you will be reviewing the patterns of selflessness in your life. This is a holy exercise in spiritual growth that matches St. Ignatius' conversion and life-transformation detailed in his autobiography and his Spiritual Exercises. In the Fourth Week of the Spiritual Exercises, the one making a retreat seeks to understand how God labors in all things for our good. You are looking at your life in light of this graced awareness and seeking to see into the future the ideal of selflessness you most want your own life to achieve.

To understand your deepest desires for selflessness is to uncover your True Heart. Approach these exercises with great interest. We become what we desire most!

Reflection Exercise:
For today, review your life to understand those selfless actions that increased your faith, hope and love of God and neighbor.

In reviewing your life briefly note below the most significant patterns that come to light that help you understand better the deepest desires you long for that move your heart toward selflessness.

LISTENING TO MY STORY—SELFLESSNESS

EXERCISE TWO

Reflection Exercise:

Today, you are writing part one of a short autobiography of your life. You are looking to the future and imagining you have lived most of your life. You are writing a "future story" as if you had fully given yourself over to a life of selflessness. You are to write between two hundred and fifty to three hundred words; about one page of a double-spaced typed page of part one of your autobiography.

The themes you are covering in part one of your selfless autobiography will deal with your education, your career(s), your wealth and your financial investments. Be very creative, bold and descriptive. Remember; you are writing as if you gave yourself over completely to a selfless life.

LISTENING TO MY STORY—SELFLESSNESS

Reflection Exercise:

Today, you are writing part two of a short autobiography of your life. You are looking to the future and imagining you have lived most of your life. You are writing a "future story" as if you had fully given yourself over to a life of selflessness. You are to write between two hundred and fifty to three hundred words; about one page of a double-spaced typed page of part one of your autobiography.

The themes you are covering in part two of your selfless autobiography will deal with your status as married or single (if married, how many marriages?), your children if you had any, your friends and social circles and a description of your charitable giving. Be very creative, bold and descriptive. Remember; you are writing as if you gave yourself over completely to a selfless life.

LISTENING TO MY STORY—SELFLESSNESS

Reflection Exercise:

Today, you are writing part three of a short autobiography of your life. You are looking to the future and imagining you have lived most of your life. You are writing a "future story" as if you had fully given yourself over to a life of selflessness. You are to write between two hundred and fifty to three hundred words; about one page of a double-spaced typed page of part one of your autobiography.

The themes you are covering in part three of your selfless autobiography will deal with your faith practice, your political views/causes if any, the most notable events in your life, any awards you received and that for which you are most famous. Be very creative, bold and descriptive. Remember; you are writing as if you gave yourself over completely to a selfless life.

LISTENING TO MY STORY—SELFLESSNESS

EXERCISE FIVE

FAITH PRACTICES TO AVOID A SELF-CENTERED LIFE

Reflection Exercise:

Briefly review all three parts of your selfless autobiography. Write down the four main spiritual habits and/or practices you would have to incorporate into your regular regime in order for you to give yourself over to a life of selflessness. Be brief but also say why these particular practices are important as spiritual paths to selflessness.

BELIEF IN JESUS FULLY PRESENT
IN THE BLESSED SACRAMENT

This prayer exercise can be used as a vocation meditation on a retreat, for an evening exercise with young adults, a prayer in the presence of the Blessed Sacrament or in many other settings.

You might employ this exercise also as a preparation for one or all of the Night Vigils, but especially the True Heart All Night Vigil, since it references the Eucharistic miracles and stories of Fr. Pedro Arrupe, Servant of God.

We know that one of the most powerful things to bring youth and young adults to Christ is Eucharistic Adoration and so our best recommendation is to use this in that context, no matter the pastoral situation you plan on creating. Tell us how you use the exercises and how it has helped people.

The meditation also links the Christ of the disciples with the living Christ in the Eucharist as the one who brings true healing to the world. In this age of super hero movies, belief in magic and supernatural events, we must remember that the holy work of Christ in his presence to us daily in the Mass is the event, the reality, that will bring the whole world healing and peace...if we allow him.

This exercise calls young adults to take a risk and believe that Jesus is real, is present to us completely in the Eucharist and that he still wants to work powerfully in our lives, the Church and the world. And yes, that he is calling us to serve him.

Yes, Lord, I belief. Help my unbelief!

BELIEF IN JESUS THE DIVINE PHYSICIAN
FULLY PRESENT IN THE BLESSED SACRAMENT

Read the following vocation story. It will ask you to believe not only in God, but to call you to faith and belief that the Jesus who walked the earth is still with us in His fullness in the Blessed Sacrament. It will invite you to believe in His presence and ask you, in faith, that he cure someone to help the cause of the canonization of Fr. Pedro Arrupe, S.J., whose own conversion as a young adult, was triggered by witnessing a miracle cure at Lourdes in France when he was a young medical student.

Dear Friend:

I was eighteen and it was March of my senior year in high-school. Sitting in the basement of our family home I was smoking a cigarette up the fireplace chimney (did not want to let my folks know I was smoking), and watching late-night television. Suddenly, an ad for the Peace Corps came on TV. The commercial showed volunteers working with youth in Africa. I was riveted and said: "That is what I want to do with my life." I never got to sleep that night.

My thoughts moved from a year of service to a life of service—to being a missionary. I was overcome with feelings of love and hope that I had never before experienced. I knew in some way that God was involved with what was happening, but I was also keenly aware that I did not really know God. But I told myself: "God is doing this."

I entered the Jesuit novitiate the following August. The year was 1973. We could only bring one small trunk of personal belongings. One of the items in my trunk was a picture of a bird flying out of a cage. It was how I felt. I had wings for the first time in my life. I was in love and a God I did not yet know had set a fire in my heart. I was on a mission.

Christ did reveal himself to me more clearly during my Ignatian Thirty Day Retreat. I remember that retreat well for its twenty-eight days of rain out of thirty. But it was the contrast of those dark, rainy days in Oregon's Willamette Valley with the brightness and warmth of Christ's love I felt in prayer that stood out the most. After the retreat, Jesus' love for me gained traction and practical expression in the Society of Jesus' devotion to the Sacred Heart of Christ.

But my time in the novitiate was not without crises. Around Easter of my first year, I was convinced I had made a mistake in entering. I told my novice director that I wanted to leave. Being wise, he suggested instead of leaving, that I go home for two weeks and think about it…no hard decisions. I only learned later that one should never make a decision in a time of spiritual desolation, and I was clearly in one at the time.

After two weeks back home, and pondering all the different careers and vocations I might engage, nothing matched the hope, peace and desire I felt in contemplating continuing my life as a Jesuit. So, I took a bus back to the novitiate and resumed by training.

Yet, struggles continued. I was not yet reconciled with the holiness of life I felt called to live, and the reality of my life that felt anything but holy. I did not feel worthy to be a religious. I faced a difficult crossroads. How could I reconcile the intense desire for Christ and giving myself to a religious vocation in light my sinfulness and weakness? God found a way to break the logjam.

I had a powerful dream one night in my second year of novitiate. I was standing, naked, in the palm of a great hand out in the depths of space. Galaxies and stars were all about me. I *knew* that it was in the hand of God that I stood—*naked, known and loved*. God loved me in spite of my failings.

It was the most powerful dream of my life and one of the most *real* experiences I had ever experienced. I woke from the dream knowing it had come from the same source who had given me the desires that night I was watching TV. But now I knew more about this God. Most importantly, I knew that God knew me. I heard the words of Jeremiah 1:5: "Before I formed you in the womb, I knew you."

Almost two years to the date after entering the Society, I pronounced my first vows as a Jesuit. I wanted to commit myself that special day to the path of love that I had experienced. It needed to be a public witness. Yes, I was professing my vows, and that was a public witness. But I felt compelled to do something more.

Each "vow man" was offered a time at the dinner to say something. Many Jesuits and family members attended these events. I decided I wanted to say something about the devotion to the Heart of Christ.

It felt some anxiety contemplating professing my conviction about the importance of the devotion. It wasn't really in style any longer or seen as a needed spiritual practice. I thought I would look foolish and possibly be made fun of. Yet, I felt compelled to say what I believed.

My time to speak came and with apprehension in my heart, I said something to the effect: "I believe it is important for the Society of Jesus that we re-dedicate ourselves to the devotion to the Heart of Christ. If we do this, I think we will be very successful in all our efforts."

I still have Jesuit friends who remind me of my statement that day. So my "witness" did make a lasting impression, and yes, I was kidded, and still am. But the call to have a devotion to the Heart of Christ was affirmed by the Jesuit General, Pedro Arrupe.

Six years after I took vows, and in the final address Arrupe would give before a debilitating stroke silenced him, he confirmed my own convictions.[114]

Jesus is calling you, my friend. He has been since before you were born. He has a plan to make your life take flight—to give you holy wings. He has a mission, rooted in his love, that only you can accomplish. The mission is for your joy. Your "yes" to His loving call can and will transform history.

We created TRUE HEART to give you a path to find your mission. You will need a childlike heart to hear the call, but it will be unmistakable when it comes. Most likely, the call will make you look foolish in the eyes of the world, and even with your friends. But your call is to transform the world with Christ, not conform to its ways.

MAKE AN ACT OF FAITH TO START YOUR JOURNEY

Are you willing to take a leap of faith at the beginning of your TRUE HEART journey? I just mentioned Fr. Pedro Arrupe, S.J, who was superior general of the Jesuits when I entered in 1973. His cause for canonization began in early 2019, nearly twenty-five years after his death. He was indeed a True Heart. He founded the Jesuit Refugee Services and he, more than anyone one, is credited for putting the Jesuits on the path to making Gospel justice part of all our works.

I believe his powerful witness of selflessness was because he had such a strong devotion to the Heart of Christ and Christ's presence in the Blessed Sacrament. He, like Mother Theresa of Calcutta, are known as true servants of justice for the poor and both were so adamant in a child-like faith in Christ the Blessed Sacrament.

After the death of his father in 1926, he soon afterward traveled with his sisters to Lourdes (France), where he witnessed more than one miraculous healing. He took part, as a medical student, in the verification process of one such healing. He witnessed a miraculous healing of a young man "twisted and contorted by Polio." As the bishop passed with the Blessed Sacrament in the monstrance, he blessed the young man who then "rose from the cart cured."

Pedro said that the very same Jesus Christ who had cured so many people in the Gospels cured that young man. The Christ of history and the living Christ in the Blessed Sacrament are one and the same. It was this miracle by the power of Christ in the Blessed Sacrament that promoted Pedro to abandon his medical career and enter the Jesuits three months later, to serve the true Divine Physician. He would later say, "I felt God so close in his miracles that he dragged me after him."

Please pray for a similar healing miracle to take place by the presence of Christ in the Blessed Sacrament to confirm Fr. Arrupe's cause for sainthood.[115] Pray the prayer on the following page for this cause. If you are

---

[114] "The Society needs the "dynamis" contained in this symbol and in the reality that it proclaims: the love of the Heart of Christ. Perhaps what we need is an act of ecclesial humility, to accept what the Supreme Pontiffs, the General Congregations and the Generals of the Society have incessantly repeated. And yet, I am convinced that there could be few proofs of the spiritual renewal of the Society so clear as a widespread and vigorous devotion to the Heart of Jesus. Our apostolate would receive new strength and we would see its effects very soon, both in our personal lives and in our apostolic activities." Pedro Arrupe, *Texts on the Heart of Christ* (St. Louis: Institute of Jesuit Sources, 1984). 151.

[115] If you have reason to believe your prayer for healing was answered for a specific person, please communicate any favor received though the intercession of the Servant of God Pedro Arrupe: Postulazione Generale della Compagnia di Gesu/Borgo Santo Spiritu, 4/1-

capable of making this act of faith in a church in the presence of the Blessed Sacrament, do it! It is a perfect way for you to begin your True Heart journey. You are making an act of faith in Jesus to confirm a True Heart and believing that with Christ, "all things are possible."

Prayer for Pedro Arrupe's Canonization[116]

Dear Lord Jesus,
I believe you are truly present
to me here in the Blessed Sacrament.
Here you are the same person who was present to your disciples
and the people you cured in the Gospel stories.
Here you are the same person in the Blessed Sacrament
who miraculously healed the young man
Pedro Arrupe witnessed at Lourdes.
Through the intercession of Fr. Pedro Arrupe,
Please cause a miraculous cure
through your Blessed Sacrament of
(say the name of the person you want healed
and be specific for the physical healing that is needed).
May this miraculous cure lead to the sainthood
of Fr. Pedro Arrupe and reveal to the world,
like Fr. Arrupe discovered, that you
are truly the living Divine Physician.
I believe that you can affect this healing for
(say the name again and the specific thing needing healing)
and affirm again your healing power and
its promise of eternal life fully present in the Blessed Sacrament.

Thank you for hearing my prayers and answering them
If it is it serves for Your own glory and praise.
May it lead to the conversion of many souls
In honor of the holy and selfless life of Fr. Pedro Arrupe.
Through Christ, our Lord.
AMEN!

Expect miracles of grace, insight and personal transformation. Ask Jesus for them. His joy is to make you a True Heart. Pray that Christ "drag you after Him," too!

Peace to you,

Fr. Bill Watson, SJ
Easter Sunday 2019

00193, ROME (Italy). Or at: postulazione@sjcuria.org. Remember, the following conditions must be met in the case of physical healings (the most common miracles in canonization cases): The healing must be completely and professionally documented (that is, physician's reports from both before and after the healing); the healing must be attributable solely to one saint's intercession (that is, if you're also praying to Sts. Francis of Assisi, Padre Pio, Francis Xavier and others, it is not going to "count"); the healing must be instantaneous; and the healing has to be permanent (that is, the physical condition cannot relapse). Please also communicate any other favors you believe you have received through the intercession of Servant of God, Fr. Pedro Arrupe, SJ.

[116] With Ecclesiastical Approval

TRUE HEART
ALL-NIGHT VIGIL

Many years ago, when I was working at Georgetown University, we renovated a crypt chapel and started using it for night-time Masses with people who had made retreats. The chapel was indeed, a crypt chapel—not bodies—but vaulted ceilings, pillars, quiet and somewhat mystical. Students loved to come there for Mass. One year, we started all-night vigils in the presence of the Blessed Sacrament. Students would sign up to come for one or more hours of prayer from 10 in the evening till 7 in the morning.

It was a very popular event. Students loved it and I can't tell you how many things happened in the hearts and minds of those young adults during the quiet hours of the evening and early morning when they were alone with Christ. The experience made a lasting impact on those who participated.

In a conversation with Curtis Martin, founder of FOCUS (Fellowship of Catholic University Students, I asked what was the one thing, more than anything else, that helped young adults today encounter Jesus and believe in him. His answer was immediate: "Eucharist Adoration."

This True Heart All-Night Vigil will be a power spiritual resource in your pastoral tool-kit. You can use it in so many ways to help young adults find Christ, choose the values of His Kingdom, search for vocation answers and simply believe that the Lord who walked the cities of Palestine, preaching and performing "signs and wonders" is the very same Jesus who is present in the Blessed Sacrament.

The story told by Fr. Pedro Arrupe, Servant of God, that forms the core of the vigil will draw them deeply into the mystery of Christ's life and plan for the world and help them access the deepest desires and dreams they have for their life and the world.

Let us know the contexts you use this exercise. It forms the "capstone" experience of the main TRUE HEART program. However, it has many uses and can help you help others find Christ amidst the crazy, digital distress of our world.

Help your people prepare for the event by following the "what to bring" very carefully. Make sure they have a Church that has a 24-hour adoration chapel or make arrangements for one. Preparation is key.

TRUE HEART
ALL-NIGHT DISCERNMENT VIGIL

PREPARATION OF THE PLACE

The TRUE HEART All-Night Discernment Vigil is an opportunity for you to conclude the TRUE HEART program and gather the graces for the ten-week journey. [117] You also seek to offer your life to the work of the Kingdom of Christ. It is common in the history of Christianity for an individual to do a "night vigil" when beginning an important mission. Entry into knighthood in medieval times began with an all-night vigil in the chapel of a castle or a major church.

St Ignatius understood this holy ritual. After his conversion, seeking to imitate Christ, he stripped himself of his worldly ways by giving his fine clothes to a poor man. Later, in an all-night vigil before the Black Madonna in the church of the Benedictine abbey at Montserrat, he hung up his sword and dagger. Effectively, his old life was over and his new life desiring only the armor of Christ, had begun.

You are asking for the graces to dedicate your life to Christ. You may discover the specific way to accomplish this goal during the night vigil. However, the general consecration of your life to the Way, Truth and the Light of Christ is your main spiritual exercise for the evening vigil. Choose this vigil—embrace its profound mysteries and be not afraid!

---

[117] Perhaps you might consider it an is a spiritual form of an Outward Bound solo adventure. On the organization's website, there is a quote from the American author, Caroline Myss: *"Always go with the choice that scares you the most, because that's the one that is going to require the most from you."*

The time frame mirrors an eight-hour workday, only think of it as night, spiritual work. Find a Catholic Church that has a 24-hour Adoration Chapel. Find the one as close to your home as possible. Plan to be there from 8, 9, 10 or 11 PM in the evening till 4, 5, 6 or 7 AM the following morning.

Choose the best eight-hour structure to accommodate your time and the locations that might be available to you. Choose the hours, too, that you think will draw you most into the holy mystery of what you are

Contact the parish and let them know who you are and that you would like to do an all-night vigil. Plan the night by including your family in the details of the vigil. Plan not to bring a cell phone. The goal is to be alone with Christ. Embrace the silence and enter the mystery! Christ is truly present to you in the Blessed Sacrament.

NOTE: *You may be doing this with others, but pledge to not engage others in conversation or any form of communication during the eight-hour period. The more you are alone, the greater chance there is that you will be open to God working in your heart.*

Pedro Arrupe in 1909

The first part of the vigil will be reflecting on some powerful memories of Fr. Pedro Arrupe, S.J. Fr. Arrupe was the head Jesuit when I entered the order in 1973. His cause for sainthood was begun in the late winter of 2019. I read this article when I was in my mid-twenties and it had a deep impact on me. As you begin your TRUE HEART Night Vigil, I ask you to enter into the mystery of Christ present to you in the Blessed Sacrament.

Believing he is real and present and that he loves you, will be the most important work you can accomplish in this life— for this vigil. I offer this reflection of Fr. Arrupe to help you realize the authentic supernatural power of God that marks Christ's imprint on the world since the time he lived, died and rose again—forever changing your life and the history of the cosmos. Embrace the silence and enter the mystery of life, of Christ and your story.

WHAT TO BRING

—Sacred Crucifix and Prayer Stole
Purchase an inexpensive small crucifix and a prayer stole. Have both of these items blessed by your parish priest or chaplain. We recommend a woven Guatemalan stole common with laity in Latin America who wear them to Mass.[118] Each baptized Catholic shares in Christ's mission as "priest,

---

[118] The best place to purchase one of these prayer stoles is from: http://thetreeoflifeimports.com/stoles.htm
You can also purchase a small cross from the same group that supports Fair Trade and Latin American families: http://thetreeoflifeimports.com/crosses.htm

prophet and king." Bring your crucifix and wear this prayer stole during your vigil. Both will become powerful holy signs of this signature spiritual event in your life.

Your TRUE HEART materials,

—Your journal entries from the program

—A pen or two

—A Bible

—A notebook for writing

—Your favorite picture/image of Jesus

— Bring some fluids and what you think you need for nourishment

—Bring a watch

—Dress comfortably (Dress knowing you will spend eight hours with Christ--classy but comfortable. What you wear will be determined somewhat by the weather too, so take that into consideration)

Your most important element is your prayer stole.

THE HOURLY STRUCTURE

Minutes 1-5

—Kneel Silently & Listen to Your Heart

—Pray the Hail Mary & Listen to Your Heart

—Pray One of the Two Following Prayers to Affirm Christ Present in the Blessed Sacrament Before You

Anima Christi [119]

Soul of Christ, sanctify me
Body of Christ, save me
Blood of Christ, inebriate me
Water from Christ's side, wash me
Passion of Christ, strengthen me
O good Jesus, hear me
Within your wounds hide me
Let me not be separated from You
From the hateful enemy defend me
In the hour of my death call me
And bid me come to You
That I may praise You with your saints
and with your angels
Forever and ever
Amen

---

[119] Prayer from the 14th century and a favorite of St. Ignatius.

Coptic Eucharistic Prayer [120]

Father, I believe and confess that before me is the living body which your only-begotten Son, Our Lord and Savior Jesus Christ, took from the Lady, Queen of humankind, and the Mother of God. I believe, I believe, I believe that this is in very truth the living body of Christ Jesus, present to me. Help my unbelief.

Minutes 6-40
—Spiritual Exercise (Follow what is presented for each hour)

Minutes 41-50
—Journal Exercise (Write all your short journal entries directed to Jesus Christ. For example: "Jesus, I want…; "Jesus help me….."; etc. Talk to Him. Ask Him for help and guidance. Let Him be Lord and Savior for you tonight.

Minutes 51-60
—Take a Break

---

[120] Adopted from an ancient eucharist prayer for the Coptic Church.

FIRST HOUR

Minutes 1-5
—Kneel Silently & Listen to Your Heart
—Pray the Hail Mary & Listen to Your Heart
—Pray One of the Two Following Prayers to Affirm Christ Present in the Blessed Sacrament Before You

Minutes 6-40
—Spiritual Exercise (Read the following story, taking your time to pause and reflect as you do. There is no need to rush).

The Eucharist And Youth[121]

Life's Prospects for the Young People of Today

Some time ago I was making a long trip on a train when three young fellows of around eighteen entered into my compartment. They were accompanied by a man who was somewhat older, and after a bit, I learned that he was the director of physical education at their school.

They were tired, and after some remarks on their winning a soccer game, they dropped off to sleep, one after the other. A couple of hours later they began to speak again and to take down a good number of Cokes and orange sodas. Their conversation became lively, and they looked at me with a certain curiosity as if they were asking themselves: Who in the world is this priest? I did not join in their conversation since I had to prepare a conference which I was to give as soon as I reached my destination

---

[121] Adapted from: Pedro Arrupe, *Other Apostolates Today: Selected Letters and Addresses—III*, ed. Jerome Aixala (St Louis: Institute of Jesuit Sources, 1981), 283-307. Original talk of Fr. Arrupe delivered at the Basilica of St Francis, Assisi September 6, 1979. *It is three o'clock in the afternoon. Some 1400 boys and girls of the "Eucharistic Youth Movement" have entered into the lower Basilica of St. Francis. They are members of the two senior sections of the Apostleship of Prayer for children and young men and women in Italy. Present in the present assembly there are some 950 from the groups of "Community 14", that is of boys and girls from ages 14 to I6; and 400 from the groups of "Witnesses", that is young men and women of 17 and over. So the target is what we could call today the "youth and young adults" that form the nexus of our pastoral outreach to the upcoming generation.* More from Fr. Pedro Arrupe can be found at The Arrupe Collection: https://jesuitportal.bc.edu/research/documents/the-arrupe-collection/ For information on the cause of Fr. Arrupe's canonization, visit: https://arrupe.jesuitgeneral.org/en/

Pedro Arrupe, High School Graduation Portrait 1924

At one point, when their talk seemed to be dying down, the teacher asked: "Now that you have finished school, what do you plan to do?" One of the boys answered without much thought: "I don't know. I suspect that my father will tell me; I have no thoughts about anything. Who knows? It's a tough problem. It is better that they tell me what to do. Besides, I don't care to be bothered."

The second then broke in: "I've thought a lot about it, and I don't know whether I should go into business or work in the stock market. I don't know which of these two pay the better without too much work. What I want is an easy and peaceful life. I don't care for much more."

The third seemed to be a bit ashamed. He said nothing, and it looked as if he wanted to avoid giving an answer. The two others looked at him with some perplexity, and after a few seconds the teacher asked him: "And you, Frank, what are you going to do?" "To tell the truth, I'm not sure myself. I have been thinking about going for some years to some spot in the Third World to see its greatest need. I could then be a help to many who are suffering in it."

The eyes of the other two started to pop out as if to ask: "Frank, are you crazy?" The teacher then queried him: "How did you get that idea?" "I don't know," Frank replied a bit embarrassed, "but the idea has been floating around in my head for some months. Do you think it a crazy idea?" "No, not crazy, just a bit strange. Still, Frank, I really admire you."

At this, I was no longer able to keep quiet. In a low voice I said what I was thinking: "It's great, Frank. Follow that tugging of your heart since it must be a heart of gold." My four traveling companions looked at me and then began to speak about soccer.

I also let go of the topic, but I began to think how these three young people clearly manifested different attitudes shared by today's youth:

There are those who are not much on thinking. They let themselves be carried along by circumstances. They don't want to be bothered. And why? You live very well if you have no worries.

There are those who have no other ambition than to make money, and this with the least effort possible. They are self-centered at heart: "I go my way, and others can think what they want." They believe that they can find their happiness in money. They let themselves be carried off by appearances, by what they see in ads, by the fascination of the world of entertainment.

But there are also those of noble heart who are moved by a desire to be of help to others, to console those who are afflicted, to be of service to others even at the cost of personal sacrifices.

My encounter with Christ

Dear members of the Youths' Eucharistic Movement, you have invited me to share in this festival of yours; and I would like to speak with each one of you about the plans which you are cherishing in your hearts for your future life. Are you waiting for someone to tell you what you should do? Do you want to make money most of all in order to be happy? Do you feel a longing to serve your brothers and sisters? There is perhaps no one of you that has ideas that are firmly fixed, but certainly you are more or less inclined to one of these three general tendencies.

To you, to your questions, and to your expectations, I am today telling you in all simplicity what I have myself experienced in meeting Jesus Christ. A few weeks ago in Rome, a group of pilgrims, boys and girls, came to pay me a visit after the Wednesday audience of the pope. At one point, one of the younger of the group asked me point blank: "Why did you become a Jesuit?" — "Because I believed that it was my vocation."

— "And why did you believe it was your vocation?" — "Because I felt that God was calling me." — "And why was He calling you?" — "Well, the Lord wished to have another who would consecrate himself completely to Him, and He chose me" — "What did you think?" — "I thought that it would cost me much to abandon my career as a doctor, but that by becoming a Jesuit I could labor even more for others. I would be able to cure not only bodies but also souls."

Another boy broke in: "Father, I have heard that different Jesuits have been killed. It must be a rather risky vocation." — "You are right. Six Jesuits have been killed in Rhodesia, four in Lebanon, one in Chad, two in Latin America." — "Why don't you defend yourselves? Why don't you use weapons?" — "There's not even a thought of that. We want to be of service to all without discrimination. We live to serve. If we are killed for our service, it is a great honor for us!"

Pedro Arrupe (second from left top) with high school friends in Bilbao, Spain ca. 1924

— "But if you are hated and you let yourselves be killed, you have to have a lot of courage. I don't get it."

— "Right you are, but the Lord gives one strength since it is done for Him, and it is He who gives us strength." — "So," the boy exclaimed in amazement, and his face showed that he had failed to understand; and the same expression could be seen on the faces of the rest, who were listening in silence.

I then tried to explain myself: "Look at it this way. We Jesuits became such and continue to be such simply out of our enthusiasm for Jesus Christ and from our desire to work for Him and for others. Jesus Christ is most faithful. He does not abandon those who are dedicated to His service. Jesus Christ lived two thousand years ago, but he still lives today in the Eucharist and in the depths of our hearts.

One of those present suddenly exclaimed: "What? I'm getting less now than I did before!" The rest began to laugh.

I believe that this conversation, simple and straight-forward as it was, revealed a whole series of feelings, questions, and attitudes that are prevalent among young people today. And I am certain that you who have already become familiar with Jesus Christ will understand me better than the boy who said: "What? I'm getting less now than I did before!" I am certain that you will understand me.

One Same Jesus: the Jesus of the Gospel and the Jesus of the Eucharist

It is a fact that Jesus Christ, especially in the Eucharist, is a source of energy for all: for us Jesuits, for you young people, for all, since Jesus Christ is present and lives for us in the Eucharist. He becomes our Friend, our Ideal, our Model, our Strength, our Way. You should know Jesus Christ. The more you know Him, the more you will love Him, since He is in addition to being God—nothing less—He is also a perfect man, one who is both simple and congenial.

During the course of history there have been, and even today there are, many leaders, many individuals who represent different ideologies and who seek to attract us and to convince us that it is worth the effort to follow them and to dedicate ourselves to their cause, but there is no one who can be compared in this regard with Jesus Christ, even from a distance. Those who dealt with him said: "No one has ever spoken as this man." "You have the words of eternal life." "Let us follow him and stay with him." "For him I have accepted the loss of everything, and I look at everything as so much rubbish if only I can have Christ."

Pedro Arrupe as a Jesuit Novice

What can we do to gain an ever better knowledge of Jesus Christ? It is really very simple. In the Gospels, we have a true picture of the historical Jesus, of the Jesus as he lived in Palestine. And in the Eucharist, we have Jesus Christ living today in the midst of us. In neither case can we see him with our eyes, but the Gospel narrative is the word of God which gives vitality to what is said. When we read the Gospels we realize that the person of Jesus, who lived two thousand years ago, is still alive; and we feel Him very close to us.

It is as though Jesus of Nazareth continues to live now as He did then. And on the other hand, the Eucharist is the same Body and Blood of the risen Christ. He is alive and present though hidden under the sacramental species. He lets himself be perceived. He speaks to us. He inspires and strengthens us.

Saint Teresa of Lisieux arrived at such a living faith in the presence of Jesus Christ in the Eucharist that she used to say: "If they told me that Jesus was in the house next to mine, I would not go to see Him since I already have Him with me in the tabernacle and He visits me daily in Holy Communion. I do not have greater faith in the eyes of my face than in those of my faith. The eyes of the body can be deceived, but not those of faith."

By bringing together the two figures, that of the Gospel and that of the Eucharist, we shall obtain the precise image of what Jesus was and is today. Do you really wish to know Jesus Christ, to be transformed by Him? Read the Gospel before the tabernacle, receive Him in Holy Communion, ask Him with His disciples: "Lord, teach us! Lord, we do not understand what you are saying. Explain it to us!"

There is no doubt that in this way each one of us can obtain a true concept of Jesus, even though He is endowed with an infinite richness which no one can completely comprehend, assimilate, or imitate. Each one of us understands or imitates some aspects of the figure of our Lord. All the saints have sought to imitate Jesus and they are all different from each other starting with St. Paul who is different from St. Peter.

Nevertheless, we should all seek to make for ourselves an image of Jesus Christ and to grasp as surely as we can His personality. The path which we follow in our lives should be one that brings us ever closer and ever more dedicated to Him, the Jesus of the Gospel and the Jesus of the Eucharist, who is the same and only Jesus, the Jesus who has risen and is alive, who loves us and seeks us as He does the whole of humankind.

To explain what I want to say, I shall relate some of my own experiences which were connected with the Eucharist and in which I recognize the hand of the Lord who led me and still leads me in my way of life. But I am sure that you also can reflect on your own experience up till now and on the way in which the Lord is guiding you on the path of your life.

Minutes 41-50—Journal Exercise for Hour One

Ponder each of the following questions. Only reflect on one question at a time and don't read ahead. Write the one thing that seems most significant to you at this point in your life from each question. Only move ahead when the Spirit prompts you, taking time to fully explore what your heart is experiencing. Remember to write your short entries directly to Jesus. If you don't complete the reflection/answer process, you will have time to do so at the beginning of the next hour. So relax and reflect peacefully.

✠ Imagine you are going to tell your closest friend about this story. What would be the first thing you shared with them? Ponder. Write in your journal no more than two sentences as a response, clarifying what you would share and why you want to share it.

✠ Fr. Arrupe described three types of responses people can have to making life-choices (see below). Pretending you don't have to tell anyone else but Christ, present to you in the Eucharist, write in your journal which type of person you are *most* like at this time in your life, and why. Write what type of person you want to become, and why. Finally, compose a two-sentence prayer to Christ asking for the help to become your True Heart.

a. *There are those who are not much on thinking. They let themselves be carried along by circumstances. They don't want to be bothered. And why? You live very well if you have no worries.*
b. *There are those who have no other ambition than to make money, and this with the least effort possible. They are self-centered at heart: "I go my way, and others can think what they want." They believe that they can find their happiness in money. They let themselves be carried off by appearances, by what they see in ads, by the fascination of the world of entertainment.*

c. *But there are also those of noble heart who are moved by a desire to be of help to others, to console those who are afflicted, to be of service to others even at the cost of personal sacrifices.*

✠ Fr. Arrupe described the honor of serving others, even at the cost of one's life. Speak to Christ present to you in the Blessed Sacrament and tell him the one thing that would be worth the price of your own life. Ponder with Christ. Write that one thing in your journal with words that begin: "Jesus, I would give my life for…" "Jesus, I would give it because…"

✠ Fr. Arrupe said: *Do you really wish to know Jesus Christ, to be transformed by Him? Read the Gospel before the tabernacle, receive Him in Holy Communion, ask Him with His disciples: "Lord, teach us! Lord, we do not understand what you are saying. Explain it to us!"* Do you want to know Christ and be transformed by him? He is present to you. Speak to and tell him how you want to know him. How do you want to be transformed by him? Write in your journal one sentence on what you told Christ about each.

✠ Fr. Arrupe affirms that each saint in the history of the Church is different. B, although transformed by the same Christ who is the same person who walked the earth as is Present in the Blessed Sacrament Before You. Ponder if you desire to be a saint. Ask Jesus if he can make you one and how you would be remembered by history. What do you hear? Write what you hear from Jesus in your journal.

Minutes 51-60—Take a Break

SECOND HOUR

Minutes 1-5
—Kneel Silently & Listen to Your Heart
—Pray the Hail Mary & Listen to Your Heart
—Pray One of the Prayers to Affirm Christ Present in the Blessed Sacrament Before You

Minutes 6-40
—Spiritual Exercise (If you did not complete the reflection/answers from the previous hour, do those first. When complete, continue reading the story, taking your time to pause and reflect as you do. There is no need to rush).

Jesus, the Worker of Miracles, the Healer of the Ill, Is Calling Me and Is Sending Me on a Mission

The first of my Eucharist experiences was closely connected with my vocation as a Jesuit, the same vocation about which those boys asked me as I observed earlier. The experience was that of a miracle which I saw at Lourdes during the procession of the Blessed Sacrament on the esplanade that lies in front of the basilica.

Some weeks after the death of my father I had gone to Lourdes with my family since we wished to spend the summer in quiet, peaceful, and spiritual surroundings. It was the middle of August. I stayed at Lourdes for a whole month; and since I was a medical student, I was able to obtain a special permission to study closely the sick who came seeking a cure.

One day I was in the esplanade with my sisters a little before the procession of the Blessed Sacrament. A cart pushed by a woman of middle age passed in front of us. One of my sisters exclaimed: "Look at that poor boy in the cart." It was a young man of around twenty, all twisted and contorted by polio.

His mother was reciting the rosary in a loud voice a from time to time she would say with a sigh: "*Maria Santissima (Holy Mary)*, help us." It was a truly moving sight, and I remembered the plea which the sick turned towards Jesus: "Lord, cleanse me from this leprosy!" She hastened to take her place in the row which the bishop was to pass carrying the Blessed Sacrament in a monstrance.

Fr. Pedro Arrupe's First Mass 1936

The moment came when the bishop was to bless the young man with the Host. He looked at the monstrance with the same faith with which the paralytic mentioned in the Gospel must have looked at Jesus. After the bishop had made the sign of the cross with the Blessed Sacrament, the young man rose cured from the cart, as the crowd filled with joy cried out: "Miracle! Miracle!"

Thanks to the special permission which I had, I was later able to assist at the medical examinations. The Lord had truly cured him. There is no need to tell you what I felt and my state of mind at that moment. I had come from the Faculty of Medicine in Madrid, where I had had so many professors (some truly renowned) and so many companions who had no faith and who always ridiculed miracles. But I had been an eyewitness of a true miracle worked by Jesus Christ in the Eucharist, by that same Jesus Christ who had, during the course of His life, cured so many who were ill and paralytic.

I was filled with an immense joy. I seemed to be standing by the side of Jesus; and as I sensed His almighty power, the world that stood around me began to appear extremely small. I returned to Madrid. My books fell from my hands. The lessons, the experiments which had so thrilled me before now seemed so very empty. My comrades asked me: "What's happening to you this year? You are like one who has been stunned!"

Yes, I was like one stunned by that impression which every day grew more disconcerting. The one thing that remained fixed in my mind and in my heart was the image of the Host as it was raised in benediction and of the paralyzed boy who had leapt from his cart. Three months later I entered the novitiate of the Society of Jesus in Loyola, Spain.

The teaching of our Lord was the same as that of the Gospel. Through his miracles and His teaching, He awakened in me a faith and love for Him so that He could finally say: "Leave everything and follow me!" The Lord of the monstrance was the same Lord as that of the Gospel. His powers were the same, and His wishes were as they had then been: "May the workers, who are few, become more numerous since the harvest is great."

Once this voice is heard today as it was twenty centuries ago, it cannot be forgotten. One is, of course, free to follow it or not, but one with judgment or reason, as St. Ignatius of Loyola says, will end with following it. There is no doubt that the force which goes forth from Jesus in the Eucharist, and which went forth on that unforgettable afternoon at Lourdes, is the same that went forth from Jesus in Gospel times.

That experience at Lourdes was a repetition of what the contemporaries of Jesus saw when the crowds surrounded him and he cured all (Mt 9:18; 14:14; Mk 2:13; 3:20; Lk 5:17-26, etc.). Certainly, it is a question of the same Jesus, now hidden under the sacramental species, but with the same love and the same power. These are experiences which leave an indelible trace and bring it about that we also can say with the apostle: "That which we have seen and heard and touched of the Word of life, that is what we preach to you." (1 Jn 1:1).

Our vocation as Jesuits is essentially missionary. It is thus normal that a Jesuit should go to one of those countries known as a mission country. From the time that I became a Jesuit in 1927 until 1937, when I was destined to Japan, I had continuously asked to be sent there, since it seemed to me that it was the place for me. This conviction had its origins in a deep feeling within me. But the Lord had confirmed it in circumstances connected with the Eucharist.

Once when I had just finished serving Mass for our superior in the novitiate, his name was Cesareo Ibero, I told him that I had received a negative answer from the General of the Society of Jesus to my request to be sent to Japan. The rector, who was descending from the altar where he had finished celebrating Mass, told me: "You will go to Japan."

At that moment I felt as if the Lord who had been offered upon the altar had said through the lips of my superior: "Your vocation is to go to Japan, millions of souls are waiting there for you. That is the field of your apostolate." It was Jesus who told me from that hour what would be officially decided ten years later. It was the same Jesus who called His disciples from among others (Jn 1:40-45) so that He might personally send each one of them on his own way.

I also remember that in October 1938, when I was sailing from Seattle to Yokohama, that as I was celebrating Mass alone in the cabin of the ship, I recalled that incident when the rector of Loyola spoke to me when I was still a young Jesuit student. At that moment, when I was now a priest, I held in my hands, in the Host which I had myself consecrated, Him who had destined me for that same country in which another great Jesuit, St. Francis Xavier, had begun to preach the Gospel four hundred years before.

There in my hands was that Savior who had said to his apostles: "Go and preach to all people; I shall be with you till the end of time." On the ship, I experienced great joy and was inspired with the thought of the work which I was about to begin in Japan. It seemed to me that Jesus Himself, whom I held each day in my hands, was teaching me as He had taught the crowds from the prow of the ship on the lake of Tiberias (Mt 13:1-3).

It seemed to me that it was that same wisdom which had then spoken in parables that had spoken also to me, but in a manner which I could not fully understand as yet: It was that "for the moment you cannot understand" (Jn 16:12), as Jesus told His disciples. There were, in fact, things that would have then been too hard and difficult for me, but He who was speaking to me was the same Master who had said: "I will give you rest" (Mt 11:28).

Minutes 41-50

—Journal Exercise for Hour Two

Ponder each of the following questions. Only reflect on one question at a time and don't read ahead. Write the one thing that seems most significant to you at this point in your life from each question. Only move ahead when the Spirit prompts you, taking time to fully explore what your heart is experiencing. Remember to direct your short responses directly to Jesus. If you don't complete the reflection/answer process, you will have time to do so at the beginning of the next hour. So relax and reflect peacefully.

✠ Pedro's family went to Lourdes after his father died. He was a medical student at the time and was permitted to investigate reported miraculous healings. This suggests that he might have believed them to be possible or that he was skeptical and wanted to verify to prove otherwise. Which do you think was his main motive before he witnessed the miracle, and why? Ponder. Then write two sentences first describing which motive seems most true to you and second, why you choose that one.

✠ Pedro witnessed a truly miraculous healing of a profoundly crippled young man. First, it brought him joy. As the weeks progressed, he became stunned and disconcerted. His friends noticed it. Why do you think he went from joy to being stunned and confused? Talk to Jesus about it and ponder. Write one sentence on why you believe this change came over Pedro.

✠ Pedro's witnessing a miracle cure through the Blessed Sacrament moved him from wanting to be a doctor to wanting to work for Jesus. It does not matter that the "call" was as a priest but that he felt "called." Have you ever felt "called" by Jesus to do something? What was it?

✠ What miracle would it take to make you want to follow Jesus? Ponder. Can you ask Jesus for this miracle? Write what miracle you want and what it would do for you.

✠ Pedro continued to have experiences of being confirmed and "called" that coincided with experiences of Christ present in the Blessed Sacrament. Including your time tonight, can you recall any events in your life connected with Christ present in the Blessed Sacrament where you were "called and/or confirmed" in something? Ponder. Write that experience in one sentence if yes.

Minutes 51-60—Take a Break

THIRD HOUR

Minutes 1-5
—Kneel Silently & Listen to Your Heart
—Pray the Hail Mary & Listen to Your Heart
—Pray One of the Prayers to Affirm Christ Present in the Blessed Sacrament Before You

Minutes 6-40
—Spiritual Exercise (If you did not complete the reflection/answers from the previous hour, do those first. When complete, continue reading the story, taking your time to pause and reflect as you do. There is no need to rush).

The Body and Blood of Jesus for the World

Fr. Arrupe elevating the Host at sunrise during Mass on Mount Fuji

The mission which the Lord entrusts to us, though it has its origins in a personal encounter with Him, is always open to others, to the entire world, since the Lord has shed His blood "for the multitude," that is for all. Every Mass is a Mass for the world and in the world. I remember the Mass which I celebrated at the top of the famous Mount Fujiyama, at a height of more than 11,000 feet.

I had climbed it with one of my religious brothers. At that time it was made almost entirely on foot. One could only go on horseback to a height of about 3,300 feet. It was necessary to reach the summit by four in the morning to be able to see the marvelous panorama since by six the peak was covered with clouds and could no longer be seen.

We arrived on time and celebrated Mass in the most complete solitude. It was shortly after I arrived in Japan. I was living through the first impressions of a new environment and my mind was bubbling with a great number of projects for the conversion of the whole of Japan. We had climbed Fujiyama so that we might be able to offer to the Eternal Father the Sacrifice of the Immaculate Lamb for the salvation of all Japan at the highest point in all that country.

The climb had been most tiring since we had to hasten in order to arrive on time. Several times we thought of Abraham and Isaac as they climbed a mountain to offer their sacrifice. Once we had reached the top, the sight of the rising sun was stupendous. It raised our spirits and disposed them for the celebration of the Holy Sacrifice. Till then I had never celebrated Mass in such conditions. Above us, the blue sky expanded like the cupola of an immense temple—brilliant and majestic.

Before us, were all the people of Japan, at that time some eighty million who did not know God. My mind ranged out beyond the lofty vaulting of the sky to the throne of the divine Majesty, the seat of the Blessed Trinity. I seemed to see the holy city of the heavenly Jerusalem. I seemed to see Jesus Christ and with Him St. Francis Xavier, the first apostle of Japan, whose hair had become white in the course of a few months because of the sufferings he had to endure. I also was being confronted by that same Japan as Xavier had been. The future was entirely unknown. If I had then known how much I would have to suffer, my hands would have trembled as I raised the sacred Host.

On that summit so near to heaven it seemed to me that I understood better the mission which God had entrusted to me. I descended from it with a renewed enthusiasm. That Eucharist had made me feel the grandeur of the everlasting God and universal Lord. At the same time, I had felt that I was an "assistant," a sharer in the labor of Jesus Christ in the great redemptive mission entrusted to Him by His Father. I could repeat with more sincerity and conviction the words of Isaiah: "Here I am, send me" (Is 6:8) or those of St. Francis Xavier: "I am! Behold me."

Our Lord also, as is told in the Gospel, went up a mountain with His disciples and was transfigured before them (cf Mt 17:4). I also experienced the longing to remain there and not to leave so that I might continue to relish those heavenly moments, as St. Peter had when he exclaimed, "It is good for us to be here. If you wish I shall prepare three tabernacles one for you, one for Moses (my companion, Moses Domenzáin, bore this same name), and one for Elias." (Mark 9:5).

That same Jesus who had filled St. Peter with joy and admiration, so much so that he had adored Him "falling with his face to the earth" (Mt 17:6), had also shown Himself to me in the sublime sight of our Eucharist—the sacred Host, illuminated by the white light of the rising sun seemed to be transfigured before my eyes, and I believed that I heard with St. Peter the voice of the Lord which said to me: "Have no fear" (cf Mt 17:7). It was a word most necessary for me as I was descending from those heights to the harsh life that was waiting for me during those years in Japan. How many things can Our Lord teach and make one feel in a single Mass?

From this, it is almost natural for me to pass on to another remembrance of the Eucharist, to a Mass celebrated in very different circumstances from those just mentioned. This Mass taught me how Jesus, who suffers and dies for us, can bring about His plan of salvation through the mysterious ways of sorrow and suffering.

The atomic bomb had exploded at 8:10 on August 6, destroying the whole of Hiroshima, reducing it to ashes and killing at one blow eighty thousand people. Our house was one of the few that remained standing, even though it was badly damaged. There were no windows or doors left, all had been torn away by the violent wind caused by the explosion. We turned our house into a hospital and assembled there around two hundred who were injured in order to nurse and assist them.

The explosion had occurred on the sixth of August. On the following day, the seventh, at five in the morning before beginning the work of helping the wounded and burying the dead, I celebrated Mass in our house. It is certain that in the most tragic moments we feel nearest to God and the importance of His assistance. Actually, the external surroundings were not much adapted for fostering devotion during the celebration of the Mass.

The chapel, half destroyed, was packed full of those who had been injured. They were lying on the floor close to each other and they were obviously suffering from the torments of their pains. I began the Mass as best I could in the midst of that crowd which did not have the least idea of what was taking place upon the altar. They were all pagans and had never seen a Mass.

I cannot forget the frightful impression I had when I turned towards them at the opening "The Lord Be With You." (Mass was then said with one's back to the congregation) and saw that sight from the altar. I was unable to move and remained as if I were paralyzed with my arms stretched out as I contemplated that human tragedy: human knowledge, technical advance used for the destruction of the human race. All looked at me with eyes filled with anxiety, with desperation, as though expecting that some consolation would come to them from the altar. It was a frightful scene! Within a few minutes, there would descend upon the altar the one of whom John the Baptist had said: "There is one in the midst of you whom you do not know" (Jn 1:26).

I had never sensed before so greatly the solitude of the pagan ignorance of Jesus Christ. Here was their Savior, the One who had given His life for them, but they "did not know who was in the midst of them" (cf Jn I:26). I was the only one who knew. From my lips there spontaneously went forth a prayer for those who had had the savage cruelty to launch the atomic bomb: "Lord, pardon them, since they do not know what they are doing." and for those who were lying before me, tortured by their pains: "Lord, grant them faith so that they may see; give them the strength to endure their pains."

When I lifted the Host before those torn and mangled bodies there rose from my heart: "My Lord and my God: have compassion on this flock without a shepherd!" (Mt 9:36; Mk 6:34). Lord, may they believe in You. Remember that they also must come to know You (1 Tim 2:4).

Certainly from that Host and from that altar there poured forth torrents of grace. Six months later, when all, already cured, had left our house (only two persons died), many of them had received baptism, and all had learned that Christian charity can have compassion, can assist, can give a consolation that is above all human comfort, can give a peace that helps one to smile in the midst of pain and to pardon those who had made us suffer so much.

Such Masses as these are moments replete with a sacramental intuition which arrives at understanding what is so difficult or so impossible to understand without faith, that is, the value of suffering, the beauty and sublimity of the sacrifice of charity.

Minutes 41-50—Journal Exercise for Hour Three

Ponder each of the following questions. Only reflect on one question at a time and don't read ahead. Write the one thing that seems most significant to you at this point in your life from each question. Only move ahead when the Spirit prompts you, taking time to fully explore what your heart is experiencing. Remember to direct your short responses directly to Jesus. If you don't complete the reflection/answer process, you will have time to do so at the beginning of the next hour. So relax and reflect peacefully.

☩ Fr. Arrupe climbed one of the iconic mountains of the world, Fuji, to celebrate Holy Mass at its summit. His faith told him Christ would be present in that Mass. In "sight" before him and his Jesuit companion, were all the people in Japan who did not know Christ. Do you know Christ Jesus well enough that you would feel passionate about bringing knowledge of Him to people? Ponder. Talk to the Lord and write to him one or two sentences. First, ask Him to give you the kind of knowledge of Him that would make you want to "tell the world" about Him. Second, talk with Jesus about with whom would you want most to share knowledge of Him.

☩ Fr. Arrupe received a powerful grace at his Mass on Mount Fuji. Yet he would later discover that suffering would enter his life and the people he came to bring the Good News. As you are present to Christ in the Blessed Sacrament, what suffering in the world do you "see" with Him that causes you to be shaken? Ponder. Write down in one sentence that form of suffering.

☩ Many of those to whom Fr. Arrupe nursed back to health after the nuclear blast became Catholic Christians. He said they discovered: *that Christian charity can have compassion, can assist, can give a consolation that is above all human comfort, can give a peace that helps one to smile in the midst of pain and to pardon those who had made us suffer so much.* Suffering is not the end of the story. Hope is. Look out into the world again with Christ and see with new eyes those you thought above. Ponder. In a sentence or two, ask Jesus to bring them peace, healing and the grace to forgive any who caused their suffering.

Minutes 51-60
—Take a Break

FOURTH HOUR

Minutes 1-5
—Kneel Silently & Listen to Your Heart
—Pray the Hail Mary & Listen to Your Heart
—Pray One of the Two Following Prayers to Affirm Christ Present in the Blessed Sacrament Before You

Minutes 6-40
—Spiritual Exercise (If you did not complete the reflection/answers from the previous hour, do those first. When complete, continue reading the story, taking your time to pause and reflect as you do. There is no need to rush).

Jesus Friend and Consoler
Another type of Eucharistic experience is that which shows us the value that the Most Blessed Sacrament has for us when we have been in intimate and prolonged contact with Him during our life and we sense the lack of this sacrament when we are not able to receive it. At such a time we appreciate the great role which Jesus, our friend, companion, and consoler has in our life if we have been and are habitually nourished by the Eucharist.

I remember a Japanese girl of around eighteen whom I had baptized three or four years earlier and who had become a fervent Christian. Every day she received Communion at the six-thirty Mass in the morning, which she promptly attended every day.

One day after the explosion of the atomic bomb, I was passing through streets clogged with masses of ruins of every kind. On the spot where her house had formerly stood, I found a kind of hut supported by some poles and covered with pieces of tin. I went up to it. A wall about a foot and half high marked off a place within its interior. I tried to enter but an unbearable stench repelled me. The young Christian woman, her name was Nakamura, was lying stretched out on a rough table raised a bit above the ground. Her arms and legs were extended and covered with some burned rags. Her four limbs had become along their whole length a single sore from which pus was oozing and falling down upon and penetrating the earth.

Her burned flesh seemed to be little else but bones and wounds.

She had been in this state for fifteen days, without being able to take care of herself or clean herself, and she had only eaten a little rice which her father, who was also seriously injured, gave her. Her back was already one gangrenous mass since she had not been able to change her position. When I sought to clean her burns, I found that the muscles were rotten and transformed into pus that left a hollow into which my hand entered and at the bottom of which was a mass of worms.

Appalled by such a terrible sight, I remained without speaking. After a little, Nakamura opened her eyes and when she saw me near, and smiling at her, she looked at me with two tears in her eyes and sought to give me her hand which was only a purulent stump and she said to me with a tone that I shall never forget: "Father, have you brought me Communion?"

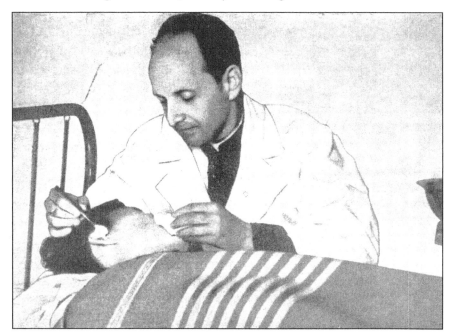

Fr. Arrupe helping a Hiroshima victim at the Jesuit Novitiate 1945

What a Communion that was, so different from that which I had given her each day for so many years! Forgetting all her sufferings, all her desires for physical relief, Nakamura asked me for what she had continued to desire for two weeks, from the day on which the atomic bomb had exploded. She asked for the Eucharist, for Jesus Christ, her great consoler, to whom she had months earlier offered her body and soul to work for the poor as a religious.

I would have given anything to have been able to hear her speak of that experience of her lack of the Eucharist and of her joy at receiving it after so much suffering. Never before had I experienced such a request, from one who had been so cruelly reduced to a "wound and ulcer," nor such a Viaticum[122] received with such an intense desire. Nakamura San died soon after, but she had been able to receive and embrace Jesus whom she had loved so much and who was anxiously waiting to receive her forever in His home in heaven.

The absence of Jesus is something like that which Martha felt when after the death of Lazarus she said to Jesus: "Lord, if you had been here, my brother would not have died" (Jn 11:32). It was precisely then that Jesus performed one of the greatest miracles of His public life. Like Martha, Nakamura also was able to feel that Jesus, though absent exteriorly, had not abandoned her and that He would come to meet her again to take her to Himself and make her completely happy for all eternity.

I have frequently thought of that scene of Nakamura San. How much it taught me! The value of the Eucharist for souls who have truly experienced it, the desire to receive it that causes one to forget every other kind of suffering and need, the joy of receiving it, all the greater the longer that one has

---

[122] The Blessed Eucharist—Communion—given to a person in danger of death.

been deprived of it, the strength that Christ gives us under the sacramental species, communicating to us His love and His incomparable joy.

A religious who, because of her work with the poorest people of Peru, could only assist at Mass every six weeks, since she had to remain far from a place of worship, told me: "It is just in this situation that I feel more what the Eucharist means for me." If we must leave our Lord to serve the souls of others, He makes Himself felt more deeply even in His physical absence since He is always living in the depth of our soul.

Fr. Arrupe (top right) with his Catholic catechists and catechism class in Yamaguchi 1941

I myself personally experienced this deep sense of pain for the lack of the Eucharist during the thirty-three days that I was imprisoned in Japan, but there was also at the same time a feeling of the faithful and consoling presence of Our Lord. The enemies of Christianity had made a thousand accusations against me. They were angry, since they saw that while they were trying to put obstacles in the way to conversions, a good number of young people were turning to the Church and were receiving baptism. The war broke out in Japan on the feast of the Immaculate Conception, 1941, with the attack of Pearl Harbor. The military police immediately put me in jail, in a cell with an area of four square meters. I did not know why they had put me there, and I was not told why for a long time, and only at the end of my confinement.

I passed the days and nights in the cold of December entirely alone and without a bed, or table, or anything else but a mat on which to sleep. I was tormented by my uncertainty on why I had been imprisoned. This provoked a kind of self-torture because of the presumptions, suspicions, and fears that I had done something that could have been a source of harm to others. But I was above all tortured by not being able to say Mass, at not being able to receive the Eucharist.

What loneliness there was! I then appreciated what the Eucharist means to a priest, to a Jesuit, for whom the Mass and the tabernacle are the very center of his life. I saw myself dirty, unshaven, famished, and chilled to the bone without being able to talk with anyone. But I felt even more anguish for my Christians who were perhaps suffering because of me. And above all, there was no Mass. How much I learned then! I believe that it was the month in which I learned the most in all my life. Alone as I was, I learned the knowledge of silence, of loneliness, of harsh and severe poverty, the interior conversation with "the guest of the soul," who had never shown Himself to be more "sweet" than then.

During those hours, those days, those weeks of silence and reflection I understood in a more illuminating and consoling way the words of Christ: "Remember what I have told you: a servant is not more important than his master. If they have persecuted me, they will also persecute you" (Jn 15:20).

I was interrogated for thirty-six hours in a row. I was asked matters that were very touchy to answer and I was myself astonished by the "wisdom" and the fitness of my replies. It was a proof of the saying of the Gospel: "Do not be concerned about what you must say to defend yourselves. I shall give you the right words and I shall give you such wisdom that all your adversaries will not be able to resist and much less defeat you" (Lk 21:14-15).

When my sufferings were becoming more cruel, I experienced a moment of great consolation. It was Christmas night. My mind went back to so many happy Christmases, to the three Masses which I was able to celebrate that night. What remembrances filled my mind! But none of all this was now possible. I was alone, without Mass. Instead of Christmas, it seemed more like Good Friday!

Just then when my Christmas was being changed into the Passion and that blessed night into a sad Gethsemani, I heard a strange sound near one of the windows. It was the soft murmur of many voices which with muted accents sought to escape detection. I began to listen. If any of you have been in prison waiting for a sentence, you would appreciate the anxiety with which I followed those sounds which were now of themselves becoming an immediate source of suspicion. Such are the fears that one feels within the four walls where one is detained.

Suddenly, above the murmur that was reaching me, there arose a soft, sweet, consoling Christmas carol, one of the songs which I had myself taught to my Christians. I was unable to contain myself. I burst into tears. They were my Christians who, heedless of the danger of being themselves imprisoned, had come to console me, to console their Shimpu Sama (their priest), who was away that Christmas night which till now we had always celebrated with such great joy. What a contrast between that thoughtfulness and the injustice of senseless imprisonment!

The song with those accents and inflections which are not taught or learned poured forth from a touching kindness and sincere affection. It lasted for a few minutes, then there was silence again. They had gone and I was left to myself. But our spirits remained united at the altar on which soon after would descend Jesus. I felt that He also descended into my heart, and that night I made the best spiritual Communion of all my life.

From then on the Eucharist became for me something new and different. I sought never to lose it. The moment when one loses something is also the moment in which its worth is best known. And so, my dear young friends, the Eucharist is a treasure, a great treasure which the Heart of Christ was able to give to humankind.

There is still another incident that has been most instructive in my life and which made me understand more fully the intimacy which we should have with Jesus in the Eucharist and that the simpler one's manner of prayer is the more profound it becomes.

I was once in Yamaguchi in charge of a group of young women and men. Among these was a woman of about twenty who, without any show, went to the chapel and remained on her knees before the tabernacle, at times for hours on end. She seemed to be absorbed, as she remained there motionless. I was struck by the fact that though she was a young woman like all the others, very charming and cheerful, she went to the chapel with such persistence, though she was living together with her companions who held her in the highest esteem.

Fr. Arrupe at Hiroshima hearings 1945

One day I met her, or rather, I made it a point to meet her, as she was leaving the chapel. We began to speak as usual and our conversation fell upon her constant and long visits to the Blessed Sacrament. She had hardly given me the chance to speak about this when I asked her: "And what do you do in so much time before the tabernacle?" Without hesitation, as if she had already prepared her answer, she told me: "Nothing."

"What? Nothing?" I insisted. "Does it seem possible to you to remain so long without doing anything?"

This sharpening of my request, which wiped out all possibility of doubt, seemed to upset her a little. This time she was a little more slow in answering me. At last she said: "What do I do before the tabernacle? Well, I am there." Then she was silent again. And we took up again our ordinary conversation.

She seemed to have said nothing, at least nothing particular. But in reality she had not concealed anything and had said everything with a word replete with content. In a single word she had condensed the whole meaning of being present before the Lord: "To be," as Mary, the sister of Lazarus, was at the feet of the Lord (Lk 19:39), or as His Mother stood at the foot of the cross.

They also *were there*. Hours of friendship, hours of intimacy, during which nothing is lost and it seems that nothing is said, since that which is given is everything—one's whole being. Unfortunately, there are too few who understand the value of this "being" at the feet of the Master in the Eucharist, of this apparent loss of time with Jesus.

Would you like to have some good advice from me? Look upon Jesus as your friend, as your confidant. Learn to go and see Him, to visit Him, to "remain" with Him, and you will see how many things you will learn. It is a wisdom which He alone can give you, the true knowledge which makes people wise, holy, and even happy. All that we need for our life is gradually attained with a pouring forth from heart to heart. "Tell me with whom you associate, and I shall tell you who you are." If you go with Jesus, if you remain with Jesus, you will certainly become, yourself, another Jesus.

Minutes 41-50
—Journal Exercise for Hour Four

Ponder each of the following questions. Only reflect on one question at a time and don't read ahead. Write the one thing that seems most significant to you at this point in your life from each question. Only move ahead when the Spirit prompts you, taking time to fully explore what your heart is experiencing. Remember to direct your short responses directly to Jesus. If you don't complete the reflection/answer process, you will have time to do so at the beginning of the next hour. So relax and reflect peacefully.

✠ Nakamura, who was suffering and on the point of death from radiation poisoning, smiled at Fr. Arrupe and asked if he came to bring her Communion. Talk with Jesus about what kind *and* depth of love someone can have to ignore suffering and focus only on His presence to them in the Blessed Sacrament. Ponder. In your own words, ask Jesus if you can know His love this deeply. Write what you asked Him in one sentence.

✠ Fr. Arrupe was imprisoned and suffering extreme anxiety not knowing what crime he caused. But mostly he was suffering because he was prevented from saying Mass and offering it for his "new" Christians. His friends risked their lives to sing him a Christmas carol and he wept for gratitude. Have you ever suffered extreme anxiety and suddenly someone risks helping you and brought you joy? Ponder, Ask Jesus if he would make it possible for you to take a risk to help someone in great need. If you know what risk you might take, write for the grace to make it happen. Write it in a single sentence request to Jesus.

✠ A young woman who would spend hours in front of the Blessed Sacrament caught Fr. Arrupe's attention. Yet when he pressed her what she did with such great amounts of time, all she said was, "I am there." You have "been here" before Christ in a similar way for about four hours. Fr. Arrupe suggests you become another Jesus by "being with" him. You have another four hours ahead of you. Tell Jesus you are happy just being with him. In a single sentence, ask him to give you the will to take time each week to simply be with him in the presence of the Blessed Sacrament, so that you become more like him.

Minutes 51-60
—Take a Break

FIFTH HOUR

Minutes 1-5
—Kneel Silently & Listen to Your Heart
—Pray the Hail Mary & Listen to Your Heart
—Pray One of the Prayers to Affirm Christ Present in the Blessed Sacrament Before You

Minutes 6-40
—Spiritual Exercise (If you did not complete the reflection/answers from the previous hour, do those first. When complete, continue reading the story, taking your time to pause and reflect as you do. There is no need to rush).

Jesus has a Special Love for the Poor
Certainly Jesus, the same Jesus of the Gospel and of Eucharist, can say profound and precious things to those who have cultivated for a long time an intimacy with him, but we should not think that he cannot speak to all people, even though they are living in the most difficult conditions and in utter poverty. Rather, it is precisely that Jesus who gave His blood for them, that can find secret and wonderful ways for reaching their hearts.

A few years ago I was visiting a Jesuit province in Latin America. I was invited, with some timidity, to celebrate a Mass in a suburb, in a "favela," the poorest in the region, as they told me. There were around a hundred thousand people living there in the midst of mud. The town had been built along the side of a depression and became almost completely flooded whenever it rained.

I readily accepted since I know from experience that visits to the poor are most instructive: they do much good for the poor, but one also learns much from them.

The Mass was held in a small structure all patched together and open. Since there was no door, cats and dogs came and went without any problem. The Mass began. The songs were accompanied by a guitar which was strummed by one who was not exactly an expert, but the results seemed marvelous to me.

The words were as follows: "To love is to give oneself, to forget oneself, by seeking that which can make another happy." And they continued: "How beautiful it is to live for love, how great it is to have to give. To give joy and happiness, to give oneself, this is love." "If you love as you love yourself, and give yourself for others, you will see that there is no egoism which you cannot conquer. How beautiful it is to live for love."

Gradually as the song went on, I felt a knot in my throat and I had to force myself to continue with the Mass. Those people, who seemed to have nothing, were ready to give themselves to share their joy and happiness.

Fr. Arrupe in a typical posture for reading and praying.

When we arrived at the consecration and I raised the Host in the midst of an absolute silence, I perceived the joy of the Lord who remains with His beloved. As Jesus says: "He has sent me to bring the good news to the poor" (Lk 4:18), "Blessed are the poor in spirit" (Mt 5:3).

Soon after, when I was distributing Communion and was looking at their faces, dry, hard, and tanned by the sun, I noticed that large tears like pearls were running down many of them. They were meeting Jesus, their only consolation. My hands trembled.

I gave them a brief homily in dialogue. They told me things which are heard with difficulty in lofty discourses. They were very simple things but at once human and sublime. One old woman asked me: "You're the superior of these priests, aren't you? Well, 'Señor,' thanks a thousand times since your Jesuit priests have given us the great treasure which we lacked, and of which we have the greatest need, the Holy Mass."

One young man said openly: "Señor padre, you should know that we are very thankful since these priests have taught us to love our enemies. One week ago I had prepared a knife to kill a comrade whom I hated much, but after I heard the priest explain the Gospel, I went and bought an ice cream and gave it to my enemy."

At the end, a big fellow, whose terrible looks could have inspired fear, told me: "Come to my house. I have something to honor you." I remained uncertain, not knowing whether I should accept or not, but the priest who was accompanying me said: "Go with him, father; the people are very good." I went to his house, which was a half falling-down shack. He made me sit on a rickety chair. From where I was seated the sun could be seen as it was setting.

The fellow said to me: "Señor, see how beautiful it is!" And we remained silent for some minutes. The sun disappeared. The man added: "I did not know how to thank you for all that you have done for us. I have nothing to give you, but I thought that you would like to see this sunset. It pleased you, didn't it? Good evening." He then gave me his hand. As I was leaving I thought: "I have met very few hearts that are so kind."

I was about to leave that street when a small woman very poorly dressed came up. She kissed my hand, looked at me and said with words filled with emotion: "Father, pray for me and for my children. I was at that beautiful Mass which you celebrated. I am running home. But I have nothing to give to my nine children. Pray to the Lord for me: He must help us." And she disappeared almost running in the direction of her house.

I learned many things with one Mass among the poor. How different from the great receptions of the leaders of this world!

Minutes 41-50
—Journal Exercise for Hour Five
Ponder each of the following questions. Only reflect on one question at a time and don't read ahead. Write the one thing that seems most significant to you at this point in your life from each question. Only move ahead when the Spirit prompts you, taking time to fully explore what your heart is experiencing. Remember to direct your short responses directly to Jesus. If you don't complete the reflection/answer process, you will have time to do so at the beginning of the next hour. So relax and reflect peacefully.

✠ Fr. Arrupe described a situation where in extreme poverty, people had a most profound faith. Have you had an experience of being with people who have next to nothing whose faith in God and Jesus is rock solid? Ponder. If you can remember a situation, write it down in a single sentence addressed to Jesus. "Jesus, I remember...etc."

✠ The poor who received communion from Fr. Arrupe had tears running down there faces, so moved that the Lord was coming to them. Jesus who is truly present in the Blessed Sacrament must have also been overjoyed to bring such hope to the poorest of the poor. Contemplate Jesus' joy at a Mass like this where he is able to touch and be present to those with nothing. Ponder his joy and ask Jesus what he felt. Listen. Write what you "heard" in a single sentence. Remember that one and same Jesus is present to you, too.

✠ A woman who had nothing to feed her nine children asked Fr. Arrupe to ask God to help her. She believed in God because of the "beautiful Mass" she experienced with Fr. Arrupe. Contemplate a situation in your own life or the world that seems impossible to resolve, and ask Jesus to make it work. Ponder. Describe in two sentences the situation and tell Jesus you "believe" he can resolve it.

✠ The presence of Christ transformed a man's hatred and desire to kill to a desire to be reconciled Has your intense anger toward "an enemy" of yours ever been similarly transformed? Ponder. Write to Jesus in a sentence or two what you remember.

✠ The most precious gift the fearful looking man could offer Fr. Arrupe was a chair at his house to watch the sunset. When can you remember being so moved by the beauty of creation that you stopped and gave thanks? Ponder. Tell Jesus in a single sentence what you saw and thank Him because "all things were made through Him and for Him."

Minutes 51-60
—Take a Break

SIXTH HOUR

Minutes 1-5
—Kneel Silently & Listen to Your Heart
—Pray the Hail Mary & Listen to Your Heart
—Pray One of the Two Following Prayers to Affirm Christ Present in the Blessed Sacrament Before You

Minutes 6-40
—Spiritual Exercise for Hour Six
(If you did not complete the reflection/answers from the previous hour, do those first. When complete, continue reading the story, taking your time to pause and reflect as you do. There is no need to rush).

The "Eucharist Person," the "New" Person Modeled upon Jesus Christ

I could go on telling you of other experiences which I have had, but the time does not permit it. Let us therefore sum up what I have sought to tell you up till now. Our Lord, through contact with Him in the Eucharist, has entered into the project of my life.

He has revealed Himself to me in different and ever new ways and He has transformed my plan of life into his own plan of life, the plan which He made known in the Gospel, for He, the Jesus of the Gospel and the Jesus of the Eucharist are the same Jesus risen from the dead and living.

He, the worker of miracles, the *Almighty Healer of the sick*, met me on the esplanade of Lourdes in the Host that was blessing the ill. He *chose me* and *sent me personally with an apostolic mission* to continue His work, when the superior of Loyola at the end of his Mass, confirmed me in my aspiration to ask for the mission in Japan, and when during the Mass on the ship, He made me feel that I was near the apostles whom He sent into all the world and to St. Francis Xavier.

He, the *Anointed-Victim* who offers Himself upon the cross to His Father for the salvation of the world, for all the people who do not yet know Him, at one with all those who suffer, offered Himself in my hands on the highest peak in Japan and in the midst of those who had been tortured and wounded by the atomic bomb. And again, He has always shown Himself to me as a most faithful friend. He, the *great consoler in suffering,* fulfilled the hunger and the longing of Nakamura as she was dying and rent with pain.

He, the *true and sole companion, able* to remain united with us even in the most absolute solitude, never abandoned me in the days when I was in prison.

He, *the friend who communicates Himself* in silence to those who "remain" near him as to that girl in Yamaguchi.

Jesuit General Arrupe shines a boy's shoes in Quito, Ecuador 1964

He who *has a special love for the poor* and knows how to fill them with joy and to bless them with great gifts that are hidden to us, as to those Christians of the Mass in the "favela" of Latin America.

We should now reflect on all this and strive to draw some practical results for our own personal lives. I shall limit myself to some brief points. Continue to ponder them.

The central ideal which your movement presents to you is that of "a person of the Eucharist," that is, of a person who, like Jesus, carries to the very end the plan of the Father, dedicating yourself totally to others, letting your heart be broken for them on a universal level open to all the world, to all people. This person of the Eucharist is the new person, the person who wishes to build a new world with Jesus. In the midst of the present culture with its advances and limitations, you wish in fact to be new, that is to be modern among those who are modern. The problem consists in knowing the criteria of this newness and in remaining constant to it.

If the newness is measured by the style of dress or of hair, by "fashion," by entertainment, the use of drugs, by confrontations and by the recourse to violence, I believe that you will certainly not be "the newest" young men and women.

But the true criterion of what is new is that which is described by St. Paul. According to him, to be old persons means to be slaves to sin, to have that hardness of spirit of one who has lost his moral sense, who lets one's conduct become disordered and delivers oneself over to the unbridled practice of every kind of impurity (cf Eph 4:22-24). According to this criterion, many young people who claim to be "modern," and "new," are precisely those who are most "old."

A person who is truly "new" is the one created by God after the model of Jesus Christ "in justice and in holiness' holiness' (Eph 4:24), "renewed (by God) to bring you to perfect knowledge and to make you like to Him who has created you" (Col 3:9-10) "with sentiments of mercy, kindness, humility, patience, and sweetness, supporting one another, pardoning one another…And above all may you have love, which is the bond of perfection" (Col 3:12).

This perfection in charity brings a great joy, the serenity which is the fruit of the Spirit. Because of this, you should always be the most cheerful of those who are young, with the joy and the smile most solid and profound, that joy which, as St. John says, no one can take from you (Jn 16:22).

The criteria for recognizing people who are "new," are those which were spoken of the first and true "new" man, Jesus of Nazareth, the Christ, the man-God. He is that charming friend who spoke in such a way that one who heard Him exclaimed: "No one has spoken as this man" (Jn 7:49), "He did everything well" (Mk 7:37), "To whom shall we go? You have the words of eternal life" (Jn 6:69), "Let us also go with him to die" (Jn II: 16). He is that friend who has so given Himself for us that He offered His life in the terrible tortures of the cross, but who, having risen, lives forever, not only at the right hand of the Father in heaven, but also much closer to us in the Eucharist.

The Eucharist gives some very precious characteristics to Christ's complete giving of Himself. They are a source of inspiration for your life as "Witnesses," and they renew you each day, making you ever more "new" and ever more "women and men of the Eucharist."

Jesus Christ becomes our food in the Eucharist, a new food, so that He may be united in the most intimate measure possible with us and to give us new strength to plan and build a new world. Jesus Christ in the Eucharist, hidden under the sacramental species, remains near us in the tabernacle as a faithful friend to encourage us and to teach us to be "new" as he was.

Strive to become intimate with, and to obtain a knowledge of Jesus Christ in the Eucharist. May He be the force which moves you along the path of the new world. Christians should not only be new for themselves but also witnesses, leaders, precursors of the truest modernity, heralds of Christ, always new and always modern.

All this that I wish to say to you can be summed up in your being friends of Christ, but true friends. He has chosen us as His friends; "You are my friends" (Jn 15:14). Now we are those who must choose Him as our friend, but as a true friend, as our best friend. And to be converted to Him, to be more closely united with him, to be identified with Him, to continue His life in ours, there is no more direct route than that which passes through the Eucharist.

Pope John Paul II and Fr. Pedro Arrupe, Jesuit General 1980

Lord, You have before You this group of young men and women who have heard Your invitation: "If you wish to be perfect, sell all that you have, and give it to the poor, then, come and follow me" (Mt 19:21). They long to be faithful to You, to follow You wherever you go and to give their lives for You. They are so filled with enthusiasm for You that they say, as Ittai, one of King David's chief captains and most faithful friends said to King David: "By Yahweh and your life, my lord king, where my lord king is, living or dead, there also will your servant be" (2 Sam 15:21).

True "people of the Eucharist," who are engaged in building a new world, are those who follow their Lord wherever he goes and who, to follow him, are nourished by his Body and Blood, and are thus transformed into "other Christs." From here, you should leave with a heart on fire, on fire with the love of Christ, who is the only one who can transform the self-centeredness of the heart of stone of the old person into the person of today.

Minutes 41-50
—Journal Exercise for Hour Six
Ponder each of the following questions. Only reflect on one question at a time and don't read ahead. Write the one thing that seems most significant to you at this point in your life from each question. Only move ahead when the Spirit prompts you, taking time to fully explore what your heart is experiencing. Remember to direct your short responses directly to Jesus. If you don't complete the reflection/answer process, you will have time to do so at the beginning of the next hour. So relax and reflect peacefully.

✠ To be a "new person" or a True Heart, Fr. Arrupe offers that fashion, entertainment and/or ideologies are really not going to help a person achieve the goal. Talk with Jesus about what challenges you face in conforming to the "fashions of the day" in order to fit in and to be accepted. Ponder. What are the specific challenges? In two sentences, write the main one(s) and ask for His help to overcome the temptation conform and instead to be a "new" True Heart—a truly "modern" person.

✠ Fr. Arrupe said: *He (Jesus) the true and sole companion, able to remain united with us even in the most absolute solitude, never abandoned me in the days when I was in prison. He, the friend who communicates Himself in silence to those who "remain" near him as to that girl in Yamaguchi. He who has a special love for the poor and knows how to fill them with joy and to bless them with great gifts that are hidden to us, as to those Christians of the Mass in the "favela" of Latin America.*

Write in a sentence or two what specific desires you have to serve others when you read these reflections.

✠ Fr. Arrupe said: *Jesus Christ becomes our food in the Eucharist, a new food, so that He may be united in the most intimate measure possible with us and to give us new strength to plan and build a new world. Jesus Christ in the Eucharist, hidden under the sacramental species, remains near us in the tabernacle as a faithful friend to encourage us and to teach us to be "new" as he was.*

How many visits per week and/or how much time do you feel called to spend in quiet prayer with Christ each week in His presence in the Blessed Sacrament? Write down what you deisre. Then in a next sentence, ask Jesus, present before you, to give you the grace to act on this desire closing with: "Thank you, Jesus, for hearing my prayer!"

Minutes 51-60
—Take a Break

SEVENTH HOUR

Minutes 1-5
—Kneel Silently & Listen to Your Heart
—Pray the Hail Mary & Listen to Your Heart
—Pray One of the Two Following Prayers to Affirm Christ Present in the Blessed Sacrament Before You

Minutes 6-40
—Spiritual Exercise

FIRST PART: The Lord Jesus, present to you in the Blessed Sacrament, desires to be your friend. He wants you to join Him in his work to heal the world. He knows there is something that only you can do for Him and He desires to lead you to the knowledge of this life mission. Pray the Triple Colloquy of St. Ignatius for the graces to be open to this knowledge. Take as much time as you want for these three conversations.

TRIPLE COLLOQUY OF SAINT IGNATIUS

First Colloquy, or conversation, will be with Mary. Speak with Mary, using your own words asking her to obtain from her Son <u>the grace to follow her Son selflessly in every act and decision of your life</u>. Pray to know more specifically what path will bring you to your True Heart—to being truly "new" and truly "modern." When you finish this conversation, pray the *Hail Mary* slowly, thinking of the words and the person to whom you are praying.

Fr. Arrupe after his stroke with Mother Theresa of Calcutta ca 1982

Second Colloquy, or conversation, will be with Jesus. Speak directly to Jesus, asking him to request his Father for the same graces as above, i.e., using your own words, He will request from His Father th<u>e grace for you to follow Him in every act and decision of your life</u>. Pray to know more specifically what path will bring you to your True Heart—to being truly "new" and truly "modern." When you finish your conversation, pray the *Anima Christi* slowly, thinking of the words and the person to whom you are praying.

Soul of Christ, sanctify me. Body of Christ, save me. Blood of Christ, fill me. Water from the side of Christ wash me. Passion of Christ, strengthen me. O Good Jesus, hear me. Within thy wounds, hide me. Permit me not to be separated from thee. From the wicked foe, defend me. At the hour of my death, call me, and bid me come to thee that with thy saints I may praise thee forever and ever. Amen.

Third Colloquy, or conversation, will be with God the Father. Ask the Father directly in your own words to give you the graces so you may follow His Son. Ask the Father for the grace for you to follow Jesus in every act and decision of your life. Pray to know more specifically what path will bring you to your True Heart—to being truly "new" and truly "modern." When you finish, pray the *Our Father,* thinking of the words and the person to whom you are praying.

SECOND PART: You have asked the Blessed Mother, Jesus and the Father for graces to know how best to find your True Heart. You have done this in the presence of Jesus in the Blessed Sacrament. Tell Jesus now: "I believe you have heard my prayers and that you will, in time, reveal all to me."

Minutes 41-50
—Journal Exercise for Hour Seven
Go back now and review all that you have written in your journal entries this vigil thus far. Read the questions and read what you spoke to Jesus in your responses. Ask for the grace "to see" and "to hear" how the Holy Spirit is working in your heart this night by "understanding with the eyes of faith" what your heart—your True Heart—is revealing to you. When you are done, write what immediately comes to your heart when you read the prompts below.

- ✠ Jesus, the challenge where I struggle most to believe you will be real and present to me in my life is...

- ✠ Jesus, what I see most about my life that gives me hope is.....

- ✠ Jesus when I look at the world, what causes me the greatest distress is....

- ✠ Jesus, I would like to help people most by....

- ✠ Jesus, what it means for me to sell all I have and follow you is....

- ✠ Jesus, if one day I might be known as one of your saints, I would be honored to be remembered most for....

- ✠ Jesus....

Minutes 51-60
—Take a Break

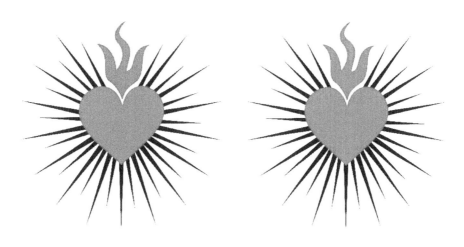

FINAL HOUR

Minutes 1-5
—Kneel Silently & Listen to Your Heart
—Pray the Hail Mary & Listen to Your Heart
—Pray One of the Prayers to Affirm Christ Present in the Blessed Sacrament Before You

Minutes 6-40
—Spiritual Exercise
—Write a personal dedication prayer that describes your desire to serve Jesus and His Kingdom. A template is provided below. You may no clue as to the shape that call will take. Yet, offer to serve Christ with your whole life by the path or vocation that will set your free you and make you a True Heart. For you to be authentically most who you are—a True Heart—will be your path to holiness. Leon Bloy wrote: *The only real sadness, the only real failure, the only great tragedy in life, is not to become a saint.* Make yourself available for the work of this Kingdom here on earth, so you can praise Him forever in the Eternal Kingdom of the Blessed. Your dedication should be no longer than 5-8 sentences! Something short enough that you can pray it briefly each day from here on out.

TRUE HEART Prayer Template

Praying the Ignatian Examen opens us to the spiritual world. It heightens consciousness so we can discern the authentic from the inauthentic in all of our thoughts, word and deeds. St. Ignatius prayed it hourly. His Constitutions require Jesuits pray it twice daily. It is the Spiritual Exercises in miniature and opens one to live life as a True Heart for the Greater Glory of God.

For the end of the True Heart journey and the close of the Night Vigil, you are creating your own unique version of this key, strategic prayer of discernment. Praying this will open you to Divine inspiration on a daily basis and "drag you" into miracles of grace!

CREATION
I believe God created everything in love and for love; I ask for heart-felt knowledge of God's love for me, and for gratitude for the general and particular graces of this day. (Add a sentence or two to personalize this grace for yourself).

PRESENCE

I believe God is present in each moment and event of my life, and I ask for the grace to awaken, see and feel where and how, especially in this present moment. (Add a sentence or two to personalize this grace for yourself).

MEMORY

I believe every violation of love committed by me and against me is in my memory, and I ask God to reveal them to me, especially those that have manifested themselves today, so I can be healed. (Add a sentence or two to personalize this grace for yourself).

MERCY

I believe that forgiveness is the only path to healing and illumination. I beg for the grace of forgiveness, and the grace to forgive, especially for the general and particular failures of this day, and from my past. (Add a sentence or two to personalize this grace for yourself).

ETERNITY

I believe the grace of forgiveness opens my heart, making my every thought, word and deed bear fruit that endures to eternity. I ask that everything in my life serve Christ's Great Work of Reconciliation. (Add a sentence or two to personalize this grace for yourself).[123]

✠ Pray your unique version of the True Heart Prayer and then pray *Foundations Prayer* afterwards. Pause at the end of the Foundations Prayer and listen to your heart before moving to the next step.

FOUNDATIONS PRAYER

For and through whom everything was made,
Is Christ Jesus. I live because he loves me.

To praise and serve him alone with all my mind, heart,
and strength is my freedom—my only freedom.

I shall not prejudice any path in following him:
for I can praise him equally in my health and sickness.

I can distinguish myself in service to his Kingdom with
great wealth, modest means, or having
nothing at all to call my own.

He is the anchor of my joy and peace
Whether I am disgraced or lauded.
In his all-embracing love I taste eternity,

---

[123] Ignatian Examen Adapted by William M. Watson, S.J.

whether my days are numbered great or small.
Christ Jesus alone is the treasure of my heart.
I shall ever listen for his call,
and follow unreservedly.

For in everything I can love and praise him,
and find my eternal joy.
Amen.[124]

✠ Pray your unique version of the True Heart Prayer and then pray the two Psalms below afterwards. Pause at the end of the Psalms and listen to your heart before moving to the next step.

PSALM 114-115

When Israel came forth from Egypt,
the house of Jacob from an alien people,
Judah became God's sanctuary,
Israel, God's domain.
The sea saw and fled;
the Jordan turned back.
The mountains skipped like rams;
the hills, like lambs.
Why was it, sea, that you fled?
Jordan, that you turned back?
Mountains, that you skipped like rams?
You hills, like lambs?
Tremble, earth, before the Lord,
before the God of Jacob,
Who turned the rock into pools of water,
flint into a flowing spring.

Not to us, LORD, not to us
but to your name give glory
because of your mercy and faithfulness.
Why should the nations say,
"Where is their God?"
Our God is in heaven
and does whatever he wills.

Their idols are silver and gold,
the work of human hands.
They have mouths but do not speak,
eyes but do not see.
They have ears but do not hear,

---

[124] A paraphrase by William Watson, SJ, of the First Principle and Foundation of St. Ignatius from the Spiritual Exercises.

noses but do not smell.
They have hands but do not feel,
feet but do not walk;
they produce no sound from their throats.
Their makers will be like them,
and anyone who trusts in them.

The house of Israel trusts in the LORD,
who is their help and shield.
The house of Aaron trusts in the LORD,
who is their help and shield.
Those who fear the LORD trust in the LORD,
who is their help and shield.
The LORD remembers us and will bless us,
will bless the house of Israel,
will bless the house of Aaron,
Will bless those who fear the LORD,
small and great alike.
May the LORD increase your number,
yours and your descendants.

May you be blessed by the LORD,
maker of heaven and earth.
The heavens belong to the LORD,
but he has given the earth to the children of Adam.
The dead do not praise the LORD,
not all those go down into silence.
It is we who bless the LORD,
both now and forever.
Hallelujah![125]

✠　Pray your unique version of the True Heart Prayer and then pray the *Teach Me Your Ways* and the *Personal Prayer of Pedro Arrupe* afterwards. Pause at the end of both prayers and listen to your heart before moving to the next step.

TEACH ME YOUR WAYS

Teach me your way of looking at people:
as you glanced at Peter after his denial,
as you penetrated the heart of the rich young man
and the hearts of your disciples.
I would like to meet you as you really are,
since your image changes those with whom you
come into contact.

---

[125] Psalm 114-115.

Remember John the Baptist's first meeting with you?
And the centurion's feeling of unworthiness?
And the amazement of all those who saw miracles
and other wonders?
How you impressed your disciples,
the rabble in the Garden of Olives,
Pilate and his wife
and the centurion at the foot of the cross. . . .
I would like to hear and be impressed
by your manner of speaking,
listening, for example, to your discourse in the
synagogue in Capharnaum
or the Sermon on the Mount where your audience
felt you "taught as one who has authority."[126]

PERSONAL PRAYER OF PEDRO ARRUPE

Grant me, O Lord, to see everything now with new eyes,
to discern and test the spirits
that help me read the signs of the times,
to relish the things that are yours, and to communicate them to others.
Give me the clarity of understanding that you gave Ignatius.

✠ Pray your unique version of the True Heart Prayer and then pray So Many Things afterwards. Pause at the end of So Many Things and listen to your heart before moving to the next step.

---

[126] Prayer of Pedro Arrupe.

SO MANY THINGS

To each one of you in particular
I would love to say –
tantas cosas: so much, really.
From our young people I ask
that they live in the presence of God
and grow in holiness,
as the best preparation for the future.
Let them surrender to the will of God,
at once so awesome and so familiar.
With those who are
at the peak of their apostolic activity,
I plead that they do not
burn themselves out.
Let them find a proper balance
by centering their lives on God,
– not on their work –
with an eye to the needs of the world,
and a thought for the millions
that do not know God
or behave as if they did not.
All are called to know and serve God.
What a wonderful mission
has been entrusted to us:
to bring all to the knowledge
and love of Christ![127]

✠ Pray your unique version of the True Heart Prayer and then pray the prayer for Fr. Arrupe's intercession for some holy favor you have afterwards. Pause at the end of I Tasted and the intercession prayer and listen to your heart before moving to the next step.

O God, loving Father: in baptism you clothed with Christ our servant Pedro Arrupe
and you called him to follow you in spiritual poverty in the Society of Jesus,
listen to my prayer benevolently.
He delivered himself to you completely, in missionary activity, and in the guidance of his
Brothers; in time of health, as in the hour of infirmity.
Moved by the Holy Spirit, you placed him at the service of faith, making him
A master of discernment and meek servant of the justice of the Kingdom.
With trust I pray, in imitation of Jesus Christ, poor and humble,
Whom he loved deeply, that Fr. Arrupe be recognized as a model of evangelical life

---

[127] A Prayer of Fr. Arrupe for Young Adults: He added at the end. *On those of my age I urge openness: let us learn what must be done now, and do it with a will. For this I offer to the Lord what is left of my life, my prayers and the sufferings imposed by my ailments.*

And prophetic witness in the world, encouraging us to become in every culture
"men and women for others."
By his intercession, and for your greater glory, I ask you now for this particular grace […]
That you grant to me, as long as it is for your service and praise.
Through Christ, our Lord, Amen

✠ Pray your unique version of the True Heart Prayer and then pray I Tasted and I Saw afterwards.
Pause at the end of I Tasted and I Saw and listen to your heart before moving to the next step.

I TASTED AND I SAW

Eternal God, eternal Trinity, you have made the blood of Christ so precious through his sharing in your divine nature. You are a mystery as deep as the sea; the more I search, the more I find, and the more I find the more I search for you. But I can never be satisfied; what I receive will ever leave me desiring more. When you fill my soul I have an even greater hunger, and I grow more famished for your light. I desire above all to see you, the true light, as you really are.

I have tasted and seen the depth of your mystery and the beauty of your creation with the light of my understanding. I have clothed myself with your likeness and have seen what I shall be. Eternal Father, you have given me a share in your power and the wisdom that Christ claims as his own, and your Holy Spirit has given me the desire to love you. You are my Creator, eternal Trinity, and I am your creature. You have made of me a new creation in the blood of your Son, and I know that you are moved with love at the beauty of your creation, for you have enlightened me.

Eternal Trinity, Godhead, mystery deep as the sea, you could give me no greater gift than the gift of yourself. For you are a fire ever burning and never consumed, which itself consumes all the selfish love that fills my being. Yes, you are a fire that takes away the coldness, illuminates the mind with its light and causes me to know your truth. By this light, reflected as it were in a mirror, I recognise that you are the highest good, one we can neither comprehend nor fathom. And I know that you are beauty and wisdom itself. The food of angels, you gave yourself to man in the fire of your love.

You are the garment which covers our nakedness, and in our hunger you are a satisfying food, for you are sweetness and in you there is no taste of bitterness, O triune God![128]

✠ Pray your unique version of the True Heart Prayer and then pray *O Most Holy Virgin* afterwards.
Pause at the end of *O Most Holy Virgin* and listen to your heart before moving to the next step.

O MOST HOLY VIRGIN

O most holy Virgin, Mother of Jesus and my mother,
I kneel in prayer at your feet in the very presence of your Son.
I join my voice to all the angels and saints in heaven.

---

[128] From the dialogue On Divine Providence (Chapter 167) by Saint Catherine of Siena, virgin and doctor.

With them, I join in praising you for your "yes" to the Angel Gabriel in giving birth to Jesus. Please intercede that I might be able this day to say "yes" in following your Son.

Dear Mary, help me with your powerful guidance in all my undertakings and toils. Protect me from all enemies and console me in all my trials.
Bring it to pass, that I might live all my life, shaped by the Way, Truth and Light of Christ until I reach the Kingdom of the Eternal Father.
Amen. [129]

✠ Pray your unique version of the True Heart Prayer and then pray *Dedication to the Heart of Christ* afterwards. Pause at the end of *Dedication to the Heart of Christ* and listen to your heart before moving to the next step.

DEDICATION TO THE HEART OF CHRIST

Heavenly Father, as Ignatius prayed in the small chapel of La Storta,
you granted by an extraordinary grace to answer the request
which he had been begging of you for a long time through the intercession of Our Lady:
To be placed with your Son.
In your words to him you assured him of your support:
"I shall be with you".
You asked Jesus carrying his cross to take him as your servant.
This he did. He turned to Ignatius with those unforgettable words:
"It is my will that you serve us."

As a follower of Jesus, I address to you the same prayer,
asking to be placed with your Son and to serve "under the banner of the Cross"
where Jesus is nailed out of his infinite love.
His side is pierced and his heart is opened
As a sign of his love for me and for all people.

I now consecrate myself to the Heart of Jesus
And promise you my allegiance.
Please give me the grace to serve your Son
with the same spirit and same intensity as Ignatius.

Through the intercession of the Virgin Mary who received the prayer of Ignatius,
and before the Cross where Jesus Christ gives to us the treasures of His open heart,
through Him and in Him, I say from the very depths of my being:
Take, O Lord, and receive all my liberty, my memory,
My understanding, and my entire heart.

---

[129] The Dedication prayer to Mary is adapted from the traditional solemn consecration of the Society of Jesus to the Immaculate Heart of Mary.

Whatever I have or hold, you have given me.
I give it back to you and surrender it wholly to be governed by your heart.
Give me only your love and your grace,
And I am rich enough, for I need or desire nothing else. [130]

Closing Minutes –The Rest of Your Life
—Journal Exercise
Write in your journal the three most significant things you desire to remember for the rest of your life from this night vigil .

---

[130] The Dedication Prayer to the Sacred Heart is adapted from Pedro Arrupe's prayer of the Consecration to the Heart of Christ.

THE REST OF YOUR LIFE EXERCISES

The final section of TRUE HEART Practices has three exercises. The first is a repeat of one of the Night Vigils which in this edition are called "Guided Gospel Meditations."

The second exercise is to incorporate the True Heart Prayer into a daily spiritual regimen. Below is the text of this special form of the Ignatian Examen created especially for TRUE HEART.

You will also find multiple audio versions of this on our website under the TRUE HEART Program that can be listened to online or download to a phone or other device. These recorded meditations are the one concession we have made to the digital age believing that listening to guided prayer on the go is a good thing!

The final exercise is an adaptation of the Abide in Me which closes the Forty Weeks program. You can use it as a reflection for a retreat, the basis for a discussion or some other good pastoral use for young adults.

As always, let us know the ways you use these exercises so we can share that with the greater TRUE HEART community that will develop around this program.

STEP ONE: Upon completion of ten weeks of True Heart exercises, I invite you to do or re-do the final I Night Vigil Week 10. Either alone or with friends who have shared the journey with you find a quiet chapel or church that has a tabernacle with the Blessed Sacrament.

STEP TWO: Do the prayer exercise and ask the Lord to guide you to a life commitment that will set your heart free, give you hope, make a difference and bring you joy. He will not be silent to such a prayer!

STEP THREE: Read "Abide in Me."

TRUE HEART PRAYER

Sacred Story Institute is dedicated to helping people find freedom and happiness and their true heart. One of the greatest spiritual tools that we use to help people is what St. Ignatius called the Examination of Conscience or simply the *Examen*. We have modified and modernized this powerful prayer discipline to fit into our many programs.

For True Heart, we created audio meditations based on a unique version of Ignatius' Examen that we call True Heart Prayer. The five movements of the prayer are short reflections on Creation; Presence; Memory, Mercy and Eternity. The text of the True Heart prayer is below.

We suggest that you do this daily for a set number of minutes. St. Ignatius' method is for fifteen minutes. You might begin with giving each of the five meditations one minute of time. Gradually, you can add minutes to meditation. You can go all the way to fifteen minutes daily, but no more than that.

The goal is to develop a sustainable habit that is not too time-consuming but that refocuses your heart, your True Heart, so that you can live more selflessly than selfishly.

Please use the words of the five movements below for this daily spiritual "true heart" discipline. After you read each part, close your eyes for several minutes to aid you in spiritual listening. We have also created recorded versions of this prayer with music and nature sounds. You can find those on the Sacred Story website under the True Heart Program.

The prayer is below. Say the words silently or vocally if you are in a place by yourself.

"Jesus, help me slow down and hear you in my heart. (Pause, listen, reflect)

CREATION: *Father, I believe you created everything out of love as a gift for me. Jesus, I ask you to help me remember the gift in your creation that brought me the most faith, hope and love today. When you help me remember, I will thank you for that gift."* (Pause, listen, reflect)

PRESENCE: *Father, I believe you are present in every moment and event of my life. I ask for a heartfelt knowledge of Jesus' love for me. Jesus, I ask you to help me know what my heart is feeling now. If I am peaceful, I will tell you why. If I am sad, I will tell you why. (Pause, listen, reflect)*

MEMORY: *Father, I believe Jesus helps me remember everything that I have done, or that has been done to me that have hurt my life of faith, hope and love. Jesus, I ask you to open my memory to these sinful things, so that your love can heal me. (Pause, listen, reflect)*

MERCY: *Father, I believe that you showed us in Jesus, that mercy and forgiveness is the greatest expression of your love. Jesus, I will tell you the things I have done for which I need your forgiveness and mercy. I will also tell you the things that others have done to me so that I can offer your mercy and forgiveness to them. (Pause, listen, reflect)*

ETERNITY: *Father, I believe you can give me eternal love, because Jesus' passion, death and resurrection opened the path to your eternal kingdom. I ask you, Jesus, to transform my every thought, word and deed, into fruit that endures to eternity. Jesus, I ask that everything in my life serve your eternal kingdom of faith, hope and love. (Pause, listen, reflect)*

CLOSING: Father, let me always be grateful for your gift of life. And let me honor the covenant relationships of all persons made in your image and likeness. Let me commit to relationships that lead to selflessness, and avoid relationships that lead to selfishness. I ask you in my own words, to lead me to the Christian vocation that will set my heart free. I know you will always be with me.

(Pray the Our Father)

ABIDE IN ME

A Daily Relationship with Christ as Savior, Divine Physician and Lord of All

I invite you to pray with the first few verses of chapter fifteen from the Gospel of St. John. Take as many minutes, hours or days as you wish to pray with St. John. There is no hurry.

I am the true vine, and my Father is the vinedresser. Every branch of mine that bears no fruit, he takes away, and every branch that does bear fruit he prunes, that it may bear more fruit. You are already made clean by the word which I have spoken to you. Abide in me, and I in you. As the branch cannot bear fruit by itself, unless it abides in the vine, neither can you, unless you abide in me. I am the vine, you are the branches. He who abides in me, and I in him, he it is that bears much fruit, for apart from me you can do nothing. If a man does not abide in me, he is cast forth as a branch and withers; and the branches are gathered, thrown into the fire and burned. If you abide in me, and my words abide in you, ask whatever you will, and it shall be done for you. By this my Father is glorified, that you bear much fruit, and so prove to be my disciples. As the Father has loved me, so have I loved you; abide in my love. If you keep my commandments, you will abide in my love, just as I have kept my Father's commandments and abide in his love. These things I have spoken to you, that my joy may be in you, and that your joy may be full. (Jn 15: 1-11)

The Ignatian *Examen* that inspires *True Heart* prayer became an active part of my Jesuit life in 1994. Having entered the Society of Jesus in 1973, I had already lived for twenty years as a Jesuit—eight of those years as a priest. My practice of this prayer was inconstant for many years. By most measures, one could say that I *had* a Christian vocation. I mean this in much the same way that one looking at a Catholic married couple with children or a single person doing service work would agree that each of these persons *has* a Christian vocation.

A life of prayer and daily Mass, a yearly eight-day retreat, and a fair amount of *theological living* (faith-oriented reading plus lots of God/Church conversations) made me feel I *had* a real religious life. And I did. The question for me had become instead: was I fully *living* a Christian vocation?

The answer to that is much more complex. For simplicity's sake, let me say that I have learned more clearly that a Christian vocation is not equivalent to simply belonging to a religious order. To use an analogy, a *Christian marriage* is different from *being Catholic and married with children*.

My Christian vocation requires that I daily open myself to Jesus and allow my actions, emotions, desires, loves, hurts, fears, and plans (especially my precious plans), to be shared with and shaped by Jesus' influence. Sharing means that I submit myself to Jesus and let Him have a say in what I am doing and who I am daily becoming, what I hold on to and what I relinquish. Acting in a Christian way means that I no longer belong to myself. Rather, I belong to Christ.

Some good friends of mine who have been married for several years recently shared with me one of the biggest adjustments they have had to make as a result of being married. They can no longer make plans in blissful isolation but have to consult with each other about practically every aspect of their lives.

This consultative sharing can be both a joy and an annoyance. Each one is called out of the prison of their own ego and invited to love, sacrifice, and make adjustments so that the other can grow and flourish. We really grow when we are called out of ourselves. But there is joy in sharing intimately in the life of the Beloved. We are created for the joy of sharing intimately in the life of the other. We are made in the image and likeness of God who *is relationship*.

A Christian vocation requires an intimate relationship with Christ. It requires making this relationship a priority on a *daily* basis. *True Heart* prayer, more than any other spiritual discipline I have encountered in my forty years in religious life, brings me face-to-face with Christ in a relationship that calls me out of myself. It is the most effective path that has enabled me to be true to the man and priest that God desires me to be.

It is not always easy and I do not want to minimize the challenge it has been in terms of my honesty and openness. It is a joy and an annoyance for exactly the same reasons as any serious relational commitment. I have had moments of aggravation and difficulty in praying *True Heart*. I have also experienced times when I did not want to pray because I knew I would be confronted with things I would prefer to ignore.

Here is a typical example. Some time ago, I was struggling internally with someone who, I judged, had wronged me. I was hurt, frustrated, and upset from what I perceived to be an injustice against myself. I discovered I was not at all upset when this person experienced misfortunes, for I felt this person *deserved* it. In prayer, I was not speaking with Jesus about this person. Instead, I found myself rehearsing conversations in my head about how I had been wronged. My focus was on myself.

One day I was awakened to my lack of Christian charity. Instinctively I understood that I needed to bring my feelings about this person to Jesus and yet, I resisted. A part of my heart wanted to simply rehearse my justified hurts. It took several *True Heart* prayer periods for me to begin to speak *from my heart* to Christ about what I was feeling. The *insight* that I needed to reach out and forgive this person came in a split-second. I was also able to accept some of the fault lines in my own personality which may have contributed to the initial difficulties. It is amazing how that clarity comes with honesty. This was a *graced* experience!

However, upon leaving the time of *True Heart* prayer, a new inspiration took hold. Perhaps it is unwise to forgive? I could lose ground. The re-emerging frustration and darkened spirit—the counter-inspiration—accompanying this new inspiration was in *marked* contrast to the peacefulness I had experienced previously in the time of *True Heart* prayer. In testing the spiritual inspirations, it was clear which inspiration was from the Divine-Inspirer and which inspiration was from the counter-inspirer.

Honestly, I was strongly tempted to *ignore* the truth of my spiritual discernment and go with the refusal to forgive. But I was being invited by God to *disarm*. I was invited to be vulnerable. It was an invitation to greater spiritual freedom, the freedom that Ignatius calls *detachment*. Freedom *sounds* good, but it is not something we always really want.

This event was a wake-up call because it clearly presented the difficult choice of forgiveness. It may sound odd, but it gave me the conviction that Jesus is interested in *everything* I am doing. Every thought, word and deed I have is important to Christ. He wants to be part of everything I experience. *True Heart*, prayed faithfully, has made me aware of what *being in relationship* with Jesus means.

I feel the effects of the surrender that is necessary for a real relationship with Jesus, and I feel it in a particularly powerful way twice a day. I have chosen to make spiritual surrender the center of my Jesuit life. And praying *True Heart* prayer has revealed how many areas of my daily life I keep off-limits from Christ.

A strong intellectual tradition is a characteristic of the Society of Jesus; it is a good in and of itself. But there is something that Ignatius wanted Jesuits to value above learning: virtue, the spiritual life, and the surrender of our will and our hearts to Christ. The human gifts we cultivate only reach their fruitfulness in light of a well-grounded spiritual life. In Section Ten of the Jesuit Constitutions, entitled "How the Whole Body of the Society is to be Preserved and Increased in its Well-being," Ignatius says:

Thus it appears that care should be taken in general that all the members of the Society devote themselves to the solid and perfect virtues and to spiritual pursuits, and attach greater importance to them than to learning and other natural and human gifts. For these interior gifts are necessary to make those exterior means efficacious for the end which is being sought. Part X [813] 2.)

This advice is written for Jesuits, and for the care and growth of the Society of Jesus. Yet it offers good pragmatic Ignatian wisdom that is applicable to any vocation or situation in the Church. Human gifts and qualities reach their perfection and the height of their potency when the bearer of those gifts and/or qualities is grafted to the vine of Christ—when they surrender to Christ.

This holds true for the talents of the athlete, the intellectual acumen of the college student, the artistic skills of the singer or architect, the healing gifts of the doctor or nurse, the ministry of religious and priests, the leadership skills of the politician and the professional business person, and the love of husband and wife for each other and their children.

The personal decision I face daily—twice daily—is how much of my life will I allow to be grafted onto the vine of Christ? How much will I allow myself to *abide* in His Love? Jesus must have been looking at grapevines when He spoke this passage from John's Gospel. The vine or stalk is the source of all nutrients. Only shoots which grow directly from it, or have been grafted onto it, bear fruit.

As I look back over my life, I can see that I have produced all sorts of fruit by my *own* effort. What has become a much more important question at this point is: how much of what I produce is the fruit of my relationship with Jesus? In other words, have I allowed myself to become a "daily disciple" of Jesus by being in relationship with Him? Am I grafted onto the vine of Christ?

The bottom line of my experience of *True Heart* is that I am being challenged to open *all* of my heart and my life to God's grace. While the commitment to the Jesuits and the priesthood always felt full-time and lifelong, the *relationship* with Jesus seemed to have an on-again, off-again feel to it.

Quite frankly, I was more in control than Christ. Now I feel that I have truly begun to commit to *Jesus*. Twice daily I need to come to Him with my ups and downs, my joys and anger, my loves and victories, my failures and grief, and my *constant* need. My *constant* need: what does that mean? It means that *True Heart* prayer makes me more aware of my weakness, my failures, and my need for redemption. I have been graced with the eyes to see the reason for Christ's redeeming sacrifice, more clearly than ever before. It is a sacrifice and grace I cannot live without.

Perhaps it is the same discovery of the alcoholic or drug addict. One day, the addict finally wakes up and realizes that the life they thought they controlled is actually out of control.

The only way to salvation is to surrender to love's sobriety and embrace. The alcoholic genuinely in touch with the truth of her/his life knows they are *always recovering* and are never *fully* recovered. One must live constantly with the knowledge of her/his vulnerability and turn to God for help and aid. It is a life of submission, humility, and holy dependence.

Is the invitation to submission, humility and holy dependence the best way for me to convince you to stay committed to *True Heart* prayer? Is this good marketing? Perhaps not, but I am convinced that while your issues may be different from mine, your experience will pull you into the same position of humility, submission, and dependency on God when confronted with the truth of your weakness and need.

What could possibly be attractive about living this way? Praying and living *True Heart* enables a person to be vulnerable, humbly submissive and dependent on God. I can rely on Jesus, who has promised to give me what I need: "If you remain in me and my words remain in you, ask for whatever you want and it will be done for you." (Jn 15: 7)

These words utterly change a person and their world view. Jesus offers this relationship so that my joy "may be full." How so? Because I experience that even in the weakest and most vulnerable condition of my life, Love does not walk away from me. Love has irrevocably committed Himself to me. He sacrificed for me so that I could be whole, and He wants the knowledge of this great love to be known by me on the most intimate level.

He has also promised that this life of discipleship gives great glory to the Father in heaven. Allowing oneself to abide in His love will bear fruit that will give glory to the Father of Jesus Christ. What an awesome reality!

At the beginning of a retreat or in my daily *True Heart* prayer, I try to commit to this relationship. The renewal of my vocational commitment to Christ in the daily engagement with *True Heart* prayer is a means to deepen the knowledge of my radical dependence on God. It fosters the joy of a personal relationship with Christ Jesus that grounds me and opens me up to the deepest yearnings of my heart—my True Heart.

The more I open my heart to a serious relationship with Christ, the more I come to understand the joy for which I have been created. You also have been created for this joy. That is why I am confident you will remain in the embrace of *True Heart* and the Lord Jesus who loves you beyond all reckoning will never let you go. The Love that grounds the universe holds you in His True Heart. Let us pray for each other that we can all find the joy and peace of living our True Heart!

Peace,
Fr. Bill Watson, S.J.

TRUE
HEART

WAYS
TO
SELFLESSNESS

find us at:

https://sacredstory.net/true-heart-young-adult-program/

ABOUT THE AUTHOR

Fr. William Watson, S.J., D.Min., has spent over thirty years developing Ignatian programs and retreats. He has collaborated extensively with Fr. Robert Spitzer in the last fifteen years on Ignatian retreats for corporate CEOs. In the spring of 2011, he launched a nonprofit institute to bring Ignatian spirituality to Catholics of all ages and walks of life. The Sacred Story Institute is promoting third-millennium evangelization for the Society of Jesus and the Church by using the time-tested Examination of Conscience of St. Ignatius.

Fr. Watson has served as director of retreat programs at Georgetown University, vice president for mission at Gonzaga University, and provincial assistant for international ministries for the Oregon Province of the Society of Jesus. He holds master's degrees in divinity and in pastoral studies 1986, from Weston Jesuit School of Theology: Cambridge, Mass.). He received his Doctor of Ministry degree in 2009 from The Catholic University of America in Washington, DC.

Sacred Story Press
Seattle, USA
sacredstorypress.com

Sacred Story Press explores dynamic new dimensions of classic Ignatian spirituality, based on St. Ignatius's Conscience Examen in the Sacred Story prayer method, pioneered by Fr. Bill Watson, S.J. Our publications are research-based, authentic to the Catholic Tradition, and designed to help individuals achieve integrated spiritual growth and holiness of life.

We Request Your Feedback

The Sacred Story Institute welcomes feedback on our programs. Contact us via email or letter (see below). Give us ideas, suggestions, and inspirations for how to make them a better resource for Catholics and Christians of all ages and walks of life. Please also contact us for bulk orders and group discounts.

admin-team@sacredstory.net

Sacred Story Institute & Sacred Story Press

1401 E. Jefferson, Suite 405

Seattle, Washington 98122

Made in the USA
Middletown, DE
10 September 2020